THE UTOPIAN NOVEL IN AMERICA, 1865-1900

by

ROBERT L. SHURTER

With a new introduction
by the author

AMS PRESS

NEW YORK

THE UTOPIAN NOVEL IN AMERICA, 1865-1900

by

ROBERT L. SHURTER

Submitted in partial fulfillment of the requirements
for the Degree of Doctor of Philosophy

Department of English
WESTERN RESERVE UNIVERSITY
May 15, 1936

Library of Congress Cataloging in Publication Data

Shurter, Robert LeFevre, 1907-
   The utopian novel in America, 1865-1900.

   Originally presented as the author's thesis, Western
Reserve, 1936.
   Bibliography: p.
   1. American fiction--History and criticism--19th
century. 2. Utopias in literature. I. Title.
PS374.U8S5 1972   813'.03   72-2944
ISBN 0-404-10710-9

Reprinted by arrangement with Robert L. Shurter

Library of Congress Catalog Card Number: 72-2944

International Standard Book Number: 0-404-10710-9

Manufactured in the United States of America

L 406611

TABLE OF CONTENTS

Introduction

One of the pnenomena of American literature which has previously been disregarded is the large number of utopian novels that appeared in the last three decades of the nineteenth century. Particularly in the last dozen years of the century, the quest for utopia resulted in more than seventy such novels, most of them inspired by the great success of Edward Bellamy's *Looking Backward* (1888). As a group, these novels shed considerable light on contemporary economic conditions by their protests against unequal distribution of wealth, the power of trusts and labor organizations, cut-throat competition, growing urbanization, the end of the frontier, and social injustice in general.

In terms of literary merit, only one or two novels have assured themselves of a permanent place in the American literary record. Bellamy's *Looking Backward* has been widely read and translated into numerous languages ever since its publication and William Dean Howell's *A Traveller from Altruria* is still known to students of American culture. The other utopias may be of interest to the cultural historian or the sociologist as reflections of the mood of the times. For the most part these novels constitute a kind of populist literature written by and for the common people and casting light on the problems of the times by the simplistic or naive solutions served up in these versions of utopia.

While no one knows better than the researcher of utopian novels the dangers implicit in forecasting the future, it seems reasonably safe to predict that we will never again see such an outpouring of utopias in fictional form. The reasons for such a prediction are worth examining since they shed considerable light on the contrast between nineteenth and twentieth century attitudes and reactions.

First of all, the realities of twentieth century science and technology have so far outstripped the imaginings of the nineteenth century uptopists that their predictions produce only brief amusement or considerable boredom for the twentieth century reader. To be specific, it is difficult to generate much excitement in tales about going around the world in eighty days in a home where the television set is showing actual pictures of Americans walking or riding on the moon. Thus the nineteenth century prediction of cars speeding at ten miles an hour or of crude radios and airplanes are hardly calculated to arouse much enthusiasm in today's readers. The result has been that the scientific marvels which the nineteenth century writer combined with his new social system to arouse interest has subsequently been lopped off to form the separate genre of science fiction in the twentieth century.

Secondly, the utopian novel of the late nineteenth century appealed to the naiveté and moral earnestness of its readers. To accept the utopists' vision of the future the reader had to accept the fact that by wearing a crystal button or by applying the principles of the Sermon on the Mount, the golden tomorrow could be achieved. One novelist even bases his better world on making sure that the conjugation of all verbs, the comparison of all adjectives, and the plurals of all nouns would henceforth be regularized. There was a feeling, as one editor described it, that "we are in the springtime of another period of awakening and advance" and that to accomplish this, reform "should engross the heart, brain, and soul of the true novelist, making him the herald of a better state, the champion of the world's helpless and oppressed millions."

While such naiveté and its concomitant crusading spirit were hardly the exclusive possession of the nineteenth century, it is difficult to imagine similar concepts having broad appeal in the increasingly cynical and pessimistic twentieth century. Our path toward social reform seems to lie not through fiction but through political activism and the organization of special pressure groups. Perhaps this is the reason why the twentieth century thus far has not produced as many American utopian novels as appeared in the last dozen years of the nineteenth century. Even the best known American utopia of the past twenty-five years, B. F. Skinner's *Walden Two* (1948), has evoked no imitators or answers as did *Looking Backward* whose attackers and defenders made their motivation clear in such titles as *Looking Further Backward, Looking Forward, Looking Beyond, Looking Within*, and *Young West* (after Julian West the leading character in Bellamy's novel). Perhaps—to paraphrase Bellamy's well known words—the era of the fictional utopia in America has ended to be succeeded by the forecasts of behavioural and social scientists and the protests of the activists.

One of the very real problems confronting the researcher is the setting of territorial limits on utopia. This land of nowhere, as Thomas More first named it, has a long and honorable history stretching from Plato and More to Huxley and Skinner and Orwell in our own time, but its boundaries have never been too clearly fixed. Where, for instance, does science fiction leave off and utopia begin? Or what demarcates the boundary between tales of faraway lands and places from utopia?

I have used two major criteria as the basis for including or rejecting nineteenth century novels in my study of American utopias. It seemed to me that to be classified as utopian fiction, a novel should contain two major elements:

1. A reasonably detailed and complete description of a new form of society. Edward Bellamy's *Looking Backward* exemplifies such detail and completeness in his descriptions of Boston in the year 2000 but his book also directs some acute criticism at life in nineteenth century America.

2. A major criticism of contemporary society combined with some kind of solution to the problems of such a society. William Dean Howells's *A Traveller from Altruria* is basically a satire on and an indictment of conditions in the United States but it also ends with a brief description of the contrasting society in Altruria.

The first type of utopia, I have labeled the utopia proper and the second, the utopian satire. This at least eliminates the possibility of including *The Wizard of Oz* among utopian fiction as one critic has done. And it clearly eliminates Mark Twain's *A Connecticut Yankee in King Arthur's Court* which appeared a year after Bellamy's novel.

To anyone who reads his way through the turgid mass of utopian novels of late nineteenth century America, certain facts about the mood and motivation of their authors become abundantly clear. All of them write from dissatisfaction with contemporary social, economic, and political conditions—and the specific source of their discontent is the unequal distribution of wealth. All of them write out of a sincere conviction that they possess the one true answer, the ultimate panacea for our social ills. What they lack in talent and literary expression, they try to compensate for with sincerity and moral earnestness.

In passing judgment on the quality of many of these American utopias, one has to concur with the opinion of a critic in *The Nation* who commented "the worst thing about the future . . . will be its novels." And an equally devastating appraisal has to be made of many of the social plans and organizations on which their utopias are based. There is, for example, Bradford Peck who would base his society on organizing it like a department store while he appeals to his reader for funds or Zebina Forbush who will put his new world into reality by having a million working men set up his cooperative commonwealth by a donation of a dime. Above all else, many of these novelists believed in the perfectability of human nature. The devices by which such a change is to be effected range from Edwin Everett Hale's *Ten Times One Is Ten* in which all agree to live by the following words:

> To look up and not down;
> To look forward and not back;
> To look out and not in;
> And
> To lend a hand.

To Chauncey Thomas's *The Crystal Button* in which all the citizens pledge themselves to live by these words:

> I will try from this moment henceforth to be true and honest in my every act, word, and thought; and this crystal button I will wear while the spirit of truth abides with me.

It is all too easy to poke fun at such 'solutions' to complex social problems, but one must not forget that for many uneducated readers these utopian novels offered hope and the possibility of change. Many of the novels appeared in the years of the Populist movement and the Bryan campaigns and they were born from the same quixotic hopes for a better world in what our current cliché labels "the foreseeable future." Even Edward Bellamy believed implicitly to the day of his death that his children would surely see the Nationalistic society which his novel described.

Actually, the study of these American utopias belongs more properly in the province of the historian or the sociologist or the economist than in that of the literary scholar. Except for the novels by Bellamy and Howells—and to a lesser extent Ignatius Donnelly's *Caesar's Column*—, they lack literary merit and deserve the obsurity which subsequent years have given them. Nevertheless, for the student of American culture, they do provide an interesting insight into the reform forces of the eighteen-nineties and they form a logical transition to the muckraking movement after the turn of the century.

From the mass of mediocre writing and simplistic solutions, Bellamy's *Looking Backward* towers like Mt. Everest for the literary scholar. It is the one great American utopian novel. It is also the most influential book of its kind in America because it has constantly been reprinted and translated since it first appeared. Despite his earlier literary work and his sequel to *Looking Backward* called *Equality*, Bellamy's reputation rests solely on this novel which has won him a permanent place in American literary history. As my study shows, it is heavily dependent upon other sources like Laurence Gronlund's *The Cooperative Commonwealth*, John Macnie's *The Diothas* and August Bebel's *Frau*. But Bellamy was able to clothe the dry bones of his economics so as to appeal to millions of readers and to convey his impassioned conviction that social justice must someday prevail. It is no exaggeration to say that his utopia has had more influence than all of the other books in my study combined. In fact, *Looking Backward* deserves to rank with *Uncle Tom's Cabin* and *Ramona* as the most influential novels of nineteenth century America.

It is my hope that the research which resulted in *The Utopian Novel in America, 1865-1900* offers new evidence about three heretofore unrecognized aspects of American culture. First, it examines in detail the large number of utopian novels produced during the years 1888 to 1900. Second, it reveals the sources from which Bellamy probably derived his novel. And third, it shows the phenomenon of some seventy utopian novels within a dozen years as being almost exclusively an American phenomenon without derivation from or dependence on European intellectual currents.

Robert L. Shurter
Cleveland, Ohio 1972

CHAPTER I

THE CHARACTERISTICS AND CLASSIFICATION OF UTOPIAS

Utopia, the land of "nowhere", has been the lodestone of men's thoughts for thousands of years. Essentially unattainable----since human society is no more than a changing organization striving to improve itself, but by very nature incapable of perfection---this land of dreams has deluded many a voyager into believing that he could reproduce it upon his return to earth. Still other travellers in utopia have held up this perfect world as a magic mirror which, by its own consummate beauty, reveals all the more clearly the ugliness, the injustice, and the maladjustment of the world in which we live. To many a man, the land of utopia has offered an instant and satisfying release from a world of troubles and has become a means of escape into a land where justice and beauty reign.

Surely this questing after perfection, whatever the motive behind it, ought to be one of the noblest sections of man's intellectual history. Yet utopianism and the utopians have, with a few exceptions, been largely ignored. One reason for this has been the fact that utopian literature is not readily classified in one or the other of the categories that scholars use in their attempts to pigeonhole all human activities. Utopias belong partly in the

province of sociology, partly in economics, and partly
in literary history; as a result, they offer rather too
wide a field for investigation. Particularly is this
true of American utopias, which have never received anything but the most superficial attention.

Another reason for ignoring utopian literature is
best expressed by the practical Macaulay: "An acre in
Middlesex is better than a principality in Utopia." [1]
No one can deny that utopias belong on the outer fringe
of literary history; they are often filled with queer ideas,
freakish panaceas that could not pass current in a realm
where common sense is the prevailing coin. Utopias are,
in short, dreams---but even as dreams they have a value,
as W.H. Hudson notes:

> Romances of the future, however fan-
> tastic they may be, have for most of us
> a perennial if mild interest, since they
> are born of a very common feeling---a
> sense of dissatisfaction with the existing
> order of things, combined with a vague
> faith in or hope of a better one to come.
> The picture put before us is false; we
> knew it would be false before looking at
> it, since we cannot imagine what is unknown
> anymore than we can build without materials.
> Our mental atmosphere surrounds and shuts
> us in like our own skin ; no one can boast
> that he has broken out of that prison. The
> vast, unbounded prospect lies before us,
> but, as the poet mournfully adds, "clouds
> and darkness rest upon it." Nevertheless
> we cannot suppress all curiosity, or help
> ·asking one another, What is your dream---
> your ideal? What is your News from Nowhere,

---

(1) Macaulay, T.B., Lord Bacon in Macaulay's Miscellaneous
    Writings, (New York, 1865), II,387.

> or, rather, what is the result of the
> little shake your hand has given to the
> old pasteboard toy with a dozen bits of colored
> glass for contents? And, most important
> of all, can you present it in a narrative
> or romance which will enable me to pass an
> idle hour not disagreeably? How, for in-
> stance, does it compare in this respect
> with other prophetic books on the shelf? [2]

Macaulay and others forget that we can learn as much from
man's dreams of perfection as from any other source. A
better understanding of the true significance of utopias
is expressed by Oscar Wilde when he states that "A map of
the world that does not include Utopia is not worth even
glancing at, for it leaves out the one country at which
Humanity is always landing. And when Humanity lands there
it looks out, and, seeing a better country, sets sail.
Progress is the realization of Utopias." [3]

August Comte has said "there is no Utopia so wild as
not to offer some incontestable advantages," [4] and as
one looks back over the history of utopianism, one becomes
convinced that the utopists have aided definitely in the
advancement of civilization. The utopian ideas of one
generation have many times become realities to succeeding
generations; hence the writers of utopias have played a
major role in social evolution. Often their ideals have

---

(2) Hudson, W.H., "Preface" to A Crystal Age, (N.Y.,1907),v.

(3) Wilde, O., The Soul of Man under Socialism, (Boston,
    1910). This book has no paging.

(4) Comte, A., Positive Philosophy, Martineau Version, II,25.

been attained only after centuries of struggle; still
more often their ideas have never become complete
realities. Thomas More, for instance, suggested universal
and compulsory education, a goal toward which we are still
struggling. In discussing his industrial organization,
Miss Vida Scudder says:

> If the industrial system on which his
> society is founded is still confined to
> Utopia, communication between that common-
> wealth and England is at least more frequent
> than in his day. One is inclined to suspect
> certain of our economists even, of occasional
> trips into that land of vision; while as for
> dreamers---Ruskin, Bellamy, Morris, Howells,--
> they have sojourned there long enough to
> bring back full reports, which differ some-
> times in detail from those of Hythloday. [5]

Thus it is that utopianism points the way to an ideal
future, which in some of its parts may be attained by
succeeding generations. In constantly pointing toward the
ideal, they have helped men to avoid many errors. By constantly reiterating the idea that society by its own efforts
could reorganize itself more justly, the utopists made
that reorganization possible.

A commendable quality in all utopianism is fearless-
ness. From Plato to Bellamy the utopists dared to suggest
ideas that were derided as "visionary" and "impossible".
Men generally prefer to live with evils that they know,
than to fly to societies of which they know nothing---but
not so the utopians. "They were the venturesome men who

---

(5) Scudder, Vida D., Social Ideals in English Letters,
(Boston, 1898), 60.

because they dared did much to achieve necessary change,
quietly and rationally." [6] Because of their courage in
advocating "visionary" ideas like equality of the sexes,
universal education, eugenics, and religious toleration,
the utopists played a major role in the gradual attainment
of these benefits.

Finally, utopias have done more than anything else
in man's intellectual history to call attention to the
state as a social organization. Writers from the time of
Plato to Bellamy have stressed the State as the method
of giving men proper environment and opportunity for
advancement. In this respect, they prepared the way for
modern philosophies of government like socialism and
communism. As one of the prominent exponents of scientific
socialism puts it, "With the Utopia modern Socialism
begins." [7]

One would not be so biased as to indicate only the
contributions of utopianism; the utopists have had their
limitations as well. They are inclined to trust too much
in the establishment of a perfect society in the midst
of the old order; they realize but vaguely that transition
from the imperfect to the ideal is effected only by long
and bitter struggle. In this respect, modern utopists have

---

(6) Hertzler, J.O., The History of Utopian Thought, (N.Y.,
    1923), 283.

(7) Kautsky, K., Die Vorlaufer des Neuren Soziolismus, 466.

become more realistic, and a basic change has come about,
as H.G. Wells suggests:

> The Utopia of a modern dreamer must
> needs differ in one fundamental aspect from
> the Nowheres and Utopias men planned before
> Darwin quickened the thought of the world.
> Those were all perfect and static States,
> a balance of happiness won for ever against
> the forces of unrest and disorder that in-
> here in things. One beheld a healthy and
> simple generation enjoying the fruits of
> the earth in an atmosphere of virtue and
> happiness, to be followed by other virtuous,
> happy, and entirely similar generations,
> until the Gods grew weary. Change and
> development were damned back by invincible
> dams forever. But the Modern Utopia must
> be not static but kinetic, must shape not
> as a permanent state but as a hopeful stage,
> leading to a long ascent of stages. Now-
> adays we do not resist and overcome the
> great stream of things, but rather float
> upon it. We build now not citadels, but
> ships of state. For one ordered arrangement
> of citizens rejoicing in an equality of
> happiness safe and assured to them and
> their children for ever, we have to plan
> "a flexible common compromise, in which a
> perpetually novel succession of individual-
> ities may converge most effectually upon
> a comprehensive onward development." That
> is the first, most generalised difference
> between a Utopia based upon modern conceptions
> and all the Utopias that were written in
> the former time. [8]

Despite this improvement noted by Wells, even the modern
utopians are inclined to lose their perspective--to regard
their particular cure-all as the only hope of the world.
"They let their desires run away with their sense of
reality." [9] The utopists have not taken into account

---

(8) Wells, H.G., _A Modern Utopia_, 16.

(9) Davis, J., _Contemporary Social Movements_,(New York,
1930), 18.

certain fundamentals of human nature----they believe that

men will work as hard for an abstract state as for in-

dividual advancement; they forget that the desire to

accumulate private property is inherent in all of us; that

the family, and not the abstract state, is the fundamental

fact in social organization. Because of these and other

deficiencies, an aura of unreality clings to almost all

utopias. As H.G. Wells puts it:

> There must always be a certain effect
> of hardness and thinness about Utopian
> speculations. Their common fault is to be
> comprehensively jejune. That which is the
> blood and warmth and reality of life is
> largely absent; there are no individualities,
> but only generalised people. In almost
> every Utopia---except, perhaps, Morris's
> "News from Nowhere"---one sees handsome
> but characterless buildings, symmetrical
> and perfect cultivations, and a multitude
> of people, healthy, happy, beautifully
> dressed, but without any personal distinction
> whatever. Too often the prospect resembles
> the key to one of those large pictures
> of coronations, royal weddings, parliaments,
> conferences, and gatherings so popular in
> Victorian times, in which, instead of a
> face, each figure bears a neat oval with
> its index number legibly inscribed. This
> burthens us with an incurable effect of
> unreality, and I do not see how it is
> altogether to be escaped. It is a dis-
> advantage that has to be accepted. [10]

One characteristic all utopias have in common---a

sense of dissatisfaction with the present order. From the

time of Plato's Republic to the latest vision of H.G. Wells,

dissatisfaction with the organization of life has motivated

---

(10) Wells, H.G., op. cit., 20.

the quest for utopia. "...Whenever men feel dissatisfied with contemporary conditions they seek change. When men of culture and intelligence sense maladjustment about them, they sometimes try to construct a blue-print of an ideal social state." [11] Thus in periods when men feel most keenly the pinch of poverty and the injustice of social organization, utopias thrive abundantly; they may be used as excellent barometers of man's discontent. Other factors naturally play a part. For instance, the discovering of new lands has apparently been a powerful incentive for utopian dreams. Hence, the voyages of the Elizabethans to new lands undoubtedly attracted mens' minds to the possibility of building a new state from which all of the vices of an older civilization would be eliminated. This may account in some measure for the large number of utopias in the first half of the seventeenth century---among them such notable works as Johann Valentin Andreae's Christianopolis (1619); Francis Bacon's The New Atlantis (published in 1627, but probably written between 1622 and 1624); Tomasso Campanella's Civitas Solis Poetica, or The City of the Sun (1637); and James Harrington's Oceana (1656).

The development of science likewise has played its part in motivating utopianism, for by its own rapid development, science has attracted men's minds to still

(11) Davis, Jerome, Contemporary Social Movements, (New York, 1930), 17.

more marvellous possibilities which are incorporated in
the modern utopias of Wells, Bellamy, and Howells.

> We are educated by our circumstances to
> think no revolution in appliances and
> economic organisation incredible, our
> minds play freely about possibilities
> that would have struck the men of the
> Academy as outrageous extravagance, and
> it is in regard to politico-social ex-
> pedients that our imaginations fail.
> Sparta, for all the evidence of history,
> is scarcely more credible to us than a
> motor-car throbbing in the agora would
> have been to Socrates. (12)

Science has also changed man's conception of utopia.
Plato conceived of a slave class to do the work of his
state----and a tradition of the joy of bodily toil in
utopia has persisted from that time on through the joys
of Ruskin's road-making at Oxford, to William Morris's
News from Nowhere. Within the last century, however,
science has become more and more an integral part of utopia,
until at present,

> Science stands, a too competent servant,
> behind her wrangling underbred masters,
> holding out resources, devices, and remedies
> they are too stupid to use. And on its
> material side a modern Utopia must needs
> present these gifts as taken, and show a
> world that is really abolishing the need
> of labour, abolishing the last base reason
> for anyone's servitude or inferiority. (13)

However, despite the influence of science and exploration,
discontent remains the most important factor in utopian

---

(12) Wells, H.G., op. cit., 103.

(13) Wells, H.G., op. cit., 106.

writing as even the most cursory examination of the
history of utopias will show.

Plato's Republic dates roughly from the time of the
long war between Athens and Sparta. Plato wrote his work
in the midst of defeat, and he must indeed have felt that
something was radically wrong in a state that could be
wrecked by war. Furthermore, Plato had witnessed the
death of his teacher, Socrates, and had learned too well
of the presence of corruption and tyranny in the state.
These things without question motivated his construction
of the ideal commonwealth of The Republic.

Nearly two thousand years after Plato, Sir Thomas
More wrote his Utopia. In the years intervening, men's
minds had been occupied with a heavenly utopia, but More,
with his imagination fired by some of the voyages of
discovery, pictured a utopia in terrestial terms. In
following the adventures of Raphael Hythloday, the reader
sees again and again the vices of the England of More's
day---the rich thriving on the labors of the poor, the
corruption and flattery of the court, the servility of
those in politics. All these are missing in his "land
of nowhere" in which all men labor alike and share equally,
where private property has been eliminated, and where
government proceeds upon the principle of the greatest
good to the greatest number.

An interval of three hundred years brings us to the
nineteenth century, when utopianism flourished again, and

as always, marked man's dissatisfaction with the existing
order.

> In this new world of falling water,
> burning coal, and whirring machinery, utopia
> was born again. It is easy to see why this
> should have happened, and why about two-
> thirds of our utopias should have been
> written in the nineteenth century. The
> world was being visibly made over; and
> it was possible to conceive of a different
> order of things without escaping to the
> other side of the earth. There were
> political changes, and the monarchic state
> was tempered by republicanism; there were
> industrial changes, and two hungry mouths
> were born where one could feed before;
> and there were social changes--the strata
> of society shifted and "faulted," and men
> who in an earlier period would have been
> doomed to a dull and ignominious round,
> perhaps, took a place alongside those whom
> inheritance had given all the privileges
> or riches and breeding. (14)

This time it was the pinch of industrialism that was being
felt in both England and America. As the stress of
economic maladjustment became greater, the number of utopias
increased.

America has always been a proving ground for new
ideas and new methods of organization. Our national
characteristics seem to include a wide popular interest
in visionary schemes and ideas. Indeed, America had been
the scene of many an attempt to put utopian ideas into
effect. The reasons for this are indicated by Morris
Hillquit:

> The causes which contributed to make
> this country the chief theater of experiments

_____

(14) Mumford, L., The Story of Utopias, (N.Y., 1922), 115.

of the utopian socialists of all nations
were many.

The social experimenters as a rule
hoped that their settlement would gradually
develop into a complete society with a higher order of civilization. For that purpose they needed large tracts of cheap
land in places removed from the corrupting
influences of modern life, and America
abounded in such lands at the beginning
and in the middle of the nineteenth century.

Besides, the industrial and agricultural possibilities of the young and
growing country, its political liberty and
freedom of conscience, had an irresistible
charm for these pioneers of the new order
of things. (15)

One characteristic these utopian idealists had in common---

the belief that all social and economic ills could be

cured by some one remedy:

The United States has been favored with
its share of reformers of the single idea
type,--the promulgators of Utopian ideals.
Many are the various reforms, fantastic
and otherwise, which have found at least
a handful of adherents upon American soil;
only three have received the support of a
majority of the nation. These three cure-
alls--the popular patent medicines for the
body politic--are manhood suffrage, universal and compulsory free public education,
and free homesteads for actual settlers. (16)

In view of these characteristics, the suprising fact

to many critics is that American utopian novels appeared

no earlier. An English writer in listing a number of

English utopias of the eighteen seventies remarks upon

what he considers to be the surprising scarcity of literary

(15) Hillquit, M., History of Socialism in the U.S.,
     (New York, 1906), 22

(16) Carlton, F.T., Organized Labor in American History,
     (New York, 1920), 9

utopias in America:

> Only one book in my list comes from
> across the Atlantic; but surely there must
> be many other such.....Our Transatlantic
> cousins have decided tendencies to set up
> "communities" of various forms and differing
> degrees of extravagence upon their soil,
> and we should, therefore, expect to find
> them as facile in imagining them upon paper. (17)

A consideration of the very factors mentioned by this critic

ought to show why literary utopias appeared no earlier.

So long as we had large territory for trying out utopian

schemes, no necessity existed for committing them to paper.

The literary quest for utopia begins on a large scale only

when circumstances forbid an actual quest for it in terms

of some sort of ideal community. The existence in America

of a large body of communities, where all kinds of panaceas

were tried out, precluded our having a large body of utopian

writing. There was no need to write of utopias when a

large part of the American continent lay ready for actual

utopian experiments.

To offset the early and negative effect of these

utopian communities, certain positive factors in American

history led to the appearance of a large group of American

utopias later in the nineteenth century. These factors

will be examined in detail in a later chapter, but a few

may be mentioned here. How largely America became committed

to industrialism in these years is perhaps best demonstrated

---

(17) Notes and Queries, Fourth Series, (July 12, 1873),
XII, 22.

by statistics on the amount of power used in industry
"collected for the first time in 1870, when it was shown
that 2,346,142 horsepower were being employed...By 1900
the number of horsepower had grown to 11,300,081." (18)
Industrialism brought an increased urbanization, an unequal
distribution of wealth, a rising hostility between capital
and labor, and a definite and widespread discontent ending
in many instances in the will to utopia. These conditions
were heightened by the fact that there no longer existed
any means of escape from them. The Census Report of 1890
pointed out that "the unsettled area has been so broken by
isolated bodies of settlement that there can hardly be
said to be a frontier line." Dreams, no longer translatable
in terms of action in the great West, were henceforth to
be committed to paper----often in the guise of the utopian
novel. More than a coincidence is the fact that the end of
the frontier and the earliest appearance of a large number
of utopian novels occurred within the same two years.

One of the most perplexing questions facing any investigator of utopian literature is the classification of
utopias. Bibliographies classify everything from the works
of Jules Verne to the social novels of Walter Besant as
"utopian." Edward Wagenknecht even includes The Wizard of
Oz by L. Frank Baum among "utopian" works and states "The
distinction between utopia and fairyland is of course very

(18) Bogart, E.L., Economic History of the American People,
(New York, 1930), 574.

thin." (19) Professor Wagenknecht goes on to elaborate
on this idea:

> I have spoken of the Land Of Oz as
> an American utopia. By this I do not mean
> that the Oz books are full of social
> criticism. Since they were written for
> children, this is obviously not the case.
> Yet the utopia element in them is strong,
> and if the children do not forget it all by
> the time they grow up, perhaps it is not
> too fantastic to imagine that it may do
> some good. It would not be a bad thing
> if American law-makers and executives were
> to imbibe a few of the ideals which actuate
> the lovely girl ruler of the Emerald City----
> Ozma of Oz. (20)

Obviously some criterion must be adopted which will reject
such books as this, unless the investigator is to find
himself hopelessly lost.

A careful analysis of all the works that can possibly
be included in the most general interpretation of the word
"utopian" reveals three more or less distinct classes:

> 1.   Utopias which describe rather com-
> pletely an ideal state of society either
> in the future or in some remote place.
> These works present the ideas of the author
> as to the desirable social and political
> conditions that the human race should attain.
> Specific examples of this type are Thomas
> More's Utopia and Edward Bellamy's Looking
> Backward.
>
> 2.   Novels which satirize existing society
> under the guise of being set in the future
> or in some strange land. Their primary
> purpose is not to point the way to a better
> future but to show what is wrong with the

---

(19) Wagenknecht, E., Utopia Americana, (University of
Washington Bookstore, Seattle, 1929), 15.

(20) Wagenknecht, E., op. cit., 30.

present by ridiculing its vices or follies.
Of this type are Samuel Butler's Erewhon
and William Dean Howells's A Traveller from
Altruria.

3.   Works projecting their characters out
into space or time for the purpose of enter-
taining the reader with their marvellous
adventures. Sometimes there is the added
purpose of conscientiously trying to depict
what the future may be like---but generally
the emphasis is on the sensational aspects
of scientific progress. These works are
hardly "utopian," although most bibliographies
list them in that category. The best examples
of this whole type are the novels of Jules
Verne---such as From the Earth to the Moon.

The difficulty with any such arbitrary classification is

that certain works have the characteristics of two of the

classes. Every utopia of the first class has in it elements

of the second class, since every utopian work indirectly

looks in two directions---at the present and at the future.

Even such a work as Looking Backward has in it a definite

satirical element concerning conditions in nineteenth

century America. However, one element is generally dominant

in these works, and it is by that dominant characteristic

that I shall classify them.

This thesis will not consider Type 3 at all. Works

with the primary purpose of narrating sensational adventure

belong mostly in the realm of boys' literature and have no

place in a study of this sort. I have included the few

novels in which constructive social criticism or satire is

offered along with sensational adventure.

My interest is primarily in the first two types of

utopias---the utopia proper, as it is sometimes called, which

offers a serious delineation of society as it ought to
be, and the utopian satire, which by painting the future
points out the flaws of society as it is. My study deals
largely with utopias proper, since that was the type most
widely written in America---because many of our works
imitated Looking Backward, which was of this type, and
because our reformers seem to have taken themselves and
their schemes so seriously that satire was hardly suitable
for their purpose. Furthermore satire to be effective must
be directed at more or less settled social institutions,
and these we did not have in the United States.

I have considered the period from 1865 to 1900 as the
outside limits of my investigation, but actually, the last
twelve years of that period have occupied most of my attention,
for in those years the first large group of utopian novels
appeared in America. Within a dozen years, approximately
sixty utopias appeared in the United States. The
significance of these books in indicating the tenor of
popular opinion has been almost completely ignored. Except
for a few scattered studies of individuals like Bellamy and
Howells and one magazine article by Allyn Forbes on the
whole group, nothing has been done to indicate the importance
of these utopias in our social and literary history. Their
value as symbols of social and industrial discontent was
first noted by Professor Goldwin Smith in an article entitled
"Prophets of Unrest" in The Forum for August, 1890:

> Among other signs of the social and
> industrial unrest of the age has been the

production of a number of Utopias such as
The Coming Race, News from Nowhere, Caesar's
Column, and Looking Backward, the last-
named being the most widely circulated
and popular of all. As the rainbow in
the spray of Niagara marks a cataract in
the river, the appearance of utopias has
marked cataracts in the stream of history.
That of More, from which the general name
is taken, and that of Rabelais, marked the
fall of the stream from the Middle Ages
into modern times. Plato's Republic
marked the catastrophe of Greek republic-
anism, though it is not a mere Utopia, but
a great treatise on morality, and even as
a political speculation not wholly beyond
the pale of what a Greek citizen might
have regarded as practical reform, since
it is in its main features an idealisation
of Sparta. Visions of reform heralded
the outbreak of Lollardism and the In-
surrection of the Serfs. The fancies of
Rousseau and Bernardin de St. Pierre
heralded the French Revolution. Rousseau's
reveries, be it observed, not only failed
of realization, but gave hardly any sign
of that which was coming. The Jacobins
canted in his phrase, but they returned
to the state of nature only in personal
filthiness, in brutality of manners, and
in guillotining Lavoisier because the
Republic had no need for chemists.
      There is a general feeling abroad that
the stream is drawing near a cataract now,
and there are apparent grounds for the
surmise. There is everywhere in the social
frame an outward unrest, which as usual is
the sign of fundamental change within. (21)

Certainly Professor Smith is correct in regarding these

utopian novels as significant sociological and economic

documents.

Yet they belong in the province of literature because

most of these American utopists adopted the novel as the

---

(21) Smith, G., Essays on Questions of the Day, (New York,
      1897), 47.

form which would reach the largest number of readers.
That these novels are not great literature is obviously
true. Most of them were written by men whose names have
passed into oblivion. The importance of these books is
discovered only when they are studied in close conjunction
with our history. One must not forget that during the
last decade of the nineteenth century, these American
utopian novels were read by millions, many of whom regarded
them as the hope of civilization.

It is my hope that this thesis will point out the
true significance of utopianism in America by studying
these utopias in the light of English and American literary
history and against the background of social forces in
America.

CHAPTER II

ENGLISH UTOPIAS PRECEDING BELLAMY'S LOOKING BACKWARD

Many trends in nineteenth century American literature begin in England. Our excessive and somewhat uncritical respect for English culture and the lack of any adequate international copyright laws, are only two of the many factors that brought about this tendency to imitate things English. Thus one naturally looks to England for the roots of the large group of utopian novels that appeared in the United States during the last two decades of the nineteenth century.

Only in a general way, however, can any connection between the English and American utopian novels be established. It is impossible to take any one English utopian novel and show that it had American imitators---a fact which can definitely be demonstrated for instance concerning Bellamy's Looking Backward. On the other hand, these American utopias are indubitably the result of the same general trend toward an awakening of social consciousness in fiction that had been going on in England since the days of Dickens. As one critic sees it,

> From Oliver Twist to Sir George Tressady,
> social pictures, social problems, fill
> the scene. Dickens and Thackeray un-
> covered and revealed the social layers
> of early Victorian England. About 1850,
> their simple reproductions gave place to
> the novel of protest and arraignment; this
> in its turn is yielding nowadays [1898]
> to the novel of constructive suggestion,

> whether in the form of avowed literary
> Utopias, or of schemes for social salvation
> in would-be realistic garb. (1)

That the American utopias of the late nineteenth century arose out of this same deepening interest in social problems, this same aim of offering constructive criticism of society in the guise of fiction, cannot be denied. That they constitute an important phase in the development of English and American social thought as revealed in fiction has too long been ignored.

An examination of some of the English utopias from about 1850 to 1888---the date of Looking Backward---may well be instructive if it is not carried on with the idea of proving that the American utopists borrowed from English sources. From a reading of English utopian novels of this period, one may learn much about contemporary English ideas on subjects like woman's suffrage, evolution, and the place of the machine in man's life. Most of these novels are now forgotten----a fate which they certainly deserve----but a few, either because they were written by some prominent man or because of their subject matter still merit attention.

In general, the chief difference between these English novelists and the American utopists is that the English are less interested in depicting a complete and serious regeneration of society as a whole. They tend more toward satire by taking some tendency in contemporary society and

---

(1) Scudder, V.D., Social Ideals in English Letters, (Cambridge, 1898), 124.

showing the absurd results if it is carried to logical ends in the society of the future. They are lacking in the earnestness which makes the American utopists almost pathetic in their belief in their own schemes; but what English utopist lacks in this respect, he gains in his attitude of skepticism toward any one idea or plan as making for the perfectability of mankind. Satire predominates---but it is somewhat difficult, as we have seen, to draw any definite line between satire and the strict utopia aiming at a complete regeneration of man. Both arise out of a desire to improve human society by pointing out the flaws in its present structure, but they differ completely as to method.

The first important English utopian novel of this period is Lord Lytton's The Coming Race (1871), the popularity of which was chiefly responsible for the large number of utopian novels that appeared in England in the seventies. Lytton was "the most versatile man of letters and the most sensitive literary barometer of his time." (2) Lytton usually followed literary trends in much the same manner as the Elizabethan dramatists, but in The Coming Race he established the trend, for in point of time The Coming Race is preceded only by Sir Arthur Helps's Realmah (1868) a novel dealing with life in southern Europe in the stone age but filled with references to English society in

---

(2) Walker, H., The Literature of the Victorian Era, (Cambridge, 1921), 648.

the nineteenth century. As Hugh Walker says:

> But The Coming Race (1871), another
> novelty, showed that he was not only capable
> of writing still, but of writing something
> perfectly new. It is one of the earliest
> and one of the best of the stories which,
> taking a hint from the New Atlantis of
> Bacon, have attempted to forecast the
> changes to be wrought in human life by
> the discoveries of science; but in Lytton's
> case the satirical tone turns the edge of
> criticism directed against the futility
> of prophecy. Lytton was fond of disguising
> himself when he made an experiment, and
> he enjoyed the bewilderment and conjectures
> of the critics as to the authorship of a
> work so unlike anything they knew to be his. [3]

The Coming Race describes the inhabitants of a sub-

terranean area who are in a highly advanced state of

civilization in which strife, pauperism, and disease have

been eliminated. Their underground world is lighted

artificially, and all work is done by mechanism. They

have developed a new power called "vril" of which Lytton

says:

> There is no word in our language which
> is an exact synonym for vril. I should call
> it electricity, except that it comprehends
> in its manifold branches other forces of
> nature, to which in our scientific nomen-
> clature, differing names are assigned, such
> as magnetism, galvanism, etc. These people
> consider that in vril they have arrived at
> the unity in natural energic agencies, which
> has been conjectured by many philosophers
> above ground....[4]

A crisis is brought about among the Vril-ya----their

---

(3) Walker, H., op. cit., 647.

(4) Bulwer-Lytton, E., The Coming Race, (London, 1871), 52.

racial name----when one of their women falls in love with
a human visitor. The race would be contaminated by such
a union because adult humans are on the same mental level
as the children of the Vril-ya. They decide to put their
visitor to death, but his beloved finally saves his life.

At first glance, The Coming Race appears to be little
more than a sensational tale of adventure set in strange
worlds, with a bit of satire thrown in. Contemporary critics
disagreed completely as to its significance. One reviewer
said "Never, indeed, was so gloomy or so impossible a
Utopia devised" (5) while another declared that "the mantle
of Swift had fallen on the shoulders of the author of The
Coming Race". (6) Lytton apparently tried to present a
serious problem, but the sensational story in which he
clothed it confused many of his readers. In The Coming
Race he describes a civilization based upon two attainments--
first the discovery of a power (the vril) that will eliminate
all drudgery and second a rigorous method of selection
that had been carried on over a long period of years. He
is apparently projecting nineteenth century ideas about
Darwinism and the ultimate place of the machine in society
out into this new world with the purpose of hinting at what
the future of humanity may be. One may infer from the novel
that Lytton felt that equality of rank----although not

---

(5) Blackwoods Magazine, CX (July, 1871), 49.

(6) The Athenaeum, (May 27, 1871), 649.

necessarily of ownership---was the natural condition of a race of rigorously selected adults all of whom enjoyed that leisure which is the privilege of only the few at present.

However ambiguous the interpretation of The Coming Race may be, its popularity is indubitably shown in the number of its imitators, all interested in predicting some phase of Man's future. It was followed in 1871 by Henry Boyle Lee's Kennaquhair; H.R.H. Mammoth Martinet's (pseud.) The Gorilla Origin of Man; John Francis Maguire's The Next Generation; and Alex V.W. Bikkers' translation of the Dutch novel by P. Harting, Anno Domini 2071. In 1872 appeared Samuel Butler's Erewhon, which seems, as Butler says, to have been written quite independently of The Coming Race; it is indeed a satire rather than a constructive attempt at prophecy, but Erewhon provoked several imitations which are more or less "utopian".

In the same year there appeared a clever and humorous satire on all works of utopian nature---Charles Mackay's Baron Grimbosh, Ph. D. and Sometime Governor of Bartaria. A Record of his Experiences Written by Himself in Exile, which was published anonymously. The novel describes the appointment of Grimbosh as governor of Barataria and his subsequent fall because of his attempt to put into effect all kinds of absurd ideas---such as having all men give up beer for one day in the week for the purpose of temperance, but having them donate the money

thus saved for building an elaborate clubhouse where beer
can be served! In the novel certain characters are
identifiable as actual personages, notably Palmerston as
"Pamfoozle" and Disraeli as "Benoni". Mackay strikes at
the heart of the problem of all utopianism by showing that
Grimbosh's motives are of the best, but that his methods
and ideas are a bit too idealistic for a practical world.
One of his favorite schemes is the High Court of Humanity,
which bears a notable resemblance to the League of Nations:

> If Emperor This the First used inde-
> corous and insulting language to King That
> the Second, and King That the Second
> complained of the offence, the High Court
> of Humanity should hear the case and compel
> the offender to apologize, under penalty
> of the united displeasure of all the rest
> of the members. If King Twopenny desired
> to appropriate a slice of King Threepenny's
> territory, and proceeded to do so by acts
> of violence, all the members of the court
> should call out the police of their respect-
> ive states, and reduce Twopenny to obedience
> and subjection to the law of the world. (7)

Because of ideas like this one, Grimbosh ends by making
salads for the royal master who succeeds him. The spirit
of the book is indicated by its dedication, "To Napoleon
the Third who lost a throne by being wiser than his people,
I Herman Grimbosh, Doctor of Philosophy, who lost mine
by believing that I could reform a nation that would not
reform itself, dedicate these pages, from my cabbage-garden
and my library, with the sincere hope that he takes his

---

(7) Mackay, C., Baron Grimbosh, (London, 1872), 186.

fall as easily as I take mine." The whole novel is done
with a humorous deftness which makes agreeable reading and
yet emphasizes the fact that utopianism may fare ill in
a work-a-day world. Its place in the development of the
English utopian novel is indicated by a review in The
Athenaeum:

> More's "Utopia", Bacon's "New Atlantis",
> Robert Landor's "Fountain of Arethusa" (1848),
> "The Coming Race", "Erewhon", and half-a-
> score of other fanciful, satirical, yet
> earnest and serious works, have been as
> surely the originators of "Baron Grimbosh"
> as "The Rehearsal" was the originator of
> "The Critic". The spirit and motive of the
> earlier works are, at least, to be traced
> in the "Baron". (8)

The vogue for depicting the future as a means either
of satire on the present or of advocating favorite remedies
continued, and six more novels of utopian nature appeared
in 1873----Edward Jenkins' Little Hodge; Benjamin Lumley's
Another World; or Fragments from the Star City of Montalluyah;
Edward Maitland's By and By; Sydney Whiting's Heliondé;
James Smith's The Coming Man, which had been written much
earlier but was published in 1873; and the anonymous Colymbia.
By this time, the reviewers were beginning to protest at
the dullness and uselessness of most of these works. A
reviewer in The Nation in 1873 remarked that "the worst
thing about the future, if we may take By and By for a fair
sample, will be its novels". (9) But a reviewer in The

---

(8) The Athenaeum, (July 27, 1872), 104.

(9) The Nation, XVII, (October 23, 1873), 278.

Athenaeum of Andrew Blair's *The Annals of the Twenty-Ninth Century* was even more specific;

> For the last two years or so, Utopian
> stories and prospective histories have been
> a weariness to our souls. They are really
> never satisfactory, though great literary
> merit or an ingeniously worked-out allegory
> may now and then---recent instances are
> not wanting---make us overlook their weak
> points. When, however, we get a book like
> the one before us, a mere dull rigmarole
> in three volumes, in which the few "happy
> thoughts" are borrowed and mangled, while
> the greater part consists of silly exagger-
> ation, which has not even the merit of
> being consistent with itself, we begin to
> hope that this style of writing, having
> got so very low, will soon drop out of
> sight, at least for one cycle of literary
> fashions. (10)

By this time, the popularity of this sort of fiction was beginning to wane, and while some twenty-five novels of a "utopian" nature---in the most general sense of the word---appeared between 1874 and 1888, very few of them gained much attention. The few that are of importance I shall examine individually. The rest of these novels can be classified as deriving from three general sources-- those seeking to imitate Lytton's *The Coming Race* such as W.H. Hudson's *A Crystal Age* (1887); satires based upon Butler's *Erewhon* such as the anonymous *Colymbia* (1873); and the largest group consisting of sensational stories set in strange lands or new worlds and obviously inspired by the popularity of Jules Verne's works---such as Percy

---

(10) *The Athenaeum*, (Feb. 28, 1874), 290

Greg's Across the Zodiac (1880), Richard Jefferies'
After London; or Wild England (1885), and Richard Whiteing's The Island (1888). Whether these last should even
be included in a discussion of utopian literature is
questionable; yet oftentimes these strange worlds are
described in order to point out the defects in or the
remedies for terrestial society.

A curious and rather specialized form of utopia began
appearing in 1871 and continues throughout this period.
This form of literature dealt with a subject dear to the
hearts of all loyal Englishmen---the prediction of what
might happen in the future if England's military defences
were not improved. It was provoked by an anonymous article
in Blackwood's Magazine for May, 1871, and afterwards reprinted in pamphlet form, called The Battle of Dorking.
Written by Sir George Tomkyns Chesney, The Battle of
Dorking vividly described the downfall of England at the
hands of Germany in the twentieth century. It revealed
an exact knowledge of military science and particularly
of the English system of volunteers, which was the ultimate
cause of England's downfall. Immediately, loyal Englishmen reached for their pens and the results are to be found
in What Happened After the Battle of Dorking; Being an
Account of, the Victory at Tunbridge Wells; After The
Battle of Dorking; or What Became of the Invaders; The
Battle of Dorking a Myth. England Impregnable, all of which
are anonymous. The Armageddon type of novel is also to be

found in Tom Greer's <u>A Modern Daedalus</u> (1885) and Louis
Tracy's <u>The Final War</u>. This type of fiction is, of course,
merely a minor tangent from the main body of utopian works---
it is interested in only one phase of man's future, although of its serious purpose no reader can be in doubt.

Of the remaining English novels, four are worthy of
consideration either by virtue of intrinsic merit or because of the prominence of their authors. These are W.H.
Mallock's <u>The New Republic</u> (1877); Walter Besant's <u>The
Revolt of Man</u> (1882); Anthony Trollope's <u>The Fixed Period</u>
(1882); and W.H. Hudson's <u>A Crystal Age</u> (1887). The work
of William Morris and H.G. Wells belongs to a later period
and had little influence on the American utopian novel.

W.H. Mallock's <u>The New Republic; or Culture, Faith
and Philosophy in an English Country House</u> is generally
classified as a novel, although it has no plot and resembles the <u>Imaginary Conversations</u> of Walter Savage Landor
more than anything else. The characters involved are
actually real persons under fictitious names---among them
are Ruskin, Arnold, Rossetti, and Pater. [11] These people
agree to talk about a set series of topics---"The Aim of
Life", "Town and Country", "Society", and "The Future",
but the other topics are soon set aside, and "The Future"
occupies the largest part of their time. They begin by

---

(11) A complete key to the characters may be found in
Baker, E.A., and Packman, J., <u>A Guide to the Best
Fiction</u>, (New York, 1932), 322.

"seeing what we really wish society to be---what we really

think that the highest and most refined life consists in,

that is most possible for the favoured classes...!" [12]

Mallock then has each character design his own ideal society

with the result that "the accuracy of the parody is simply

astonishing". [13] The following statement of "Allen", a

fictitious character, is typical of the spirit and method

of the whole work:

> What I should want in a Utopia---would
> be something definite for the people to
> do, each in his own walk of life. What
> I should want would be some honest, definite,
> straightforward, religious belief that
> we might all live by, and that would
> connect what we did and went through here
> with something more important elsewhere.
> Without this to start with---all life seems
> to me a mockery. (14)

As one may infer from this excerpt, The New Republic is

a highly philosophical and literary utopia which, with-

out offering any complete system for man's regeneration,

yet aims to point the way toward a better society in the

future.

Typical of the utopian novel which aims at improving

contemporary society by projecting one of its evil tendencies

out into the future and showing the consequences, is Walter

Besant's The Revolt of Man (1882). Intended as a satire

on the women's rights movement, it depicts a society two

---

(12) Mallock, W.H., The New Republic, (N.Y., 1878), 153.

(13) The Athenaeum, (March 24, 1877), 377.

(14) Mallock, W.H., op. cit., 211.

hundred years in the future in which women have actually gained control of all things---they run the government, institute a religion consisting of worship of the Perfect Woman, and propose marriage to the men. A revolt is brought about because young men resent having to marry old women of fifty or sixty---an obvious satire on nineteenth century marriages of convenience---and finally men come back into power. The story is rather dull generally because of the absurd lengths to which Besant goes in order to satirize female suffrage. Yet occasionally there are flashes of that high-minded social sympathy, that hatred of class injustice, which crystallized in <u>All Sorts and Conditions of Men</u> (1882). It is not alone of the difference between man and woman, but of the difference between man of the present and the man of the future, that Besant is thinking when he writes:

> There is one point of difference between man's and woman's legislation which I would have you bear in mind. Man looks to the end, woman thinks of the means. If man wanted a great thing done, he cared little about the sufferings of those who did that thing. A great railway had to be built; those who made it perished of fever and exposure. What matter? The railway remained. A great injustice had to be removed; to remove it cost a war, with death of thousands. Man cared little for deaths, but much for the result. Man was like Nature, which takes infinite pains to construct an insect of marvellous beauty, and then allows it to be crushed in thousands almost as soon as born. Woman, on the

other hand, considers the means. [15]

There is a larger purpose than mere satire on woman's rights, when he contrasts the ideal society of the future with that of the nineteenth century:

> ...You see how pretty and quiet a place
> it is; yet in the old times it had a pop-
> ulation of half a million. It was per-
> petually black with smoke; there were
> hundreds of vast factories where the men
> worked from six in the morning until six
> at night. Their houses were huts---dirty,
> crowded nests of fever; their sole amusements
> were to smoke tobacco and to drink beer
> and spirits; they died at thirty worn out;
> they were of sickly and stunted appearance;
> they were habitual wife-beaters; they
> neglected their children; they had no
> education, no religion, no hopes, no wishes
> for anything but plentiful pipe and beer.
> See it now! The population reduced to
> twenty thousand; the factories swept away;
> the machinery destroyed; the men working
> separately each in his own house, making
> cotton for home consumption. [16]

The spirit that motivated Besant in passages like these in All Sorts and Conditions of Men is the same as that which produced utopian novels of a more serious nature than those merely satirical.

Much more amusing than Besant's novel, is Anthony Trollope's The Fixed Period, a highly diverting satire on the numerous panaceas being offered by contemporary novelists for attaining a perfect society. Trollope proposes euthanasia---putting to death of all people when

---

(15) Besant, W., The Revolt of Man, (Edinburgh, 1882), 147.

(16) Besant, W., op. cit., 148.

they become 65---as the basis of his utopia. The story tells of one Neverbend, Governor of Britannulia, who with a group of young men and women emigrated from England to Britannulia in Australia, where they founded a republic based upon the principle that anyone who attained the age of 65 should be put to death after being "deposited" in a luxurious college for his last glorious year. The advantages of this as explained by Neverbend are as follows:

> We should save on an average 50 pounds for each man and woman who had departed. When our population should have become a million, presuming that one only in fifty would have reached the desired age, the sum actually saved to the colony would amount to 1,000,000 pounds a year. It would keep us out of debt, make for us our railways, render all our rivers navigable, construct our bridges, and leave us shortly the richest people in God's earth. [17]

All goes well until 1980, when Crasweller, the first man to reach 65, is "deposited" for his last year. A fury of opposition develops toward Neverbend, engendered because most of the people in the colonies are approaching the age of 65. Finally Neverbend is carried off on a British warship, still hoping that he will find someplace where he may try out his plan.

The last of these English utopias before the period dominated by Morris and Wells, is W.H. Hudson's <u>A Crystal Age</u> (1887), a work as idyllic and as charming as Morris'

---

(17) Trollope, A., <u>The Fixed Period</u>, (London, 1882), I, 8.

own lovely description of the future in <u>News from Nowhere</u>.
The society described has made considerable progress
toward perfection through a long process of natural
selection. Simplicity is the key to this new life---all
the burdensome complexities of "civilization" like cities,
money, machinery, and private ownership have been eliminated.
It is a world in which Thoreau would have found himself
very much at home. Hudson describes a sort of naturalist's
paradise inhabited by a people of strong bodies and healthy
minds. Sexual love has been eliminated in this world---
except in the case of certain individuals who are chosen
to carry out the propagation of the next generation.
Perhaps this is the most "impossible" of all the utopias
that we have considered, but its simplicity, its emphasis
on life's real values, make it one of the most memorable.

These, then, are the English utopian novels that
immediately preceded the work of Bellamy and Howells in
America, and of Morris and Wells in England. To search in
them for any sources of the later works is futile; to
seek any close connection between the English and American
utopists is time wasted. As will be shown in a later chapter,
the American utopian novels arose out of social and economic
factors in American history; they show little influence
of English works in which the satirical element is more
often predominant than that of constructive planning for
the future.

Several reasons may be offered for the absence of any wide utopian interest in England in the late nineteenth century to parallel that in America. Social ranks had stratified in England a century or more before this time; consequently by the late years of the nineteenth century, English writers saw no great social injustice in class distinctions to which they had long been accustomed, but which were for the first time making themselves apparent in America. Furthermore, industrialism had dominated English life from the early part of the century; the first effects were felt fully fifty years before this period, and Englishmen had somewhat adjusted themselves to this new way of life. In America industrialism did not swing into full stride until after the Civil war, and the process of social and industrial adjustment was consequently more acute. The older civilizations of Europe had been urbanized for generations, whereas, in America, this trend to the cities was a comparatively new phenomenon. The whole difference lay in the fact that the United States was suffering the growing pains which Englishmen had either grown accustomed to or had forgotten. Class tradition brought about by years of social and economic stratification had given the stamp of authority to social and economic arrangements. The difference is shown by one critic of America's Gilded Age:

> In a general way, of course, there
> was nothing new about the juxtaposition

> of mammon and poverty in American cities
> but there were features in the situation
> that distinguished it from the urban life
> of other civilizations. Especially striking
> was the fact that the masses in the great
> cities of the United States were not
> slaves of the submerged offspring of
> slaves; neither were they the descendants
> of twenty generations of urban starvelings.
> They were free men, a large portion of
> whom had wandered into the cities from
> the farms bearing with them the notions
> fitted to rural economy; others had come
> straight from the fields of Europe. Even
> the oldest of American cities were new by
> comparison with those of England or the
> Continent. They had no traditions of royal
> patronage, noblesse oblige, or princely
> aesthetics. The feudal nexus had been
> dissolved; the cash nexus substituted. (18)

Yet in a general way, despite the differences we have noted, both English and American novelists wrote from a feeling of social injustice, an awakening interest in the problems of society. The significance of the utopias of both nationalities lies in their being barometers of a growing discontent on both sides of the Atlantic, and in their presentation of the popular ideas of how economic and social problems might best be solved.

---

(18) Beard and Beard, The Rise of American Civilization, II (New York, 1930), 394.

ENGLISH UTOPIAS PRECEDING LOOKING BACKWARD

1859

Lang, Hermann, The Air Battle: A Vision of the Future.

1868

Helps, Sir Arthur, Realmah.

1871

Bikkers, A.V.W., (translator) Anno Domini 2071.

Chesney, Sir George Tomkyns, The Battle of Dorking.

Other books on the same subject:

> Anonymous, What Happened After the Battle of
>   Dorking; Being an Account of the Victory
>   at Tunbridge Wells.
> Anonymous, After the Battle of Dorking: or What
>   Became of the Invaders.
> Anonymous, The Battle of Dorking a Myth. England
>   Impregnable.
>
> Louis Tracy, The Final War.
> Tom Greer, A Modern Daedalus.

Lee, Henry Boyle (pseud. Theophilus McCrib), Kennaquhair.

Lytton, Bulwer, The Coming Race.

Mammoth Martinet (pseud.) H.R.H. alias Moho-yoho-me-oo-oo,
    Gorilla Origin of Man; or the Darwin Theory of
    Development confirmed from Travels in the New World
    Called Myn-me-ae-nia or Gossipland.

Maguire, John Francis, The Next Generation.

1872

Butler, Samuel, Erewhon.

Published Anonymously by (Charles Mackay, L.L.D.), Baron
    Grimbosh, Ph.D. and Sometime Governor of Barataria.
    A record of his Experiences Written by Himself in
    Exile, and Published by Authority.

1873

Jenkins, Edward, Little Hodge.

Lumley, Benjamin (pseud. "Hermes"), Another World; or Fragments from the Star City of Montalluyah.

Maitland, Edward, By and By, (published anonymously).

Smith, James, The Coming Man.

Whiting, Sydney, Heliondé.

1874

Blair, Andrew (Published anonymously), Annals of the Twenty-Ninth Century; or the Autobiography of the Tenth President of the World Republic.

1875

Anonymous, Etymonia.

Davis, Ellis J. (Published anonymously), Pyrna, A commune; or Under the Ice.

1876

Davis, Ellis J., Coralia; a Plaint of Futurity.

1877

Cobbe, Miss Frances Power (pseud. Merlin Nostradamus), The Age of Science. A Newspaper of the Twentieth Century.

Davis, Ellis J., In Front of the World.

Mallock, W.H., The New Republic.

1878

Wright, Henry, Mental Travels in Imagined Land.

1880

E.M.H., The Octagon Club; A Character Study.

Greg, Percy, Across the Zodiac.

1882

Besant, Walter, The Revolt of Man.

Trollope, Anthony, The Fixed Period.

--------------, The Dawn of the Twentieth Century.

1883

Anonymous, Politics and Life in Mars: A Story of a Neighboring Planet.

1884

The Socialist Revolution of 1888 by an Eye-Witness.

Maitland, Edward, How the World Came to an End in 1881.

1885

Greer, Tom, A Modern Daedalus.

Huder Genone (pseud.), Inquirendo Island.

Jefferies, Richard, After London.

Reade, Compton, Under Which King ?

1886

Burnaby, Fred, Our Radicals: a Tale of Love and Politics.

1887

Hudson, W.H., A Crystal Age.

1888

Besant, Walter, The Inner House.

Morris, William, The Dream of John Ball.

Whiteing, Richard, The Island, or Adventures of a Person of Quality.

CHAPTER III

CHARACTERISTICS OF EARLY UTOPIANISM IN AMERICA

The examination of English utopian novels of the
nineteenth century shows only that we must look elsewhere
for the roots of American utopias. One must go to
American social and economic forces if he is to find the
motivating force for so large a body of utopian writing.
The present chapter attempts to offer a brief account of
earlier utopian writings and to weigh the influence of
those writings on the novelists of the eighties and nineties.

The three decades before the Civil War had seen the
rise of numerous minor reform movements aiming at changing,
among other things, the dress, the food, the drink, and
the religion of the American people. Of major importance
were the abolition movement and the attempts at land reform.
Along with these reform forces, there developed a type of
utopianism, which was aimed not at one specific evil, but
was designed to offer a plan for the regeneration of humanity.
These ideas emanated from the writings of Fourier, Owen,
and Cabet, and found willing interpreters like Albert Brisbane in America. Their most tangible result was a large
number of idealistic communities [1] like the Owenite
Communities at New Harmony, Yellow Springs, Ohio, and Nashoba,

(1) For an excellent guide to the literature concerning
these communities see Raymond Adams, _A Booklist of
American Communities_, (Chapel Hill, N.C., 1935).

Tennesee; the Fourieristic Communities at Red Bank, N.J., known as The North American Phalanx, the Brook Farm group, and others in Wisconsin, New York, and Ohio; the Icarian Communities based on Cabet's Voyage in Icaria and located at Nauvoo, Illinois, Cheltenham, Missouri, and various other places. Although these Icarian communities were on American soil, they consisted mostly of Frenchmen and had little influence in this country. Finally there were the religious communities, comprising by far the largest number of colonists, like those of the Shakers and Zoarites in Ohio, the Amana Community in Iowa, and the Perfectionists at Oneida, N.Y., under John Humphrey Noyes.

By the time of the Civil War, most of the purely secular and social communities had foundered on the rocks of disharmony, lack of leadership, or general impracticability. The religious communities were notably more successful, but they are less important from our point of view because their settlements were not primarily established as object lessons for the rest of the world but as religious retreats for their members. At any rate, the Civil War acted as a "counter-reformation" and drew off most of the utopian or idealistic forces of that generation.

In view of this widespread idealism, it is essential that we examine in some detail the characteristics of this earlier movement in order to compare or contrast it with the utopists of the eighties and nineties.

The first difference that may be noted is that the

ideas of the forties and fifties derived largely from European sources, [2] whereas, as will be shown later, the later movement grew out of political, social, and economic conditions in America. To be sure, the ideas of Fourier and the others had found reflection in the writings of Emerson, Thoreau, and Alcott, but their source was European; America's chief contribution to this earlier movement lay in actually trying the ideas out.

> The three decades before the Civil War had seen the rise and fall of a form of Utopianism which in its prime had drawn into it a considerable number of the American people. Its inspiration was European, coming from the writings of men like Cabet and Fourier and from American interpreters like Brisbane in his "Social Destiny of Man". Its application was the contribution of the United States, where the vast extent of cheap public lands afforded conditions ideal for carrying out the foreign theories. [3]

As has been shown before, the United States in addition to its vast public land, offered great industrial and

---

(2) One exception to this derivation from European sources is pointed out by Professor F.T. Carlton in "An American Utopia" in The Quarterly Journal of Economics, (February, 1910), XXIV, 428-433. Professor Carlton mentions land reform as being a native American idea as expounded in the works of Lewis Masquerier, George Evans, and Horace Greeley. "The communistic schemes of Owen and Fourier were of European origin. The Utopia of Masquerier and Greeley was necessarily that of a frontier community living upon the soil in an independent fashion." (432).

(3) Forbes, Allyn B., "The Literary Quest for Utopia", Social Forces, VI, (December, 1927), 181.

agricultural opportunities along with religious freedom----
all of which were essential to the founding of communities.

Second, the earlier writers were ethical and moral in
their attitude toward man; the later writers were economic
in their interpretation. An examination of the ideas of
Fourier will show this fact. It was his belief that God
created the universe on a uniform and harmonious plan:
he endowed man with certain passions and instincts which
are useful; hence society ought to afford all its members
a full opportunity to gratify these passions. Fourier then
proceeds to an analysis of human passions and finds that
they break down into three general groups---the "five
sensitive passions", sight, hearing, smell, taste, and touch;
the "four affective passions", friendship, love, ambition,
paternity; the "three distributive or directing passions",
emulative, alternating, composite. All of these, argued
Fourier, impel man toward a collective tendency or universal
unity. The free play of these passions ought to lead to
the formation of groups---hence Fourier arranged his ideal
state with various units, called groups, series, and
Phalanxes. These last, being the very corner-stone of his
theory, are described by him in great detail. Consisting of
1800 or 2000 members, the Phalanx occupies a building
called the Palace; all members work on a cooperative plan
although all are not paid equally. The basic idea is that
everyone shall do the work for which he is best fitted.

Fourier was firm in his belief that once the first phalanx was established, others would follow in rapid succession until ultimately the whole world would be covered with them. Typical of his passion for detail and accuracy was his estimate that the world would hold exactly two million phalanxes. [4] Despite this detail, one must not lose sight of the fact that Fourier's ideas are at bottom, philosophic or moral rather than economic. His basic idea is the concept that man is naturally good, and the society which would let him express himself most fully is the best. As one critic has pointed out in connection with this earlier group of thinkers,

> One and all believed that with proper environment man would be actually perfect. He was naturally good, but existing en- 'vironment with its overwhelming imperfections and maladjustments destined him to evil and woe. Hence their utopianistic activities consisted mostly in educating man to a knowledge of this congenial environment and the devising of means to bring it to pass. As thinkers ahead of their time, they all saw the great value of education, and all with the ex- ception of Babeuf, gave universal and com- pulsory education a very significant place in their methodology. [5]

This difference between the moral and ethical analysis of the mid-century writers, and the economic motif lying behind the later group, can be seen very obviously in the development of American socialism which was an important

---

(4) For the best discussion of Fourierism, see Morris Hillquit's History of Socialism in the United States, (New York, 1906), 78-88.

(5) Hertzler, J.O., The History of Utopian Thought, (New York, 1923), 222.

phase of this whole idealistic trend:

> Socialism before 1850 was a humanitarian rather than a political or economic movement. The utopian socialists did not understand the new industrial system, and acted upon the general principle that the evils arising from it were "arbitrary deviations" from natural law due to the acts of the dominant powers in society. They believed, with the eighteenth century philosophers, that governments were made and unmade by the deliberate acts of men, as described by Rousseau in his Social Contract, and they therefore usually planned a form of society which would be free from the evils of the existing system and urge its adoption. Frequently, the plan was presented in the form of a description of an imaginary country with a government and manner of life free from the evils of the contemporary social organization. The Utopia of Sir Thomas More was the model for many of these reformers, and they hoped by a limited test of their plans in a small community to convert gradually the entire world to their proposed systems. Hence the utopian socialists frequently were responsible for the establishment of such communities as social experiment stations. In fact the principal concrete manifestations of this phase of socialism are to be found in a great number of communities that were undertaken both in Europe and the United States from 1820 to 1850, as the result of the activities of Robert Owen, Charles Fourier, Etienne Cabet, and other utopian socialists. [6]

The same difference is noted by the best historian of

socialism in America, Morris Hillquit:

> Utopian socialism was built on purely moral conceptions, and derived its inspiration from the teachings of Christ or other codes of ethics; its existence was equally justified in the eighteenth century

---

(6) Haynes, F.E., Social Politics in the United States, (New York, 1924), 22.

> as in the nineteenth, and in this country
> as on the old continent.
> Modern socialism, on the other hand,
> is primarily economic in character, and
> can not take root in any country before
> its social and industrial conditions have
> made it ripe for the movement. (7)

A third difference between the mid-century group of
American utopists and their successors in the eighties
and the nineties is to be seen in their method of procedure in attaining the millenium. As we have seen, the
community was the most concrete manifestation of the
idealism of the forties and fifties. These communities
existed to attain the isolation which their members
desired; to be sure, Fourier hoped and believed that his
ideas would spread from the original Phalanx until the
whole world would be organized according to his plans.
Owen felt much the same way:

> He confidently predicted that the truth of
> his principles and the blessings of communism
> would in the near future manifest themselves
> in the new colony, and spread "from Community
> to Community, from State to State, from
> Continent to Continent, finally overshadowing
> the whole earth, shedding light, fragrance
> and abundance, intelligence and happiness
> upon the sons of men," and with his character-
> istic enthusiasm and broadness he invited
> "the industrious and well-disposed of all
> nations" to come to New Harmony, as he re-
> christened the settlement. (8)

Despite all these confident hopes for the future, the
practical emphasis remained upon the single, isolated

---

(7) Hillquit, M., op. cit., 150.

(8) Hillquit, M., op. cit., 62.

community, whereas the later utopists never bothered with
so small a concept----their plans all show a whole world
reorganized as they wanted it to be. So limited a territory
as a single community would decidedly hamper their plans,
most of which hinged upon the idea of mutual cooperation
among the nations. In a word then, the later utopias are,
in general, world-wide; the earlier ones isolated----and
this isolation was the chief reason for their failure.

> The founders of all communities pro-
> ceeded on the theory that they could build
> up a little society of their own, eliminate
> from it all features of modern civilization
> which seemed objectionable to them, fashion
> it wholly after their own views of proper
> social relations, and isolate themselves from
> the surrounding world and its corrupting
> influences.
> But the times of the Robinson Crusoes,
> individual or social, have passed. The
> industrial development of the last centuries
> has created a great economic interdependence
> between man and man, and nation and nation,
> and has made humanity practically one organic
> body. In fact, all the marvelous achieve-
> ments of our present civilization are due
> to the conscious or unconscious cooperation
> of the workers in the field and mines, on
> the railroads and steamships, in the factories
> and laboratories the world over; the in-
> dividual member of society derives his power
> solely from participation in this great
> cooperative labor or its results, and no man
> or group of men can separate himself or
> themselves from it without relapsing into
> barbarism.
> This indivisibility of the social
> organism was the rock upon which all com-
> munistic experiments foundered. They could
> not possibly create a society all-sufficient
> in itself; they were forced into constant
> dealings with the outside world, and were
> subjected to the laws of the competitive
> system both as producers and consumers. Those
> of them who learned to swim with the stream,

> like the religious communities, adopted by
> degrees all features of competitive industry,
> and prospered, while those who remained
> true to their utopian ideal perished. [9]

A fourth point of difference in the utopian ideals
of the 1840's and the 1880's is a significant one. In the
earlier period there seems to have been little concept of
the power of applied science to relieve man's drudgery;
anyone who has read about Brook Farm, for instance, will
remember the way in which the menial tasks were allotted---
all of them to be done by hand labor. By the late period,
the utopists had devised a far simpler system. They had
already been introduced to the first rudimentary attempts
at electric lights, telephone, and telegraph---and these
served to launch the imaginations of these novelists on
the sea of the undreamed of comforts and luxuries that
applied science might bring to man. Consequently, all of
the later American utopias rest upon the fundamental idea
that science as man's slave would permit him numerous hours
of leisure, would do all the unpleasant work, and would
free him from drudgery. Hence it was, that these later
novelists in their imaginations "invented" devices like
the radio, the automobile, the airplane, long before those
things were actualities.

A fifth and final distinction lay in the form in which
the ideas were presented. A few of the earlier utopias are
in novel form, but the larger number are presented in the

---

(9) Hillquit, M., op. cit., 140-141

fashion of economic treatises. The growing popularity
of the novel in nineteenth century America is nowhere
better shown than in the almost universal acceptance
of that form as the best means of presentation for utopian
ideas in the 1880's and 1890's. After Looking Backward,
if a writer wanted his ideas to gain acceptance, he knew
that he must clothe them in some kind of story; Fourier,
Owen, and Brisbane had let their ideas carry their own
appeal.

To sum up then, there are five major differences
between the utopianism of the early group of writers whose
work gained attention in the United States prior to the
Civil War, and the novelists who wrote in the last two
decades of the nineteenth century. The work of the earlier
group derived from European sources, it was moral and
ethical in its attitude, its chief concept was isolation
as embodied in the community, it paid little attention to
the possibilities of science, and it was seldom clothed
in novel form. In view of all these things, one can hardly
see any dependence of Bellamy and his fellows upon the
earlier utopists popular in America.

CHAPTER IV

THE HISTORICAL BACKGROUND OF THE UTOPIAN NOVEL IN AMERICA,

1865--1900

The Civil War cut across the idealism of the 1840's
drawing off the forces of reform and concentrating them
upon the issues involved in the war.

> There was emerging in the forties a
> class of idealists and a spirit of social
> progress more promising even than those
> of other nations. This idealism was ex-
> hausted in the Civil War, and it needed
> another generation to come upon the scene
> and to learn anew the social problems which
> the intervening years had intensified. [1]

Not until a generation after the war did utopianism again
flourish in this country, but one must turn to the post-
bellum period in order to find the motivating forces of
the late nineteenth century utopian novels. In the political,
social, and economic trends of the 'seventies and
'eighties are the roots of the ideas of Bellamy and his
successors.

Charles Dudley Warner and Mark Twain aptly termed the
years following the Civil War the Gilded Age, and in their
superficial ostentation and their thinly veiled corruption,
those years justify the name all too well. The Gilded Age
saw industrialism beginning to swing into full stride,
bringing new social and economic problems; it saw the end

(1) Haynes, F.E., op. cit., 16.

of the frontier; new developments in science appeared; urbanization increased tremendously; almost every year from 1877 on was marked by clashes between capital and labor. These are the forces from which emerged the outburst of utopian novels of the last two decades of the nineteenth century---and in a detailed examination of these forces one finds that the utopian novel has a real significance, since it grew not alone out of men's dreams but out of reality too unpleasant to endure.

Chaos is the keynote of this whole era, extending from the uncertainty of the Reconstruction period to the dissatisfaction and unrest of the 'eighties and 'nineties. Professor Beard has aptly remarked that "the decades following the Civil War were characterized by economic anarchy---laissez faire with a vengeance." [2] Speaking of the latter years, Professor David R. Dewey says:

> The years from 1885 to 1897 cover a period of unsettlement. Action and re- action followed in quick succession. The period lacks definiteness either of purpose or of progress: there was no unanimity of opinion as to the facts of economic life or as to national policy. Old political platforms were not applicable to the new problems. Party politics became confused, and shrewd political leaders were at a loss which way to turn. The result was un- certainty, vacillation, and inconsistency..." [3]

The same unrest, uncertainty, and discontent is noted by

(2) Beard, C.A., Contemporary American History, (New York, 1915), 38.

(3) Dewey, D.R., National Problems, 1885-1897, (New York, 1907), 3.

other writers:

> The score of years between the panics
> of 1873 and 1893 marked an extremely pe-
> culiar period in American history. It was
> an epoch of great unrest and discontent.
> The panic of 1873 was followed by an extra-
> ordinary amount of unemployment, suffering
> and unrest. In the latter part of the
> seventies, many secret organizations of
> working men appeared. Labor difficulties
> culminated with the railway strikes of 1877. [4]

But let us proceed to an examination of some of the specific

causes producing this unrest, of which the utopian novel

is but one expression.

First, there was the growing distrust of labor toward

capital---a feeling of hostility between employer and

employee which broke loose in strikes. The gap between

employer and employee was widened by the increase of in-

dustrialism throughout this whole period. No longer

apparently could the industrialist and the laborer work

for common interests.

> In the old days both belonged to the
> craft guild and viewed matters either as
> workers or former workers, or as employers
> or prospective employers. Today each has
> his organization----to fight the other. It
> is a rare thing for the modern John Treat
> to labor alongside his employer, much less
> to woo and win his daughter. If his em-
> ployer is a corporation, the employer has
> no daughter. Even if he be an individual
> he is often a man of vast interests which
> he commits to the care of others, so that
> John Treat may not in his whole lifetime
> so much as set eyes upon him. Under such
> conditions there can be little community

---

(4) Carlton, F.T., Organized Labor in American History,
(New York, 1920), 36.

of interest or understanding. Instead
there is lack of sympathy and often down-
right hostility. (5)

One cause of this hostility was indubitably new machinery:

The invention of new and perfected
machinery reduced many skilled mechanics
to the ranks of common laborers, and de-
prived many more of work and wages permanently, or at least during the long and
tedious process of "readjustment". (6)

Another reason for the antagonism between capital
and labor lay in the very vastness of corporate enterprises, which gave the laborer no feeling of being a
vital part of the organization:

The employer in many industries no
longer came into personal touch with his
employees; and the old personal relations
no longer existed to soften and humanize
the treatment of his employees. (7)

To meet these conditions, laborers attempted solidarity
through the labor union, and the epoch is characterized by
the rise of the Knights of Labor and the decline because
"it became entangled in politics", (8) and the formation
of the American Federation of Labor. American Socialism,
as we conceive of it today, emerged out of these same
conditions:

---

(5) Haworth, P.L., _America in Ferment_, (Indianapolis,
    1915), 160.

(6) Hillquit, M., _op. cit._, 15.

(7) Carlton, F.T., _op. cit._, 35.

(8) Bogart, E.L., _Economic History of the American People_,
    (New York, 1930), 613

> The present socialist movement depends
> for its support upon the existence of a
> large class or working men divorced from
> the soil and other means of production,
> and permanently reduced to the ranks of
> wage labor. It also requires a system of
> industry developed to a point where it
> becomes onerous upon the working men,
> breeds dissatisfaction, and impels them
> to organized resistance. In other words,
> the movement presupposes the existence of
> the modern factory system in a high state
> of development, and all the social contrasts
> and economic struggles incidental to such
> a system. [9]

With the organization of the laboring class into unions,

came strikes which were increased and enhanced by factors

like immigration and unplanned production resulting in

the panics of 1873 and 1893. This unrest reached its

climax in the decade between 1880 and 1890:

> In no decade of our history has there
> been such wide-spread evidence of discontent.
> Not only did workmen in the mills, factories,
> and mines, and on the railways protest
> against the existing conditions of employ-
> ment, but there was profound disappointment
> and unrest on the part of the sections of
> society which lie between the artisan and
> the rich. Organized labor struck and boy-
> cotted; legislators passed factory laws
> and established boards of arbitration; men
> of property and intelligence, with gospel
> zeal, advocated the seizure by the state
> of economic rent; while others turned
> sympathetically to socialism as presented
> in the attractive guise of "nationalism". [10]

The years from 1884 to 1886 were particularly bad in this

respect.

Frequent railway strikes were a feature

---

(9) Hillquit, M., op. cit., 150.

(10) Dewey, D.R., op. cit., 40.

of the labor movement during the years
1884 to 1886. Some early successes of
the Knights of Labor in the conduct of
these struggles served as a powerful
advertisement of the organization. The
result was that strikes were declared and
the strikers joined the Knights after they
had struck. The almost unavoidable
outcome of such a method was a second
strike after a short interval in order
to protect the existence of the new union.
A strike on the Wabash Railway in August,
1885, was of this character. A lockout of
the members of the Knights of Labor, under
the guise of a reduction of forces compelled the general executive board to issue
an order which would have caused a general
strike affecting Jay Gould's Southwestern
railway system.

The outcome of the Gould strike of
1885, the exaggeration of the power of
the Knights by the press and the public,
and their success at Washington provided
the setting for the great labor upheaval
of 1886. This upheaval marked the appearance of a new class in the labor movement---
that of the unskilled. They felt that they
had found a champion who could curb the most
powerful capitalists in the country. Their
accumulated feelings of bitterness and resentment now caused a rush to organize
under the leadership of the Knights. The
rapid pace at which the order grew, the wave
of strikes, particularly sympathetic strikes,
the use of the boycott, the violence of
the movement----1886 was the year of the
Chicago anarchist outbreak---all were
evidences of the rise of a new class----the
unskilled worker. The outburst bore the
aspect of a social war. A frenzied hatred
of capital was shown in every important
strike. (11)

These strikes reached their culmination in violence and in

number in the years just prior to the flood of utopian novels,

---

(11) Haynes, F.E., op. cit., 92.

which in many cases were motivated by a desire to solve
this most perplexing of all labor difficulties:

> The number of establishments in which
> strikes occurred in 1886 was 10,053, or
> over four times as many as were affected
> in 1885. This number was not exceeded
> until 1900; and the number of employees
> thrown out of work in 1886 by strikes was
> not exceeded until 1894. The big strike
> on the Missouri Pacific system took place
> in 1886. The anarchist episode in Chicago,
> known as the Hay-market riot, occured in
> May of the same year. This is also the
> year of the Henry George campaign in New
> York City. In 1887, many "anti-poverty"
> societies were formed. (12)

That these conditions bulked large in the minds of Bellamy,
Howells, and the other utopists, goes without saying; each
one of their novels attempts some specific reform of labor
difficulties.

Closely connected with the marked hostility of capital
and labor, was the development of the huge corporations and
trusts;

> American genius and enterprise displayed
> itself not only in ceaseless activity, in-
> vention, and the rapid development of agencies
> of transportation, but also in forms of
> commercial organization. After the depression
> of 1873, corporations began to take the place
> of individual or partnership undertakings.
> The size of the industrial establishment
> was enlarged, and in many instances an increased
> output was made by a smaller number of mills
> and factories. In 1880 there were 1990
> wollen-mills; in 1890 but 1311; the number
> of iron and steel mills decreased by a third,
> but yielded a product one-half greater. The
> number of establishments engaged in the
> manufacture of agricultural implements fell
> from 1943 in 1880, to 910 in 1890, although

---

(12) Carlton, F.T., op. cit., 38.

the capital was more than doubled. (13)

That these gigantic organizations brought on class hatred and social unrest, is obvious:

>The tendency toward concentration of industry had never before been so marked. "Not less than $500,000,000 is in the coal combination," reported Lloyd in 1894, "that in oil has nearly, if not quite, $200,000,000 and the other combinations in which its members are leaders foot up hundreds of millions more. Hundreds of millions of dollars are united in the railroads and elevators of the Northwest against the wheat-growers. In cattle and meat there are not less than $100,000,000; in whisky $35,000,000, and in beer a great deal more than that; in sugar, $75,000,000; in leather, over $100,000,000; in gas, hundreds of millions....There are in round numbers $10,000,000,000 claiming dividends and interest in the railroads of the United States. Every year they are more closely pooled."
>
>These immense combinations of capital had the effect of uniting vast armies of labor in each of the lines of industry mentioned. The gigantic trusts called forth formidable trade-unions. The class lines were drawn more distinctly, and the class struggles grew more embittered and assumed larger proportions. Hardly a year passed without witnessing one or more powerful contests between capital and labor. (14)

The effect of this type of business organization was above all else to increase competition; social ideals were sacrificed to the driving urge for profits, and both the small producer and the laborer suffered in the process:

>The eighties were years of great industrial

---

(13) Dewey, D.R., op. cit., 188.

(14) Hillquit, M., op. cit., 307.

development. The number of wage earners
engaged in manufacture increased from
nearly two and three-fourths in 1880
to four and one-fourth millions in 1890,--
an increase of about fifty-five per cent.
in ten years. The railway mileage of the
United States expanded from 93,296 in
1880 to 163,579 in 1890,---an increase
of over seventy-five per cent. in one
decade. This was the era of "tooth and
claw" competition. The trust appeared on
the scene; and the small business was engaged in fighting for its life,---and
losing on many industrial fields. Independent industries and proprietors were
being ruthlessly crushed in order that a
comparatively small number of big bus-
inesses might survive and flourish; and
in the process the employee inevitably
suffered. (15)

This intense and often reckless competition caused

over-production and waste; the evils of industrial war-

fare were intensified; popular indignation was aroused

against big business as more and more of its unscrupulous

and ruthless methods became known in the investigations

of trusts like the Standard Oil Company, the American

Cotton Oil Trust, and the Distillers' and Cattle Feeders'

Trust. Popular judgement took an ethical view toward such

practises.

This tendency to regard economic
phenomena as moral problems was heightened
by the early disclosures of business
practices by railroads such as the Erie
or by "trusts" such as the Standard Oil.
Although there were few codes of ethics
by which to judge such behavior, it offended
common decency and fairness. The opposition
to big business had, therefore, the spirit and

---

(15) Carlton, F.T., op. cit., 34.

fervor of a crusade. But it had no
thorough and logical dogma. In Europe
socialism, Marxian and otherwise, arose
to supply a formula of explanation and
policy. In this country a few might adopt
these European beliefs, and others, like
Henry George, might forge a consistent
philosophy of their own. But on the whole
the American crusade was opportunistic.
It dealt with single abuses as they appeared.
Such an outcome was not surprising. For
the American crusaders generally owned
property which they did not want threatened
by radical theories. (16)

Out of such an attitude, one can easily see how the fervid
reform of the utopian novelist developed. The whole social
theory of men like Bellamy rested upon the assumption that
the trusts should be carried through to their logical
conclusion---until there was just one trust, the government,
which controlled all organs of production and distribution.
This method theoretically eliminated the competition of
privately owned big business and offered a planned economy
which was supposed to end panics and unemployment---in other
words, it did away with all of the elements in the social
and economic organization which were regarded by the late
nineteenth century thinkers as undesirable.

Closely connected with this ethical attitude toward
big business was the popular opinion of the men who ran
it. The contrast between the few men who possessed large
fortunes and laboring classes who barely existed was all

(16) Kirkland, E.C., A History of American Economic Life,
(New York, 1932), 613.

too obvious. With America more and more committed to industrialism, there came a general belief that the cards were stacked in favor of a few. While the United States might still seem to offer opportunity, it was no longer an opportunity equal to all.

> "Born an employee, die an employee" has become the general rule in a great number of industries. Occasionally, to be sure, a workingman does make the passage to the employer class, but where one succeeds, a thousand fail. (17)

The difference between the America before the Civil War and that after the war in this respect is described by one of our economic historians:

> The growth of the industrial state was sure to create perplexity and a formless discontent. The old America was passing away. It had been an equalitarian America, where rich men were neither numerous nor often millionaires, and where the open frontier had directly brought about in the west an approach to an equality of economic conditions and, through its opportunities of escape, indirectly guided the east in the same direction. Now there was an America where the frontier was passing, and where men were amassing great fortunes in transportation, marketing, manufacturing, and banking. The sheer novelty of these changes stimulated diverse action. On the one hand, attempts were made to preserve the old days by prolonging the era of the frontier. Indian reservations were opened to settlement, the lavish granting of land to the railroads stopped, and in the first decade of the twentieth century this nostalgia for the old America was transmuted into the reclamation and

---

(17) Haworth, P.L., _America in Ferment_, (Indianapolis, 1915), 159

> conservation policies of the Roosevelt
> adminstrations. At the same time the
> great fortunes which were "widening the
> gulf between Dives and Lazarus" were
> subjected to scrutiny. Their novelty
> aroused the suspicion that they were
> somehow unrighteous. (18)

Here was indeed a subject that could be brought home to
the masses in dramatic terms---the contrast of the "bloated
millionaire" with the workingman who lived in abject poverty.
"To the earlier dissatisfaction with the money system, the
tools of exchange, and the instrument for measuring values,
was now added dissatisfaction far deeper, extending to a
demand for a different division of wealth." (19) The
socialists saw in this their great appeal to the workingmen--
"a new era was introduced in the national life of America---
the era of multimillionaires and money-kings, of unprecedented luxury and splendor, but also the era of abject
poverty and dire distress." (20) As Professor Parrington
says, many people were coming to feel that,

> Something was wrong with a progress that
> augmented poverty as it increased wealth,
> and with the alarmist cry in their ears--
> the rich are growing richer and the poor
> poorer--the untutored democracy of the
> seventies and the eighties turned to question
> the drift of tendency that quite evidently
> was transforming a democratic people into
> a vast engulfing plutocracy. An older
> agrarian America was confronted by a
> younger capitalistic one, and the conflict

---

(18) Kirkland, E.C., op. cit., 613.

(19) Dewey, D.R., op. cit., 41.

(20) Hillquit, M., op. cit., 152.

of ideals and purposes was certain to bring
on a bitter debate. (21)

The novelists likewise saw in this unequal distribution
of wealth the source of all evil; they presented vivid
pictures of the few living in luxury at the expense of
the many, and they described their utopias in which all
men were absolutely equal with respect to ownership of
private property. Many and ingenious were their plans
for curing this distressing state of affairs.

Industrialism brought with it, as always, a great
increase in urbanization. The extent of this trend to
the cities may be seen in the following statistics:

> The growth of municipalities continued
> unabated; the number of cities with eight
> thousand or more inhabitants nearly doubled
> between 1880 and 1900. In 1880 the urban
> population constituted less than a quarter
> (22.6 per cent) of the total population;
> by 1890 it had increased to nearly thirty
> percent of the total, and by 1900 to a
> full third. In the North Atlantic division
> of states, covering New England, New York,
> New Jersey, and Pennsylvania, the city
> growth was even more marked, embracing in
> 1890 more than half of the population. (22)

The result of this was that large sections of our population lived in conditions of squalor and congestion. "At
the same time, the flow of working men to the industrial
centers caused a congestion of population in some cases
comparable only to that of China; slums and tenement-houses

---

(21) Parrington, V.L., The Beginnings of Critical Realism
in America, (New York, 1930), 257.

(22) Dewey, D.R., op. cit., 12.

became as much a feature of our principal cities as their magnificent avenues and mansions." [23] Unchecked immigration aggravated these conditions. "Between 1880 and the beginning of the new century, twenty-six million people were added to the population or more than the entire number of inhabitants in 1850." [24] Naturally, most of these newcomers were members of the laboring class, so that the proportion of that group to our total population was constantly increasing. "In 1860 there were about one and a third million wage earners in the United States; in 1870 well over two million; in 1880 nearly two and three-quarters million; and in 1890 over four and a quarter million. The city sucked them in from the country; but by far the larger augmentation came from Europe; and the immigrant, normally optimistic, often untaught, sometimes sullen and filled with destructive resentment, and always accustomed to low standards of living, added to the armies of labor his vast and complex bulk." [25] Thus there existed a growing audience willing to listen to any fantastic idea that might improve their lot. What better way to reach these masses than through the attractive picture of a better life framed in an exciting story?

_____

(23) Hillquit, M., op. cit., 152.

(24) Dewey, D.R., op. cit., 4.

(25) Orth, S.P., The Armies of Labor, (New Haven, 1921), 69.

The year 1890 marked the end of the frontier, according to the reports of the United States Census Bureau. This fact is of the utmost significance, for the frontier had always acted as a "safety-valve" to carry off unrest. Those who were discontented with their lot could find actual escape from it by moving to the free public lands in the West. The unprecedented increase in our population had exhausted the public domain at a much earlier date than anyone could have predicted. Land became an object for commerce and speculation instead of something to be had for the asking from an endlessly generous government. Thus the end of the frontier eliminated the one solvent that might have lessened the discontent engendered by the competition, the unequal distribution of wealth, and the unpleasant life in cities. But it did more than that.

We have seen that earlier utopian ideas developed around the community, whose very existence depended upon a large body of unsettled land to which a group could go to put into application their ideas of an ideal society. Thus earlier utopian ideas had been "practical" in the sense that they were intended for application. With the end of desirable public lands, this outlet was exhausted. Hence, this "applied Utopianism" vanished, and the last two decades of the nineteenth century saw the birth of literary utopianism. When men could no longer transform their dreams into actualities, they committed them to paper in the form of utopian visions. There is more than concidence in the fact that the same years that marked the end of the frontier, saw the highest point in the development of the utopian novel in America.

A similar situation existed with regard to the major political parties of the period. Had they offered any real outlet for the zeal of idealists, there would have been little occasion for the individual to offer his own "political platform" in a utopian novel.

> For a long time an increasing number of voters had been growing dissatisfied with conditions in both the old parties. They were tired of the persistent stand-pat conservatism of certain leaders of the one, and distrustful of the talents and tenets of leaders of the other. They believed that neither party had shown a consistent determination to deal with the vital problems confronting the country, and they feared that no progress could be made by either party so long as it contained a powerful reactionary wing seemingly capable of blocking any real forward movement. They realized that old issues were dead or dying. They were beginning to regard party names as mere hobby-horses on which politicans rode into office. They had come to believe that there existed an "invisible government" exercising a sinister influence in behalf of a favored few against the interests of the many. Repeated questionable circumstances had led them to surmise that not infrequently ostensible party enemies were in reality secretly allied in a "bipartizan combine" whose influence was inimical to real popular government. (26)

That there was little real difference between the Republican and Democratic parties in the twenty years prior to the campaign of 1896, is evidenced by the mushroom growth of

-----

(26) Haworth, P.L., op. cit., 370.

third parties, each intended to present the desires of some section of the populace which found no expression in the two major parties.

> The accumulation of vast fortunes, many of which were gained either by fraudulent manipulations, or shady transactions within the limits of the law but condemned by elementary morals, and the massing of the proletariat in the great industrial cities were bound in the long run to bring forth political cleavage as deep as the corresponding social cleavage. The domination of the Federal government by the captains of machinery and capital was destined to draw out a counter movement on the part of the small farmers, the middle class, and the laborers. [27]

The Populist Revolt of 1892 is only one of many such attempts.

Another factor which ought not to be forgotten, is the rapidity with which all of these changes in our social, economic, and political structure came about. Science was making rapid changes in our industrial and social life; within the decade from 1875 to 1885, four important inventions were put into practical operation----Bell's telephone, the Brush arc light, Edison's incandescent lamp, and Edison's electric street car. All of these affected the everyday life of man. The nation in 1900 was changed far beyond the most fantastic dreams of anyone in 1850:

> In 1850 the population of the United States was but little over 23,000,000; half a century later it rose to over 75,000,000. In 1850 the wealth of the

---

(27) Beard, C.A., Contemporary American History, (New York, 1915), 143.

> country amounted to little over
> $7,000,000,000, and was pretty evenly
> distributed among the population; in 1890
> the "national wealth" exceeded
> $65,000,000,000, and more than one-half
> of it was concentrated in the hands of
> but 40,000 families, or one-third of one
> percent of the population. In 1850
> fifty-five percent of the wealth of the
> United States consisted of farms; in
> 1890 the farms made up less than twenty-
> four percent of the wealth of the country.
> In 1860 the entire capital invested in
> industries in the United States was little
> over $1,000,000,000; in the space of the
> following thirty years it had increased
> more than sixfold. (28)

This transition from an agricultural to an industrial era

occurred with bewildering speed. The distribution of the

nation's goods produced in this machine era might well seem

to the common man to be unjust---hence the way was prepared

for some prophet to offer his plan for the future. And

because of the very fact that so many changes had taken

place in a half century, no dream of what might occur in

the future could be considered as absolutely fantastic.

Who in 1850 would have believed a novelist that prophesied

the actual conditions of 1890? Was it correct to assume

that Bellamy's picture of life in 2000 A.D. was absurd,

when one considered the changes that had taken place in an

equal period of years from 1776 to 1887? Thus it was that

the very existence of rapid change in the late nineteenth

century made the accounts of the novelists at least plausible.

(28) Hillquit, M., op. cit., 152.

and by many readers they were assumed to be true.

In addition to this speculation about science, the time was ripe for economic theories, and both self-appointed amateurs and professional economists took advantage of the opportunity. So many changes had occurred in so short a period that economic and political theories had not had time to coalesce into formal laws with the weight of tradition behind them. As Professor Parrington says,

> There was much speculation on the disturbing phenomena of the great change, and current economic theory was slow to settle into the conformities of a school. It divided sharply, not only between the advocates of capitalism and agrarianism, but between those who accepted the classical English theory and those who believed that economic conditions in America warranted an independent American school. The first group of professional economists--Henry C. Carey, Francis A. Walker, David A. Wells--made its appearance, and a very considerable group of amateurs--free-lance economists and fireside theorists--contributed to the speculation of the times in the measure of their intelligence. These latter have received scant attention, since the battle went against them; nevertheless they do not deserve to be forgotten, for most often they were an expression of the social conscience of the times--a homely protest against the exploitation of farmer and workingman by the rising capitalism. [29]

Among these "free-lance economists and fireside theorists," the writers of utopian novels played a large part, and by virtue of their stories succeeded in reaching a larger

---

[29] Parrington, V.L., The Beginnings of Critical Realism in America, (New York, 1930), 103.

audience than most of the other theorists.

Here then are all the forces out of which rose the utopian novel---the growth of big business, the cut-throat competition, the unequal distribution of wealth, the hostility of capital and labor, the crowded life in cities with escape to the West no longer possible, and the failure of the major political parties to supply a medium for the expression of idealism. The connection between the novels and these social forces is definitely shown by the dates of publication of the former. Beginning in the late 1880's and coming to a climax in the early years of the nineties, these novels appeared at the time when economic distress and social injustices were being most keenly felt by the mass of the people. Considered from this point of view, Edward Bellamy's Looking Backward (1888) was one of the most opportune novels ever published in America, deserving to rank in this respect with Uncle Tom's Cabin and Ramona.

Just as the Civil War had drawn off into other channels the reform forces of an earlier generation, so in the late eighties and early nineties there were set in motion a series of events that acted as a "counter-reformation" --- that is, events which either reformed rank abuses or gave reformers a practical outlet for their zeal. Some of the earliest attempts at conciliation of the reform groups by legislation are to be seen in the Interstate Commerce Act of 1887, the law of 1888 providing for the voluntary ar-

bitration of railway labor disputes, the Sherman Anti-
Trust Act of 1890, and the Income Tax Law of 1894. By
the turn of the century, this counter-reformation was in
full swing; as a result the utopian novelist found much
of his material useless.

> Just as the Protestant Revolt during
> the sixteenth century was followed by a
> counter-reformation in the Catholic Church
> which swept away many abuses, while re-
> taining and fortifying the essential prin-
> ciples of the faith, so the widespread and
> radical discontent of the working classes
> with the capitalist system hitherto
> obtaining produced   a counter-reformation
> on the part of those who wished to pre-
> serve its essentials while curtailing some
> of its excesses. (30)

In preparing the way for these reform forces, the utopian
novel had accomplished much by educating the popular mind
to the possibilities of an ideal social system.

The spectacular campaign of Bryan in 1896 gave an
outlet for the reform forces. To many, it seemed as if
another young Lochinvar had come riding out of the West,
this time to champion the cause of human rights against
the encroachments of special privilege and capitalistic
greed. Professor Beard sees in this first Bryan campaign
a definite struggle of class against class.

> It does not require historical perspective,
> which is supposed to be necessary for final
> judgements, to warrant the assertion that
> the campaign of 1896 marks a turning point
> in the course of American politics. The
> monetary issue, on which events ostensibly

---

(30) Beard, C.A., op. cit., 303.

> revolved, was, it is true, an ancient one,
> but the real conflict was not over the
> remonetization of silver or the gold stan-
> dard. Deep, underlying class feeling found
> its expression in the conventions of both
> parties, and particularly that of the
> Democrats, and forced upon the attention
> of the country, in a dramatic manner, a
> conflict between great wealth and the lower
> middle and working classes, which had hither-
> to been recognized only in obscure circles.
> The sectional or vertical cleavage in
> American politics was definitely cut by
> new lines running horizontally through society. (31)

Much more important than any of these factors, however,
was the economic recovery that followed the depression of
1893. That year saw the worst of the panic. The Spanish
American War played its part in diverting popular attention
from domestic affairs. With the approach of the new century
came better times, higher prices and wages. The effect was
to pacify both industrial and agricultural laborers.

> With the defeat of the Democratic party
> in the spectacular campaign of 1896, and the
> beginning of the long era of rising prices,
> the discontent of the farmers became less
> and less acute. Restless and radical Kansas,
> for example, was gradually transformed into
> prosperous and contented Kansas; and the
> epoch of greenback and populist agitation
> drew to a close. As the end of the century
> approached came an extraordinary period of
> gigantic business combinations. (32)

As prosperity returned, the utopias became fewer and the end
of the movement is marked by the end of the century. The
next phase, which need not concern us here, is the muck-raking

---

(31) Beard, C.A., *op*. *cit*., 164.

(32) Carlton, F.T., *op*. *cit*., 40.

of the early years of the twentieth century---a reform
movement which offered plenty of realism in contrast to
the romantic dreams of the utopists.

The factors discussed in this chapter show above all
that the American utopias were opportunist. Seizing upon
some one evil, the utopist wrote his novel to demonstrate
how some one flaw could be eliminated from the social
structure; in doing this, he apparently believed that he
had indicated the only way to a perfect commonwealth.

CHAPTER V

AMERICAN PREDECESSORS OF BELLAMY

Edward Bellamy had few American predecessors in depicting a complete new society of the future. A few
scattered novels present one phase or another of the future;
others offer a satire on various social and economic trends;
and in the decades after the Civil War, the number of
stories dealing with contemporary social problems increases
definitely---but these three phases of the utopian novel
were seldom offered in the same work. Yet a gradual
evolution in this type of fiction can be traced, although
the chain is by no means complete.

In 1868, The Philosophers of Foufouville by "Radical
Freelance" appeared. This, the first novel of the post-
war period that may be remotely considered as "utopian",
is a satire upon communities based upon Fourieristic
principles. This type of satirical utopia has been rather
rare in America. Actually The Philosophers of Foufouville
offers no constructive criticism and its satire on idealistic
communities is both vague and fatuous; it has little or
no significance in the development of the utopian novel
in America. In 1869, Edward Everett Hale published Sybaris
under the pseudonym of Col. Frederic Ingham. The book
was a collection of several shorter pieces that had appeared
earlier in the Atlantic Monthly. Sybaris is a vague sort
of utopia describing the visit of a Colonel Ingham to the

land of Sybaris where life is ideal, but the organization
of the whole thing is described only in generalities.
Typical of Hale's method is the following excerpt:

> They have here but few very large
> fortunes transmitted from father to son.
> They have no such transmissions by will....
> Then they give every man and woman who is
> over sixty-five a small pension,---enough
> to save anybody from absolute want. [1]

In the years following the Civil War, speculation about
the future had a completely religious cast. The interest
was not in man's future life in earthly society, but in
describing what his future in heaven would be. This grew
naturally out of the Civil War which had brought personal
losses to many and had turned their thoughts to speculation
about the hereafter. Of the novels catering to this rather
morbid interest, Elizabeth Stuart Phelps's The Gates Ajar
(1869) was one of the most popular and may be taken as
typical of the whole class. The Gates Ajar describes the
sufferings of a young girl who finds all her religious
beliefs swept away by the intense disillusionment resulting
from her brother's death. To alleviate this sad state of
affairs, Miss Phelps offers a rather surprising remedy. The
reason why people sorrow without hope and why their faith
slackens is that the external life is not painted in
sufficiently attractive colors. Hence, someone ought to
present a more attractive picture of heaven than had hither-

---

(1) Hale, E.E., Sybaris, in Hale's Complete Works,
    (Boston, 1900), IX, 69.

to been given, and The Gates Ajar is the novel that attempts
this. The novel offered great consolation to the wives
and mothers of men killed in the war. "Appearing soon after
the Civil War, when many were mourning relatives, the book
leapt into popularity." (2) In the years following, other
works of the same nature appeared---among them William H.
Holcombe's In Both Worlds (1870), the anonymous Lifting
The Veil (1870) and others. A critic in The Nation
analyzed the reason for the success of this type of fiction
in one of his reviews:

> They give comfort to the bereaved, we are
> told, and we are not going to deny it; but
> their principal object appears to be the
> throwing of sops to a morbid and illegitimate
> curiosity....There is always likely to
> remain that hungry crowd of inquisitive and
> curious readers who make the production of
> books like this...a very profitable occupation. (3)

That the popularity of these novels endured for some time
is shown by the fact that Elizabeth Phelps wrote a sequel
to The Gates Ajar as late as 1883. This novel, entitled
Beyond The Gates, describes the community of heaven in the
following terms:

> In this new community to which I had been
> brought, that old effect [loneliness] was
> replaced by a delightful change. I per-
> ceived, indeed, great intentness of purpose
> here, as in all thickly-settled regions; the
> countenances that passed me indicated close

---

(2) Baker, E.A. and Packman, J., A Guide to the Best
    Fiction, (New York, 1932), 383.

(3) The Nation, X, (Feb. 10, 1870), 94.

conservation of social force and economy of
intellectual energy; these were people
trained by attrition with many influences,
and balanced with the conflict of various
interests. But these were men and women,
busy without hurry, efficacious without
waste; they had ambition without un-
scrupulousness, power without tyranny,
success without vanity, care without
anxiety, effort without exhaustion....(4)

This excerpt shows how remote from all practical social

problems these fictionized religious utopias were.

The application of religious ideals to earthly problems

was the next step in the evolution and is obviously closer

to the utopian novel than the descriptions of heaven had

been. Earliest and most prominent of this type was Ten

Times One is Ten; the Possible Reformation (1870) which

Reverend Edwin Everett Hale wrote under the pseudonym of

"Colonel Frederic Ingham". This is a utopian sketch of

the effect which might be produced on mankind by the

widening influence of a single good life. Harry Wadsworth,

the hero of the book, is a young freight agent of manly

and helpful character. He dies, and at his funeral ten of

the people whom he has been able to teach and cheer, form

themselves into a society to perpetuate Wadsworth's memory

and accomplish his work. They agree to preserve his motto----

"To look up, and not down;

To look forward, and not back;

---

(4) Phelps, E.S., Beyond the Gates, (Boston, 1883), 119.

To look out and not in;

And

To lend a hand."

Each of the original ten, pledges himself to get ten other members, and the movement grows in this way until in 1882 the whole world is converted to Wadsworth's ideas and becomes utopia indeed. After the publication of Ten Times One is Ten, Lend A Hand Societies were organized in connection with Y.M.C.A.'s; curiously enough, the same method of getting converts to Bellamy's ideas is now being utilized by Bellamy Societies throughout the world. As to the practicability of these ideas, one can only say with a reviewer in The Nation: "The methods by which these reforms are brought about are most comically possible and most pathetically improbable, and the reader is left sighing in vain over the rose-colored vision." [5] Yet, at least, Ten Times One concerns itself with a terrestial rather than a heavenly paradise and with social rather than spiritual problems.

In the eighteen seventies, novelists began using their medium for advocacy of various reforms. The Nation noticing this tendency, remarked:

> Even the socialist has so far bowed
> down to custom that he has joined the
> abolitionist and the woman's right ad-
> vocate and the temperance-preacher, and
> in fact most other people with hobbies,

---

(5) The Nation, XI, (November 17, 1870), 335.

and written a novel in support of his views.
The inflationist will be the next to come,
we suppose. (6)

One of the earliest of these novels of purpose was Ca Ira

by William Dugas Trammell, an obscure writer of Waverly

Hall, Georgia. Although it is not cast in the form of a

utopian novel, Ca Ira indicates a definite trend toward

the form and the ideas of the later utopists. It tells of

the adventures of a young southerner who goes to France,

gets involved in a revolution there, and then returns to

the United States. The plot is chaotic and almost im-

possible to follow, but in its prophecies of the future

greatness of America and the ardent sympathy with the cause

of labor, Ca Ira indicates a trend toward utopianism. The

novel is dedicated "To the Workingmen and to the memory of

all who have ever suffered in their cause, hoping that the

energies of the living, and the inspiration of the dead,

may unite to peacefully accomplish that Great Revolution

to which all Humanitarians must look with the greatest

concern, The Emancipation of Labor." In its prophecies of

an International Association of all men of all nations in

a condition of equality, Ca Ira is definitely a forerunner

of the ideas of later utopias:

> We look forward to the Universal Re-
> public, which, indeed, seems a dream of
> enthusiasm and worthy to be laughed at only
> to tyrants and their either ignorant or
> designing abettors. Under the Universal

---

(6) The Nation, XIX, (July 2, 1874), 9.

Republic wars shall cease; love of country
shall give place to love of Humanity;
imaginary State lines shall not be
sufficient to make people enemies; all
shall acknowledge the whole human family
to be a Common Brotherhood, having
common interests, a common sympathy in a
common struggle, a common glory, and a
common destiny. This is the ultimate
aim of the International Association,
with which the Commune was certainly in
the warmest sympathy. That the International Association will finally succeed
in its mission, I will not suffer myself to
doubt for an instant. The time will surely
come when all the world shall unite to
raise a monument to its founders. (7)

Ca Ira takes exactly the same point of view that Bellamy

and others were later to manifest in its attempt to show

unequal distribution of wealth as the root of all evil:

Let some prophet rise up and say to
the people, and let them be taught to
understand and obey him: "The world has
plenty, and to spare. Behold on every side
enough for the whole human race! But on
every side the people dies of hunger and
wretchedness! By an unjust system, all
comforts, and all luxuries, have been given
to one-tenth of the human race. They cannot
consume the comforts. The luxuries waste
before their eyes! And yet there is enough
for all! Enough, and to spare! Let the
people rise up and crush the system which
oppresses it and reduces it to despair.
The people starves! And yet it dare not
reach forth its hand for the bread that
rots within its grasp! Down with the system!
Let property be universalized." And this
is precisely what will be done, sooner or
later. (8)

Here we have the novelist donning the prophet's mantle and

---

(7) Trammell, W.D., Ca Ira, (New York, 1874), 265.

(8) Trammell, W.D., op. cit., 285.

pointing the way to a better future. Ca Ira marks a
definite step along the pathway to utopianism in America.

Literary critics of the period were blind to the
growing tendency to use the novel as a medium for presenting
social and economic problems. An editorial in The Nation
of March 1, 1883 deplores "the decline of the novel of
'purpose', i.e., the novel which aims at effecting the
reformation of some wrong or injustice...Neither in England
nor in America does any novelist of the first rank attempt
to use the novel as a means of reform in public opinion,
of stirring up enthusiasm or indignation on social subjects.
..." (9) The editorial writer then goes on to give his
reasons for this "ignoring" of the novel of purpose here
and in England:

> One [reason] is that the subjects in
> this generation which interest persons of
> a reforming turn of mind are subjects which
> hardly lend themselves to fiction...There
> is no tyrannical social system to which the
> novel reader can attribute abuses. The
> questions which have arisen in this country,
> while of equal importance, are not of the
> same value for purposes of fiction with
> those of an earlier day. You can fill a
> reader's mind with indignation at slavery,
> but it is difficult to imagine a novelist
> basing a successful story on the evils of
> the protective system as illustrated by the
> duty on steel blooms. Civil service reform,
> biennial legislatures, the fee and salary
> question, codification, copyright, seats in
> the House for cabinet ministers---all these
> are important matters, but they are trouble-
> some to use in fiction. (10)

---

(9) The Nation, XXXVI, (March 1, 1883), 185.

(10) Ibid., 185.

Yet Bellamy, Howells, Besant, Morris, Wells, and others were soon to find in these and allied subjects, material for fiction that won popular acclaim however "troublesome". To them there seemed indeed to be a tyrannical social system which the novelist could use. The writer then goes smugly on to give as his final reason for the decline of purpose, the complete freedom of the press which seemed to him to offer a ready outlet for any reformer:

> Besides all this, the ventilation the press now gives all abuses, as a matter of business, helps to take the wind out of the sails of the novelist of "purpose". Fifty years ago the press was itself much more closely connected with the class which was interested in the perpetuation of abuses than it is now. It kept silent or threw cold water upon reform schemes. Now it is the reformers' regular means of agitation, and he must be a very feeble agitator who cannot get a hearing through it. It furnishes to reformers a more immediate and certain vehicle than the novel. [11]

The next seventeen years were to show the fatuousness of this view.

In the same year that this short-sighted editorial appeared, there was published the first complete utopian novel of the period, The Diothas, or A Look Far Ahead (1883) by "Ismar Thiusen". The novel was written by Professor John Machie, Professor of Mathematics in the University of North Dakota, but he never acknowledged it as his production---perhaps because of disparaging reviews.

---

(11) Ibid., 185.

> So well did Professor Macnie guard
> his authorship of this book that it was
> never generally known. A copy of the
> book was secured by the Library of Congress
> soon after its publication. In accordance
> with the cataloging procedure of that
> library it made inquiry, through the
> publisher, as to the true name of the
> author. This request was forwarded to
> Professor Macnie by Putnams but was
> returned with the penned notation, "The
> author is not willing to give real name at
> present, even to the publisher," signed
> I.T., the pseudonym initials. (12)

Despite the fact that the novel "went through two editions

in this country and sold 150,000 copies in England", (13)

it has been completely ignored by critics and is now very

obscure. The Diothas is of some importance because it is

a possible antecedent of Bellamy's Looking Backward, a fact

which will be discussed more definitely in a later chapter,

but which even the following brief summary will indicate.

The Diothas is the account of one Ismar Thiusen who

is projected from the nineteenth century into the ninety-

sixth century by means of a mesmeric dream. He finds himself

in New York City in a world which has changed radically,

but in every respect for the best. A conventional love

story runs through the book, Ismar Thiusen having fallen

in love with Reva Diotha, who is the reincarnation of his

nineteenth century sweetheart, Edith Alston. The novel ends

---

(12) Carlson, W.A. "Professor Macnie as a Novelist" in
The Alumni Review of The University of North Dakota,
(December, 1934), 4.

(13) Carlson, W.A., op. cit., 4.

on a sensational note when the two lovers plunge over
Niagara Falls in a boat, and the hero wakes from his dream
to find himself back in the nineteenth century.

The civilization of the ninety-sixth century is described in great detail, and many of its features are
significant. Writing in 1883, Professor Macnie was able
to foretell many inventions and scientific developments
with a startling accuracy. In fact, this dependence upon
scientific achievement is one of the important characteristics of his ideal civilization. Machines do man's work,
science brings him comfort, luxury, and a large amount of
leisure. The discovery of the potentialities of electricity
is largely responsible for all this:

> "Electrical as well as chemical science,"
> said my companion, "has made such progress
> since your period, that many things then
> regarded as difficult or impossible have
> become matters of every-day use. It re-
> quires, indeed, some effort on our part to
> conceive how the way to their discovery
> was so long missed. The great discovery of
> the principle that enables us to store a
> large amount of electric force in a small
> space was long missed by a hair's-breadth,
> as it were. Yet this discovery brought
> about even greater changes in the social
> condition of mankind than did the improve-
> ment of the steam-engine. Electricity
> completed, in some cases, what steam had
> begun. Such, for example, was the gradual
> disuse of animal power, first for draught,
> at last for any purpose whatever. In
> other cases, electricity reversed the
> effect of steam. Such was the utter
> abolition of the factory system, with all
> its attendant evils." (14)

---

(14) Macnie, J., The Diothas, (New York, 1883), 21.

A sort of crude prototype of modern radio but much
less marvellous is described:

> "The telephone is the magician," said
> Utis. "The concert you heard this morning
> was performed in a great city of Central
> Europe, at an hour there belonging in the
> afternoon. Each continent has its own
> great musical centre, toward which gravi-
> tates whatever arises of genius, talent,
> or vocal endowment. In that city are
> produced musical performances on a grand
> scale. By means of the telephone, these
> are reproduced at the ends of the earth,
> in the homes of all willing to pay a small
> annual sum for the privilege. A whole
> continent, at times all the continents,
> will thus, at the same moment, sit in
> judgment on a new piece or a new singer." (15)

Other phases of the scientific development of this ninety-
sixth century civilization are "curricles"--that is, crude
predecessors of the automobile attaining a top speed of
twenty miles an hour--, malleable glass, a universal system
of irrigation, rapid communication with all parts of the
globe, and a widespread use of aluminum, which has replaced
all other metals. New York is now a stately and beautiful
city. Its sidewalks are covered with arcades, one for each
story, upon which the populace walk to and fro. The buildings
are devoted to warehouses and offices and the lower streets
carry the heaviest traffic. The upper stories contain the
shops and residences.

The social structure of this civilization is completely
changed, although Macnie is quick to repudiate anything which
smacks of communism:

---

(15) Macnie, J., op. cit., 83.

"We have no aristocracy," was the reply, "if by that you mean a class living in idleness by the toil of others. Nor have we any working-class, if you mean a class that spends its life in toil that leaves no leisure for their development as intellectual beings. Such as these you so greatly admire compose the only class among us. You may call them an aristocracy if by that you mean a cultivated and ruling class, for such they are. You may also call them the working-class, for all support themselves by their own exertions."

"What!" I exclaimed. "That must imply Communism, or something like it."

"No: Communism, in the sense you mean, does not exist among us. Each is the owner of whatever property he acquires, whether by gift or his own exertions. But public opinion stigmatizes idleness as the meanest of vices, the fruitful parent of other vices, and of crime also. Now, it has been ascertained, by careful computation and by experiment, that if every able-bodied person in a community works between three and four hours every day, at some productive employment, the result will supply all with every necessary and comfort of life, with something to spare. Allowing other ten hours for sleep and refreshment, there remain still other ten for mental improvement and such unproductive pursuits as individual taste may prefer.

"If any live in idleness, it is evident that others must toil to support them. Time-honored custom, therefore, requires that all children, whether boys or girls, shall acquire some handicraft. For the present, I must defer a full account of our social arrangements to some other occasion. I shall merely remark, that we consider the body as well as the mind to stand in need of due exercise to preserve it in sound condition. It has been found, that no physical exercise is so beneficial and pleasing as labor skilfully directed toward some definite object. All, therefore, whether possessing much or little, men and women, young and old, spend a certain number of hours each day in some productive employment, and no more dream of having their work done by others than of having eating, sleeping, or digestion performed by deputy. In universal industry has been found a panacea for the worst of the evils that for long ages were the curse of society and the despair of legislators. Our labor,

> however, is not drudgery. A few steps
> will take us to a window where you may see
> and judge for yourself to what perfection
> machinery has been brought. We merely
> guide: the real work is performed by
> forces once allowed to go to waste."(16)

Education has assumed a new importance in this ideal civili-

zation:

> Our main reliance, after all, is upon
> education. The training of the young is
> regarded as the one great duty, both of
> the family and of the State. Having no army,
> no navy, no expensive hierarchy of public
> functionaries, we are able to devote a
> great part of our energies and resources
> to this most important of duties. (17)

Through the introduction of machines, the period of labor

has been shortened to three or four hours a day----this is

done by a conscripted army of labor:

> Although, as before stated, there was
> neither army nor navy to maintain, there
> was, nevertheless, a sort of conscription
> in force that exacted for public purposes
> the service of all young men between the
> ages of seventeen and twenty-five. By
> these conscripts, called zerdars, were
> performed those labors which, however useful
> or indispensable, are not attractive as
> life employments to those not compelled
> to follow them.
> At seventeen each young man was ex-
> pected to report for duty at a certain
> place. There, unless allowed to return
> home for another year, he was at once
> assigned to some duty, always at a dis-
> tance from his home. According as exigency
> required, any zerdar might become a sailor,
> a miner, a member of the sanitary police,

---

(16) Macnie, J., op. cit., 11.

(17) Macnie, J., op. cit., 114.

and so on. The nature of the training they
had received rendered them fully competent
for the management of the machinery that
had superseded muscular labor in every
department of life.

The younger were first assigned to
comparatively light tasks. I had already
remarked, with some surprise, that the
conductors of the city railroads, and other
similar officials, were all very young.
After a year or more at such light tasks,
they were.drafted to heavier labors in
some other division of the world; regard
being had, as far as possible, to the
preferences of the young men. In order to
give the zerdars the educational advantage
of becoming familiar, in turn, with every
great division of the world, its climate,
and its productions, the various nations
had established a sort of universal labor
exchange, somewhat on the plan of the postal
unions of the present. In this way, during
his seven or eight years of service, each
zerdar would visit every part of the world,
and certainly gain an extensive knowledge of
mankind; no impediment existing in the way
of difference of language, or class feeling,
to prevent free social or intellectual
intercourse. (18)

The Diothas follows the conventional device of most

utopian novels in its contrast of the ideal society with

the society its readers lived in. The instability of the

nineteenth century is regarded as particularly deplorable:

> The society of your days, as compared
> with that now existing, was unstable as
> ocean compared with land. All was fluct-
> uating, and individuals were largely at
> the mercy of circumstances. Some, with-
> out effort on their part, were born to
> virtue, happiness, and honor: others,
> through no apparent fault of theirs, seemed
> born to vice, misery, and degradation.

(18) Macnie, J., op. cit., 156.

Yet, all imperfect as it was, the civilization of your day was far in advance of
that of any former age. Amid much wrong,
there were genuine aspirations after justice;
amid darkness, an earnest, though blind,
groping toward light; amid much selfishness,
much self-sacrifice and heroism. I believe,
indeed, that could men have become convinced,
even at that early period, of a permanently
beneficial result from their self-sacrifice,
the possessors of what the world had would
have been willing to share equally with
their less fortunate brethren. Such a
partition would then, it is true, have
resulted merely in disappointment. The
baser elements of society had first to be
sifted out. It was chiefly the dim per-
ception of this that rendered many so
hopeless of improvement. The gradual advance
perceptible, in spite of many fluctuations,
in the history of our race since that time,
was the effect, not of any far-reaching
plan, but of the earnest endeavors of
earnest men to combat evils immediately
pressing on their attention. At last came
a time when so much had been effected, that
the task would be completed on a prescribed
plan, and has since been carried towards
completion with minimum waste of effort. (19)

Its social injustice, its inequality of classes, were the

worst features of the nineteenth century:

Some of these were in a condition not
greatly raised above that of the lower
animals, and were treated, in fact, as such
by the more favored races. The latter had
attained to some knowledge of the rudiments
of science, and made a fair beginning of •
subduing to their use the forces of nature,
but were themselves a prey to monstrous
moral evils. A few of the more favored
by nature or fortune appear to have lived
a life approximating to that now lived by all.
But even they must have found any rare

---

(19) Macnie, J., op. cit., 106.

> share of happiness difficult to attain,
> surrounded, as they were, by every form
> of misery and degradation, the fault of
> man himself, not of the world in which
> he has been placed....Many things then
> lingered that were soon to pass away
> forever. It was a period of fermentation
> and incipient corruption, from which
> society emerged at last, so fundamentally
> altered in its outward form, and many
> of its aims and views, as to bear scarcely
> any resemblance to that existing but a few
> generations before. [20]

The long evolution from which this ideal society of

the ninety-sixth century emerged, is described in detail.

Two sets of nations developed along divergent lines---one

group, known as the Absolutists [Fascists ?], believed "that

the rule of an intelligent despot is the highest type of

government." [21] Opposed to these advocates of dictator-

ships were the Liberals who believed in an adequate repre-

sentation of all the people in any form of government.

Finally, after centuries of conflict, the Absolutists had

been repulsed chiefly by the United States, and by the

time Ismar Thiusen appeared upon the scene, an equitable

system of government was in effect.

> Since then, the progress of mankind
> in good government has been peaceful and
> continuous. The stern temper generated
> by the long struggle between rival prin-
> ciples gradually softened away; through
> the maxims, "Resist the beginnings of

---

(20) Macnie, J., op. cit., 60.

(21) Macnie, J., op. cit., 112.

evil," and "Mercy to the bad is cruelty
to the good," have become settled principles
of action. (22)

The Diothas is an important book in the history of
utopianism in America. It contains a complete new society
presented in all of its details; it shows an exceptional
knowledge of science in all its possibilities; it presents
these features in the guise of a story which has interest
enough to carry the reader along through the details of
the social structure of the ninety-sixth century. It is
significant that in his "Preface" to the second edition
of The Diothas, Professor Macnie disavowed any leanings
toward communism:

> It will be seen that the author is
> not deeply imbued with the communistic ideas
> now so attractive to many. To become the
> well-fed slaves of an irresistible despotism
> with its hierarchy of walking delegates
> seems hardly the loftiest conceivable
> destiny for the human race. (23)

It has been rather definitely established that Professor
Macnie "believed Bellamy borrowed heavily from his own
book" (24) but the nature and extent of these borrowings
will be shown in a later chapter. One may note in passing
that Macnie came to believe that the ideal society might
be attained earlier than the ninety-sixth century although

(22) Macnie, J., op. cit., 113.

(23) "Preface" to the second edition of The Diothas
(New York, 1890), iv.

(24) The Alumni Review of the University of North Dakota,
(December, 1934) 16.

possibly not as early as Bellamy predicted:

> If man continues to increase his
> control over the forces of nature in the
> same ratio as during the past century, the
> material conditions requisite for such
> a state of society as that described may
> be realized ere the close of the twentieth
> century. But judging by the past, it would
> require the moral progress of a thousand
> years at least to render such a society
> possible. (25)

A much less important utopia appeared the year after
The Diothas. Utopia, or the History of an Extinct Planet
by Alfred Denton Cridge is little more than a pamphlet
describing the history of a smaller and more advanced planet
than the earth. The narrator is transported to it by
"psychometry", and once there, describes the history, people,
and social institutions of this ideal society. Private
enterprise has been eliminated and the worker becomes a
part owner in all things. Idleness is a disgrace in this
new society. Equal wealth is the chief characteristic of
this most advanced civilization, and the constitution contains a clause providing that "no private debt shall ever
be considered binding or have any standing in law or justice..." (26) The novel offers no complete social system,
but puts great emphasis on spiritualism, life after death,
and religious speculation. It is vague as to the methods
by which utopia was attained, although science played a

---

(25) "Preface" to the second edition of The Diothas,
(New York, 1890), v.

(26) Cridge, A.D., Utopia, or the History of an Extinct
Planet, (Oakland, Calif., 1884), 19.

major part in it, as the following excerpt shows:

> With science as a servant, they turned
> every possible thing to advantage, and
> lived in ease and even luxury. All shared
> alike and no one shirked or monopolized.
> Money was unknown and greed forgotten.
> Equality, liberty, and justice reigned amid
> them all. (27)

The next American utopia was Henry F. Allen's
pseudonymous work, The Key of Industrial Cooperative
Government (1886) by "Pruning Knife". The theme of this
work is the futility of the attempt to reconcile the
principle of isolated selfish endeavor with a peaceful
society. Such reconciliation is declared impossible because
individual interests always conflict with group interests.
Hence, in the new order described, every form of competitive
enterprise has disappeared, and the state has taken over
all functions of production and distribution. Labor in
the new state is compulsory, and its results are put into
one common fund from which all the citizens are supplied
with their needs. Money is thus eliminated, and with it
ends the concentration of wealth in the hands of a few.
All of these changes are described as taking place peacefully, but as usual, the author is vague as to the specific
methods.

Much more significant is The Republic of the Future,
or Socialism a Reality (1887) by Anna Bowman Dodd, the

---

(27) Cridge, A.D., op. cit., 29.

author of <u>Old Cathedral Days</u>. Written as a series of

letters by a Swedish nobleman visiting New York to a

friend in Christiana, <u>The Republic of the Future</u> describes

New York in 2050 under a socialistic government. Its

importance lies in anticipating many of the same things

that Bellamy was to use in his romance---but <u>The Republic</u>

<u>of the Future</u> takes a completely different view of the

socialistic state. Life in the New York of 2050 is so

monotonous that the people are perishing from ennui. The

deadly regimentation accompanying socialism has eliminated

all initiative and ambition; uniformity is the keynote of

this future New York:

> The total lack of contrast which is
> the result of the plan on which this
> socialistic city has been built, comes,
> of course, from the principle which has
> decreed that no man can have any finer
> house or better interior, or finer clothes
> than his neighbor. The abolition of
> poverty, and the raising of all classes to
> a common level of comfort and security, has
> resulted in the most deadening uniformity.
> Take for example, the aspect of the shop-
> windows. All shops are run by the govern-
> ment on government capital. There is, con-
> sequently, neither rivalry nor competition.
> The shop keepers, who are in reality only
> clerks and salesmen under government
> jurisdiction, take naturally, no personal
> or vital interest either in the amount of
> goods sold, or in the way in which these
> latter are placed before the public. The
> shop-windows, therefore, are as uninviting
> as are the goods displayed. (28)

The author has made a curious error in ascribing to the

---

(28) Dodd, A.B., <u>The Republic of the Future</u>, (New
     York, 1887), 21.

ideas of Henry George, the founder of this new state,
most of the blame for this social scheme. In fact the
only religion of the future republic is a worship of
Henry George:

> Inside, in the center of the building
> was a colossal statue--a portrait it is
> said--of the founder, Henry George. Around
> the sides of the wall, were niches where
> portrait busts of the martyrs stand--the
> nihilists, early anarchists, and socialists
> who endured persecution and often death
> in the early days of socialism. A book
> I noticed was placed near the Henry George
> statue. It was the socialistic bible
> "Poverty and Progress" which with a number
> of other such books forms the chief lit-
> erature of the people. Once a year, my
> young friend told me, there is a sacred
> reading to the people from this book. [29]

Machinery plays a prominent role in the new era; only two
hours of labor a day are required of the inhabitants, a
fact which accounts for their boredom. Mrs. Dodd agrees
completely with the late utopists in her attacks upon
machinery as "the true cause of the hostility between capital
and labor." [30]

In reading The Republic of the Future one has the
feeling that it is offered as a refutation of Bellamy's
ideas; since it antedates Looking Backward by a year, this
feeling is obviously incorrect. It anticipates in a general
way, everything that Bellamy was to do more specifically---

(29) Dodd, A.B., op. cit., 82.
(30) Dodd, A.B., op. cit., 46.

and offers a shrewd criticism of socialism. In fact
the following excerpt sounds very much like the criticisms
of Bellamy's society:

> Well, if some of the ineradicable, in-
> destructible principles in human nature
> could be changed as easily as laws are
> made and unmade, the chances for an ideal
> realization of the happiness of mankind
> would be the more easily attained. But
> the Socialists committed the grave error
> of omitting to count some of these deter-
> mining human laws into the sum of their
> calculations. (31)

Possibly the appearance of Laurence Gronlund's Cooperative
Commonwealth a few years before influenced Mrs. Dodd and
others to think seriously of the virtues and defects of
the socialistic state.

American utopias might have remained of this general
and intermittent type, had not Edward Bellamy's Looking
Backward given a directing force to the movement. As we
have seen, social and economic conditions were of a sort
that impelled men to a literary quest for utopia. Without
Looking Backward, there would unquestionably have been
scattered sporadic attempts at using the utopian novel as a
literary medium; but the success of Bellamy's novel spurred
other novelists to imitation or to criticism of his social
structure. For the next ten years, readers grew accustomed
to having their heroes or heroines fall asleep to waken in
some future era where strange sights, strange people, and

(31) Dodd, A.B., op. cit., 56.

ideal societies occupied a large part of the novelist's
attentions.

A CHRONOLOGICAL BIBLIOGRAPHY OF AMERICAN UTOPIAS

1868 - 1887

Radical Freelance (pseud.) The Philosophers of Foufouville, (New York, 1868).

Hale, E.E., Sybaris, (Boston, 1869).

Phelps, E.S., The Gates Ajar, (Boston, 1869).

Holcombe, W.H., In Both Worlds, (Philadelphia, 1870).

Anonymous, Lifting the Veil, (New York, 1870).

Hale, E.E., Ten Times One is Ten, (Boston, 1870).

Trammell, W.D., Ca Ira, (New York, 1874).

Dooner, Pierton W., Last Days of the Republic, (San Francisco, 1880).

Gaston, Henry A., Mars Revealed, (San Francisco, 1880).

Macnie, J., ("Ismar Thiusen"), The Diothas, (New York, 1883).

Phelps, E.S., Beyond the Gates, (Boston, 1883).

Cridge, A.D., Utopia, or the History of an Extinct Planet, (Oakland, Calif., 1884).

Allen, H.F., The Key of Industrial Cooperative Government by "Pruning Knife", (St. Louis, 1886).

Dodd, A.B., The Republic of the Future, (New York, 1887).

CHAPTER VI

EDWARD BELLAMY

Any record of the career of Edward Bellamy must
necessarily trace his intellectual development, rather
than the events of his life, since his life was for the
most part quiet and uneventful. In fact, his present
biographer, Mr. Arthur Morgan, complains constantly to
surviving members of the Bellamy family that "there is nothing of glamour or human interest" in Edward Bellamy's
career---a fact which makes the task of writing a full
length biography difficult.

Edward Bellamy was born on March 26, 1850, in the little
village of Chicopee Falls, Massachusetts, where he was
to spend the major part of his life except for short periods
of residence in Boston, New York, and Colorado. He was
the third son of the Reverend Rufus King Bellamy and Maria
Louisa Putnam Bellamy, his father having been the Baptist
minister in Chicopee Falls for thirty-five years. The fact
that he was of clerical descent on both sides---his mother's
father was the Reverend Benjamin Putnam; one of his paternal
ancestors was Dr. Joseph Bellamy a prominent theologian of
Bethlehem, Connecticut, and the teacher of Aaron Burr---
and the fact that he was brought up in a religious atmosphere undoubtedly combined to make him an idealist. A
friend writes that the Reverend Rufus Bellamy "was a man
of strikingly tender, sympathetic nature, with heart ever

responsive to human suffering. This same nature has
proved a priceless heritage to the son, for sympathy may
be said to form the keynote to all that he has written." (1)
While it is certainly true that sympathy directed toward
social problems is the motivating force of Looking Backward
and Equality, one can hardly see this quality in Edward
Bellamy's earlier and more purely literary work.

We get a definite idea of the youthful Bellamy's
imagination, his dreaminess, his love of reading, and his
rather abnormal religious fervor, in the following attempt
at an autobiography, which he wrote later in life and which
has never before been published:

> The lad sitting on the floor in the
> dim book-walled library is very busy, and
> if you looked over his shoulder you would
> not disturb him. What is the book he is
> so intently pouring over? Well I warrant
> it to be the life of Napoleon or Mahomet
> or Nelson, or very likely some plutarchic
> demi-god of the foreworld. Over such
> great stories he spends his leisure time,
> that is, all the time he can spare from
> play. It is interesting to watch the
> expression on his face as he reads. Now
> surely he is charging over the bridge over
> the Lodi with the Corsican. Before such a
> look the Austrian gunners quailed. Now
> pride, now courage, now self-sacrifice, now
> shame, now admiration transforms his face.
> It is a peculiarity with his reading that
> with every hero he measures himself. Every
> deed of high emprise challenges him with the
> question "Would I do likewise?" Sometimes
> he frankly answers "No.", and blushes with
> shame as he reads, but with youth's innocent,

(1) Baxter, S., "The Author of Looking Backward" in The
New England Magazine, (September, 1889), I, New
Series, (VII Old Series), 93.

nay noble self-conceit he mostly answers
"Yes" and so honest is he that the triumph
of the hero almost seems his own. A dozen
times this hour has he already led terrible
charges, once has he quailed, and several
times he has mentally shared the laurel
wherewith the thankful people have crowned
his hero. Such reading is brave sport indeed.
No wonder the boy prefers it to play. The
conceit of youth which instantly concludes
it would have done the noble thing it hears
of, we find laughable. Rather respect it
and regret it.

Growing years disclose to us our growing
weaknesses of character which bring us into
self-contempt. Let us then cherish the
testimony of our childhood's undoubting
self-confidence as evidence at least of the
nobility of our instincts ere our fatal
inability to realize their behests has been
experienced.

And now mingles with the roar of artillery
a still small voice sounding through the
library doors, "Hugh, Hugh, tea is ready."

"Hugh, Hugh" comes in more urgent tones
and adding the crafty suggestion "Hot
biscuits and syrup. There won't be any left
for you."

Hugh glances hastily ahead to see how
much longer the battle lasts. A column at
least. He can't wait. The fate of Europe
is in the balance. So are the biscuits.
Europe licks the-...With a sigh the tome
is laid away and the lad obeyed the oft repeated summons and experienced in feeling,
if not in thought as he walked along, the
strangeness of the sensation when we are called
by a trivial yet imperative necessity of
our physical needs and material natures to
descend out of a lofty realm of thought,
and the contrast between the two qualities
of our natures is sometimes bizzarre even
to grotesqueness. But not even the fast-
dissappearing biscuits can at once recall
the boy's mind from the clash of arms and
the trembling fate of empires. His hand
wanders aimlessly over the table, taking
biscuits for butter and butter for biscuits.

CHAPTER 2

His age at this time was about fifteen.

The scene of the last chapter may be taken
as a fair sketch of his mental life for
the preceding five or six years. An insatiable
reader since he first learned his letters,
his interest had been, by the common taste
of children, attracted towards adventurous
tales and great men's histories. The child's
feeling of unlimited, because untried powers,
which makes this sort of reading interesting,
because it makes it seem probable and rational,
was peculiarly developed in him, as indeed,
we have previously intimated. But he did
not merely listen and allow the tales to
titillate his mental retina. His imagination
was always busy putting himself in the space
of the characters and comparing his probable action with theirs. The tales were
thus in reality mere projections of himself
in the space of the characters and comparing
his probable action with theirs. The tales
were thus in reality mere projections of
himself in imagination. He enjoyed them
subjectively, not as the world of children
objectively. On this account they took
hold on him more deeply. Other children might
listen open-mouthed and saucer-eyed to some
story of daring deeds and then turn about and
roll marbles. But not so Hugh. He would still
sit with flushed face and pouting mouth, gaze
afar, fighting over the fight with himself
the hero. This sounds as if he were very
egotistical, but he was not so in any other
sense than those may be said to be who occupy
themselves with the task of approximating
their conduct to some high ideal. So exacting
and even wearing was this habit of Hugh's that
he would sometimes avoid hearing such tales.
They excited him too much. He did not like to
feel his eyes glazing with tears, his throat
gripped with convulsive emotion. The intense
luxury of this ecstasy of sympathy for noble
deeds he felt a thing almost sacred and not
to be indulged in for the pleasure of it like
a common thing. Thus nourishing youth sublime,
Hugh grew up. He never doubted but that he
too should do some great thing like those he
read of. I never knew what his plans were
nor do I think any of his friends did but I
knew that he had them and that they were as
definite as they were prodigious. Nor does
this mean that the boy was vain, he was simply

permeated through and through by the in-
toxicating aroma of glory exhaled from the
pages, for so many years his daily recourse.
His only views of life and action in the
world about him he regarded with a serene
contempt, or rather a total indifference.
They seemed to him merely the lay figures
of the world. From his intercourse with
heroes and kings he had gained a royal air
in regarding the common herd. When he came
to go out in the world it was with profound
surprise and bewilderment that he found these
common people quite capable of obstructing
his course. Thus, with his head in the
clouds, the boy grew up. Thus as utterly
out of joint with the world as Don Quixote
in his library he drew near his maturity.
At an early age this aspirant of a grand
destiny had not failed to perceive the
necessary and utter pettiness of all achieve-
ments undertaken in the selfish spirit as
contrasted with the infinite scope of unselfish aims. He was therefore greatly
troubled in his mind lest his own lofty
aspirations might spring from a selfish love
of fame or personal credit. This point he
never fairly got over. At times he felt
that the service of humanity was his chief
motive, and at other times he explained his
ambitions if not on an unselfish, yet on a
neutral basis, by ascribing them to the natural
passion of human nature to fully expand,
exert and express itself in great activities.

In this desire to escape self he became
greatly captivated by the idea of service.
He would be the servant of God, of humanity.
The motto of the blind king of Bohemia, and
robbed by the Prince of Wales, "Ich Diene"
had a great attraction for him. He would,
in fine, shuffle off the responsibility of.
being selfish upon somebody else, either God
or humanity, by devoting himself to them. He
did not see that God must be very unselfish
to be so selfish as to allow himself to be
served. In order that he should fill the
highest ideal, someone else must fill the
lower one. Lord, Lord, what a poor makeshift
morality is ours.

CHAPTER 3

Such was the childhood of the boy.
This period seemed to close with a religious
experience. That this may be understood
it is necessary to premise that Hugh was of
an old New England family with Calvinism in
its blood. His life as a child had been one
of entire conformity to rules of propriety.
The great dreams that dominated his mind had
a restraining effect upon his conduct so that
even of boyish peccadiloes he committed
scarcely his share. He had been taught to
believe that he was a grievous sinner, accursed
from God with whom he must make peace or
suffer the most terrible consequences. He
had never thought at all upon such subjects,
but had accepted this statement of the case
as an undoubted reality. Accordingly he
submitted to the emotional experience of
a religious conversion. He came to feel a
sense of intimacy, an indescribably close
communion with what seemed to him a very real
and sublime being. The mental and moral
revolutions of later years never blotted
from his mind the strange and touching experiences of this epoch. In prayer he took
a deep and careful pleasure. It was to him
a sensation of almost sensuous happiness as
of ineffable sublimity, when at such times
his heart seemed to throb of diety and his
soul seemed fused and melted in perfect union
with the divine. A love more tender and
passionate than that to which human charms
ever moved him, then seemed to bind him to
the infinite. From school he hastened home
to pray, not that he wanted anything, save
only to be with God. In after years he used
to preserve an old chair which had been his
oratory, and no moment did he so cherish as that,
for it recalled the most ecstatic moments
of his life. He saw the world with new eyes.
There seemed no other business in it save
God's service, no other reward save communion
with him. He ceased to feel any interest in
any reading which did not relate to this subject.
It seemed to him that the only bond of
brotherhood between men must be their brotherhood in Christ. His earlier ambitions he did
not renounce, but they were in suspense. Death

which had always been an unpleasant thought
to him, now became a delightful occasion
of faith, an ecstatic experience, which it
were a pity man could not undergo more than
once. The relation established by Christianity
between the believer and Christ makes a woman
of the former, tending as it does peculiarly
to cultivate the feminine graces of trust-
fulness and confidence in protection to be
repaid by love. It is better adapted to
women that men on whose minds it has an effect
to degenerate the masculine virtues of self-
reliance and valor. Hugh used to go to sleep
with a feeling of exhultation at the thought
that he might die before morning. No thought
so calmed and prefaced his mind for slumber.
In these days so complete seemed his dependence
upon Christ for support, courage, inspiration,
that he naively wondered how he had formerly
gotten along at all or how the rest of the world
managed to exist in their prayerless, godless
state. There were now always two to consult
at every step, himself and his deity. The effect
of these experiences on his conduct was also
noteworthy. (2)

Edward Bellamy received his education in the local

school at Chicopee Falls, followed by one year in Union

College. His highly reticent temperament seems to have de-

prived him of the social benefits a college education might

have conferred; perhaps this explains his general attitude

of contempt for the formal education that colleges offered.

Throughout Looking Backward and Equality are numerous de-

rogatory remarks about college education in the nineteenth

century. In his own journal he suggested that it would be

"a good idea if men could be made to work until thirty and

then went to college, when their minds are stronger than as

(2) This material was sent me in typewritten form by
Mrs. Marion Bellamy Earnshaw, Mr. Bellamy's daughter.

boys." (3)

At the age of eighteen, he went abroad with his
cousin Mason Green. In Germany he was impressed for the
first time with a sense of social injustice. He later wrote,
"It was in the great cities of Europe and among the hovels
of the peasantry that my eyes were first fully opened to the
extent and consequences of 'Man's inhumanity to man'." (4)
His eyes might well have been opened to the same consequences
of "Man's inhumanity to man" had he carefully examined
conditions in the mills of his own native state; maturity
was to bring him a definite realization of all this and,
what is more, a driving urge to do something about it.
Aside from this awakening of interest in social affairs,
European travel seems to have affected Bellamy little.
Social philosphies so widely discussed in Europe at the
time apparently influenced him not at all. He was above
all else American in both background and interest. "Bellamy
was essentially a New-Englander. His background was that
of Boston and its remote suburbs. And when he preaches the
necessity of the co-operative commonwealth, he does it with
a Yankee twang. In fact, he is as essentially native American
as Norman Thomas, the present leader of the Socialist Party
in this country." (5)

---

(3) From material sent me by Mrs. Earnshaw.

(4) Dictionary of National Biography account of Edward
    Bellamy.

(5) Broun, H., "Introduction," to Looking Backward,
    (New York, 1926), iii.

During this period, Bellamy began what came to be
a confirmed habit of setting all his thoughts down on
paper. His earliest production is apparently the following
sketch which shows him as a dreamer trifling with fantastic
ideas---the same sort of thing that was later to appear
in his short stories:

> The best of life are its dreams; they
> are its volatile quintescence. The hours
> in which as if from a gentle fermentation
> of the mind the fumes of memory rise to
> the brain are the most golden of life.
> Reverie may truly be called the intoxi-
> cation of the intellect, wherein the
> thoughts are full of wine and like glowing
> Bacchantes are woven in the mazes of the
> dance.
>   It is as if a ball were given to all
> the denizens of the mind, both new and old,
> both dead and living. Through the ivory
> portal, wide open thrown, throng the
> thoughts of today and the memories of
> "auld lang syne", the associations of the
> past breathing an odor as if wrapped in
> lavender. The hopes of the future and the
> reminiscences of the past jostle and mingle.
> There is no distinction of time. These
> have as good a right, the dreams that were
> realized, and those fairer, more majestic,
> that were never mocked by the distorted
> reflections of fulfillment. Regrets for
> sin and failure and the recollections of
> success are here on equal ground, for all
> alike are dreams.
>   Oh, the strange commingling, the face
> of the wife, who this night will lie in your
> bosom, comes hand-in-hand with your love of
> long ago. There is no jealousy, for all
> are dreams. Your sainted mother leads your
> boy whom she has never seen. Here are
> grouped together the anticipations and the
> memories of some event long past, a strangely
> contrasting company, viewing which you are
> as a god who sees at once past and future.
>   Many, many are the guests that frequent
> the reveries of some of us. And how fares

the host? He is as one who views from a
place apart a brave spectacle. The
thoughts come of themselves; their strange
tableaux they spontaneously arrange. He
merely furnishes the page. Nay, rather,
they take possession of it. The man
overcome by reverie is not overcome by his
thoughts. His past has risen up against
his present and for the time has put it
out of possession. And when the ball is
over and the quiet company has silently,
one by one, glided away, how drear and odd
seem the stage. It is as a banquet hall
deserted. The host is left lonely and
desolate, and the house erst so well filled
aches with emptiness.

There are men who know not what it is
to entertain these guests of reverie. There
are those whose inhospitable doors are shut
on their past. Not so ever shall it be with
me, but rather so wide open shall our soul
stand that past, present, and future shall
go in and out and commingle as they will.
To him who makes these welcome, they will
come as ministering angels in hours of depression.

In revery the man of gentle and catholic
mind takes a peculiar delight for there all
acerbities are sweetened, the passions which
so tempestuously rage in the present world
are here all hushed.

The present, indeed, is narrow and bigoted,
the past is calm, passionless, infinitely
charitable. For my part, it is in retro-
spection that I would fain enjoy my experiences rather than in present realization.
This latter is always deceiving. The thing
seems ever less than we had thought.

Oh, where are they gone, those dear
dreams? Oh where shall we gain the wings to
follow them? and where they are be evermore? (6)

These sentiments are hardly natural for the ordinary boy's

mind. They show the youthful Edward Bellamy as an introvert

more interested in his own fantastic imaginings than in

---

(6) Material from Mrs. Bellamy.

anything else.

At approximately this same time he began his "Note-books" and "Journals" in which he recorded his random thoughts. These give an excellent insight into the mind of this young dreamer. Sometime in 1871, he wrote in a mood of melancholia which he probably considered very picturesque:

> I am a bit weary this evening. I have just met with one of those disappointments which have become such a bitterly old story with me lately. Were the ambition which spurs my labors one of the ordinary ones as for self or fame, I fancy I should be well content to let it go and earn my daily bread in some plodding business such as men ply all about me. But I cannot turn my heart from the great work which awaits me. It is a labor none other can perform. (7)

What this "great work" was, no one knows. It may have been some literary work, for by this time he was beginning to think of becoming a writer, and the year before he had confided to his notebook:

> All writers are fishermen in the sea of their own minds, as it were sitting by the current of their own thoughts and angling therein. All's fish that comes to my net and I shall not reject any sort for another.

Probably at the same time he was recording these sentiments:

> Let every aspirant for literary fame make it a rule to write nothing until all itching for fame has died out of him. Then, if he still desires to write, it is likely

---

(7) This and the following quotations are from the un-published "Journals" of Edward Bellamy. I received the material in typewritten form through the kind-ness of Mrs. Bellamy.

that he has something in him.

There are times when I feel like writing. There are other times when I feel like being taught, and then I lay aside my pen and sit at the feet of some author, it may be a great author or a small one, but I never fail to feel a sense of humility and teacheableness.

On September 15, 1874, he is concerned with dying; this is the first mention of the poor health which was to afflict him throughout his life.

...I think I have got my death. I had always supposed the hour when this conviction impressed itself in my mind would be marked by strange experience. But I don't find it so. The idea of near death gives a not unpleasant shock when first entertained, but for an abiding sensation it is no more reliable than other notions. It soon ceases to excite the mind, and too much dwelt upon is quite capable of becoming a bore. My philosophy I find has not been wholly without fruit. It has at least bred a certain faculty of regarding death almost indifferently, which now stands me in good stead.

I may recover from my present ailment, but to me it somehow seems a foregone conclusion that I shall not. Nor should I much care but for the bitter blow of death would be (sic.) to my parents. For their sake I do wish to live. For their sake I shall obstinately fight a disease with which, otherwise, I should have no serious controversy. The most common tragedy is the fight of a man against a disease. Herein is Laocoon daily repeated all about us.

Here at this desk I have sat and idled away in vain revery many an hour that might have been spent writing for fame or money. Do I regret it? No. I regret nothing, and especially this. Who knows what is best and most profitable. Let others number the tongues that echo their name. For me I prize more the vague and wavering images that visit my soul in hours of revery than any other encitations of the mind.

Everyone to his taste. Mine runs rather

> to dreaming than to dollars--rather to
> fancy than to fame. "My mind to me a king-
> dom is" to which none other can compare.
> If these pleasures be unsubstantial, away
> with all substance; if they be unreal,
> away with all reality.

The following excerpt on his twenty-fifth birthday
is typical of the general attitude of this young dreamer:

> Today is my twenty-fifth birthday.
> In the past year the most I have gained
> is some aptitude for enjoying a sunrise,
> but it is enough. One sunrise a day is
> enough to live for.

These qualities---this preoccupation with death, this
interest in reverie, this impractical attitude---are all
to be found in his earlier short stories. His later keen
interest in social problems has as yet little expression.

Upon his return home from Germany, he took up the
study of law and was admitted to the bar in Hampden County,
Massachusetts. Characteristic of his idealistic nature
is his refusal to practise law because of a feeling that
as a lawyer he would have to take a hypocritical attitude
by defending people in whom he did not believe. Perhaps
it was at this time that he wrote in his Journal, "So
today the lawyers guard with invisible ranks the money
kings, whose group is strangling the modern liberties of
America. Such lawyers are the worst foes of our civilization. No men deserve so badly of their fellows as these
bull-dogs of the money kings." This attitude he maintained
through life; in Looking Backward he completely banishes
lawyers from his ideal commonwealth.

A career in journalism appeared more attractive
than law, and in 1871 Bellamy became a member of the
staff of the New York Evening Post. In 1872 he became
an editorial writer and book reviewer for the Springfield
Union, a post which he held until 1876, when he resigned
to devote all his time to writing. Before entering upon
this phase of his career, he took a trip to the Sandwich
Islands by way of Panama, returning on the Pacific Railways.

In the years from 1876 to 1886, Edward Bellamy came
to be known as one of the most promising young writers
in America. His first efforts were short stories which
he contributed to all of the leading magazines including
The Atlantic Monthly, Scribner's, Harper's, The Century,
and Lippincott's. Within ten years he published some
twenty or thirty short stories, the best of which were
collected in 1898 after his death in "The Blindman's World"
and Other Stories with an Introduction by William Dean
Howells. The eminent characteristic of all of these stories
is imaginative power, a quality in which Bellamy was the
literary descendant of Poe and Hawthorne, with whose work
some of Bellamy's tales may be creditably compared. Howells
recognized this power in Bellamy's work when he wrote:

> Whether his ethics will keep his aesthetics
> in remembrance, I do not know; but I am
> sure that one cannot acquaint one's self
> with his merely artistic work, and not be
> sensible that in Edward Bellamy we were
> rich in a romantic imagination surpassed

only by that of Hawthorne. [8]

Many of Bellamy's stories were woven about some unusual phenomenon or some strange thought. For example, he
was greatly intrigued by the idea that the same personality
is made up of separate individualities at various periods.
As one of his characters in The Old Folks Party remarks:

> There are half a dozen of each of us, or
> a dozen if you please, one in fact for each
> epoch of life, and each slightly or almost
> wholly different from the others...The
> different periods of life are to all
> intents and purposes different persons, and
> the first person of grammar ought to be
> used only with the present tense. What
> we were, or shall be, belongs strictly to
> the third person. [9]

Around this unusual idea, Bellamy wrote several of his
stories: notable among these are The Old Folks Party, [10]
Lost, [11] and Miss Ludington's Sister. [12]

Miss Ludington's Sister presents a situation so unreal,
so fantastic, that at first blush it seems impossible even
for romantic fiction. An elderly spinster, Miss Ludington,

(8) Howells, W.D., "Edward Bellamy," The Atlantic
    Monthly, LXXXII, (August, 1898), 256.

(9) Bellamy, E., "The Blindman's World" and Other Stories,
    (Boston, 1898), 64.

(10) Published originally in Scribner's Monthly, XI,
    (March, 1876), 660-669.

(11) Published originally in Scribner's Monthly, XV,
    (Dec., 1877), 219-224.

(12) Published serially in The Literary World (Boston),
    in 1884; later issued in a separate volume.

becomes convinced that she is a separate individual from what she had been in her youth; consequently, by means of a spiritual medium she attempts to converse with her "sister"; that is, her younger self. The séance seems successful, and by ingenious means, it appears that her "sister" has come to life, until the climax is reached in a discovery of the fraudulent methods of the medium.

In The Blindman's World [13] still another bizarre situation is presented. An astronomer has studied Mars so long and so intently that he suddenly finds himself by some sort of thought transmission, actually upon that planet. He finds that the inhabitants possess "foresight"; that is, the ability to foretell the future. Here Bellamy's imagination is given full rein in the description of this planet and its inhabitants. A similar situation is presented in To Whom This May Come, [14] in which a sailor is shipwrecked on an island in southern waters whose inhabitants are all mind-readers.

Many other examples might be given of Bellamy's imaginative power revealed in strange situations and fantastic speculations. When the plots of the stories are thus baldly presented, they are likely to seem rather ludicrous; yet it ought to be noted that Bellamy's real power lay in his

(13) Originally published in The Atlantic Monthly, LVIII, (Nov., 1886), 693-704.

(14) Originally published in Harper's Magazine, LXXVIII, (Feb., 1889), 458-466.

ability to make the unreal seem real. Howells, a realist
himself, was greatly impressed with this artistry in
Bellamy's work:

> The art employed...was the art which Bellamy
> had in degree so singular that one might
> call it supremely his. He does not so much
> transmute our every-day reality to the
> substance of romance as make the airy stuff
> of dreams one in quality with veritable
> experience. (15)

To this same effect of apparent reality may be attributed
much of the popularity which Looking Backward attained
later in Bellamy's career.

While Bellamy was thus engaged in writing short stories,
he was also turning his attention to the more substantial
novel form. His first venture Six to One: A Nantucket
Idyl (1878) was in the realm of light romance. The story
concerns a New York editor who goes to Nantucket to re-
cruit his broken-down health. There he meets six delightful young ladies, who begin to torture him by promising
each other not to hold any private tête-à-têtes with him.
However two of them fall in love with him and he falls in
love with the shyest of the entire group. The editor has
once been rejected by Addie---that is the heroine's name;
finally however they are brought together by their mutual
love of the sea, whose varied moods are the occasion for
many of Bellamy's best descriptions. The novel is very

---

(15) Howells, W.D., op. cit., 254.

melodramatic at times, and occasionally Bellamy strains hard for witty effect in the conversations of the lovers. Six to One was published anonymously and met with little success. Although, as a reviewer in The Nation commented, "the book has much merit, and may while away a couple of hours by the sea", [16] it is of little significance in Bellamy's career except for the fact that it is his first novel.

His second novel The Duke of Stockbridge is a more ambitious attempt to present an accurate account of the rebellion that broke out at Stockbridge, Massachusetts, in conjunction with Shays's Rebellion. The story begins just prior to the Revolutionary war, showing the soldiers going off to battle with expressions of hope at the improved conditions that are sure to follow when the British yoke is thrown off. Then going over to post-war days and continuing from that point, Bellamy shows the deluded patriots complaining at conditions which are even worse than before the war. The story centers around Perez Hamlin, a Captain in the Revolutionary army, who returns home just in time to assume leadership of the Stockbridge farmers who rise in protest against the imprisonment of debtors, the high taxes, and the unscrupulous methods of lawyers. The rebellion is finally quelled by troops, and Hamlin,

(16) The Nation, XXVII, (August 22, 1878), 118.

who has come to be known as "The Duke of Stockbridge,"
is killed while leading a group of men to a safe refuge
in New York State. Complication is added to the plot by
having Hamlin fall in love with the beautiful Desire
Edwards, the daughter of one of the town's leaders, or
"silk-stockings," as they are called. This romance is impossible because of the difference in social stations of
the two.

The Duke of Stockbridge is an excellent historical
romance presenting the social conditions of the period
with a great deal of accuracy. Bellamy's sympathies are
obviously with the oppressed debtors who are beginning to
wonder if they weren't better off under King George before
they won this new "freedom". One rustic character expresses this idea in the following words:

> "Wal," said Abner, recovering speech,
> "live an' larn. In them days, when I went
> a-gunnin' arter Jobez (a notorious Tory of
> the district) I use ter think ez there
> wuzn't no such varment ez a tory; but I
> didn't know nothin' 'bout lawyers and
> sheriffs them times. I calc'late ye could
> cut five tories aout o' one lawyer an'
> make a dozen skunks aout o' what was left
> over." (17)

This marks the earliest expression of an interest in social
problems in any of Bellamy's works and is quite obviously
a foreshadowing of the social sympathy that motivated
Looking Backward and Equality.

---

(17) Bellamy, E., The Duke of Stockbridge, (New York,
      n.d.), 28.

His next novel, <u>Dr. Heidenhoff's Process</u> (1880), is
deservedly the most widely known of Bellamy's early work.
In it he describes graphically the psychological effect
that evil has upon the mind of the evil-doer. The tale
describes the fate of Madelin Brand, a fine sensitive
young woman who has been seduced by a worthless clerk. Her
true lover, Henry Burr, finds that Madeline's sin is preying
on her mind and that she longs for some sort of "lethal
bath" by which her memories of the past may be completely
erased. Burr apparently finds such a process invented by
a Dr. Heidenhoff, who, by applying an electric current to
a certain portion of the brain, can eradicate all evil
memories. The process is tried on Madeline with apparent
success, until Burr wakes up to find that he has only
dreamed about this process, because of his intense longing
for such a cure. Hastening to Madeline, he finds that she
has committed sucide. The excellence of the novel is perhaps best indicated by the unstinted praise of Howells:

> The first book of Edward Bellamy's which I
> read was <u>Dr. Heidenhoff's Process</u>, and I
> thought it one of the finest feats in the
> region of romance which I had known. It
> seemed to me all the greater because the
> author's imagination wrought in it on the
> level of average life, and built the
> fabric of its dreams out of common clay...
> Nothing from romance remains to me more
> poignant than the pang that this plain,
> sad tale imparted. (18)

(18) Howells, W.D., "Edward Bellamy," <u>The Atlantic
Monthly</u>, LXXXII, (August, 1898), 253.

In 1880 with his brother Charles, he founded the Springfield _Daily News_, but apparently took little active part in its management. He was still assiduously engaged in writing short stories of the same fantastic and imaginative character that typified his earlier work and his novel, _Dr. Heidenhoff's Process_.

In 1882, Bellamy married Emma Sanderson of Chicopee Falls. The birth of his two children---Paul in 1884, Marion in 1886---brought an added sense of responsibility and a very definite change in his literary interests. Up to this time he had published three novels and numerous short stories all marked by ingenuity of plot and vividness of imagination. Because of his excellence in lending an air of reality to impossible situations, he had been praised by Howells and others as a fine literary craftsman, and his work had been favorably compared to Hawthorne's. His whole character as revealed in his intimate confessions to his "Notebooks" was that of a dreamer, unskilled in the practical affairs of life and uninterested in mundane speculations.

With the birth of his second child, his interests changed. He began thinking of social organization with the desire of insuring his children some security in life. Apparently he had never hitherto conceived the idea that it was impossible for him or anyone else to guarantee absolute social security. He began reading widely in economics and government with the idea of finding some ideal organization---and finally he wrote <u>Looking Backward</u>, which was sent to the publishers, B.H. Ticknor and Company, in October, 1887.

One can say with great accuracy that Bellamy's dominant interest changed from literature to economics in 1887. After that time he published only two short stories--- <u>To Whom this May Come</u> in <u>Harper's Magazine</u> for February, 1889, and <u>An Echo of Antietam</u> in <u>The Century</u> for July, 1889. He himself has described how he came to write <u>Looking Backward</u> and of the changes that he made to transform it from the realm of belles lettres to a serious social document. The following explanation published in the first issue of <u>The Nationalist</u> is so significant and so little known that I quote it entire:

> In undertaking to write <u>Looking Backward</u> I had, at the outset, no idea of attempting a serious contribution to the movement of social reform. The idea was of a mere literary fantasy, a fairy tale of social felicity. There was no thought of contriving a house which practical men might live in, but merely of hanging in mid-air, far out of reach of the sordid and material world of the present, a cloud-palace for an ideal humanity.
>
> In order to secure plenty of elbow room for the fancy and prevent awkward collisions between the ideal structure and the hard facts of the world, I fixed the date of the story in the year A.D. 3000. As to what might be in A.D. 3000 one man's opinion was as good as another's, and my fantasy of the social system of that day only required to be consistent with itself to defy criticism.

Emboldened by the impunity my isolated
position secured me, I was satisfied with
nothing less than the whole earth for my
social palace. In its present form the
story is a romance of the ideal nation, but
in its first form it was a romance of an
ideal world. In the first draft of <u>Looking</u>
<u>Backward</u>, though the immediate scene was laid
in America (in Asheville, North Carolina,
instead of Boston, by the way), the United
States was supposed to be merely an administra-
tive province of the great World Nation,
whose affairs were directed from the
World Capital which was declared to be the
city of Berne, in Switzerland. The action
of the story was made to begin in the
thirtieth century.

The opening scene was a grand parade
of a departmental division of the industrial
army on the occasion of the annual muster
day when the young men coming of age that
year were mustered into the national and
those who that year had reached the age of
exemption were mustered out. That chapter
always pleased me and it was with some
regrets that I left it out of the final
draft. The solemn pageantry of the great
festival of the year, the impressive
ceremonial of the oath of duty taken by the
new recruits in presence of the world-
standard, the formal return of the thanks
of humanity to the veterans who received
their honorable dismissal from service, the
review and march past of the entire body
of the local industrial forces, each
battalion with its appropriate insignia,
the triumphal arches, the garlanded streets,
the banquets, the music, the open theatres
and pleasure gardens, with all the features
of a gala day sacred to the civic virtues
and the enthusiasm of humanity, furnished
materials for a picture exhilarating at
least to the painter.

The idea of committing the duty of
maintaining the community to an industrial
army, precisely as the duty of protecting
it is entrusted to a military army, was
directly suggested to me by the grand object
lesson of the organization of an entire
people for national purposes presented by

the military system of universal service
for fixed and equal terms, which has been
practically adopted by the nations of
Europe and theoretically adopted everywhere else as the only just and only
effectual plan of public defense on a great
scale. What inference could possibly be
more obvious and more unquestionable than
the advisability of trying to see if a
plan which was found to work so well for
purposes of destruction might not be
profitably applied to the business of
production now in such shocking confusion.
But while this idea had for some time been
vaguely floating in my mind, for a year or
two I think at least, I had been far from
realizing all that was in it, and only
thought then of utilizing it as an analogy
to lend an effect of feasibility to the
fancy sketch I had in hand. It was not
till I began to work out the details of the
scheme by way of explaining how the people
of the thirtieth century disposed of the
awkward problems of labor and avoided the
evils of a classified society that I per-
ceived the full potency of the instrument
I was using and recognized in the modern
military system not merely a rhetorical
analogy for a national industrial service,
but its prototype, furnishing at once a
complete working model for its organization,
an arsenal of patriotic and national motives
and arguments for its animation, and the
unanswerable demonstration of its feasibility
drawn from the actual experience of whole
nations organized and manoeuvred as armies.

Something in this way it was that, no
thanks to myself, I stumbled over the destined
corner-stone of the new social order. It
scarcely needs to be said that having once
apprehended it for what it was, it became
a matter of pressing importance to me to
show it in the same light to other people.
This led to a complete recasting, both in
form and purpose, of the book I was engaged
upon. Instead of a mere fairy tale of
social perfection, it became the vehicle of
a definite scheme of industrial reorganization.
The form of a romance was retained, although
with some impatience, in the hope of inducing
the more to give it at least a reading.

Barely enough story was left to decently
drape the skeleton of the argument and
not enough, I fear, in spots, for even
that purpose. A great deal of merely
fanciful matter concerning the manners,
customs, social and political institutions,
mechanical contrivances, and so forth
of the people of the thirtieth century,
which had been intended for the book, was
cut out for fear of diverting the attention
of readers from the main theme. Instead
of the year A.D. 3000, that of A.D. 2000
was fixed upon as the date of the story.
Ten centuries had at first seemed to me
none too much to allow for the evolution
of anything like an ideal society, but
with my new belief as to the part which the
National organization of industry is to
play in bringing in the good time coming,
it appeared to me reasonable to suppose
that by the year 2000 the order of things
which we look forward to will already have
become an exceedingly old story. This
conviction as to the shortness of the time
in which the hope of Nationalization is to
be realized by the birth of the new, and the
first true, nation, I wish to say, is one
which every day's reflection and observation,
since the publication of Looking Backward,
has tended to confirm. (19)

The publication of Looking Backward marks the end

of Edward Bellamy's interest in literature other than as

a means of propaganda. He was now engaged in advocating

the social system that he had "stumbled upon" in writing

Looking Backward. He felt compelled to carry on the work

that he had begun to the exclusion of all else. In 1890,

Horace E. Scudder, Editor of The Atlantic Monthly, had

written offering the chance of writing a serial for The

Atlantic. Bellamy's answer to that letter is the clearest

(19) The Nationalist, I, (May, 1889), 1-4.

exposition of his new interest:

August 25, 1890

Dear Mr. Scudder:

The dangerous illness of my little
girl has for some weeks occupied my mind
to the exclusion of anything else and
made me neglect correspondence. She is
better now and I am beginning to answer
my letters.
So it happens that I am now just
acknowledging your response to my expression of regret at having to miss the
chance of writing the next Atlantic serial.
It would indeed be a delight to me to
revert to those psychologic studies and
speculations which were the theme of my
earlier writings. But since my eyes
have been opened to the evils and perils of
our social state and I have begun to
cherish a clear hope of better things, I
simply can't "Get my consent" to write or
think of anything else. As a literary
man I fear I am a "goner" and past
praying for. There is a sense in which
I am very sorry for this, for I had much
work laid out to do, and should have greatly
enjoyed doing it. There is one life which
I would like to lead and another which I
must lead. If I had only been twins. [20]

The regret that Bellamy expresses at not being able to go

on with purely literary work can hardly have been very

deep, for he was now actively engaged in the exciting

business of lecturing and forming a new party based upon

the ideas of his utopian novel. Henceforth he was a social

reformer, a propagandist for nationalist ideas. Yet the

genuine excellence of his earlier work ought not to be

obscured, as it has been, because of the eminence of Looking

---

[20] A typewritten copy of this heretofore unpublished
letter was given me by Mrs. Marian Bellamy Earnshaw,
Mr. Bellamy's daughter.

Backward. With respect to this utopian novel, Howells wisely doubted whether Bellamy's "ethics would keep his aesthetics in remembrance"; but he had no such doubt about the earlier literary work of Bellamy when he said, "I am sure that one cannot acquaint one's self with his merely artistic work, and not be sensible that in Edward Bellamy we were rich in a romantic imagination surpassed only by that of Hawthorne." [21]

The success of Looking Backward forced Bellamy to emerge somewhat from his secluded life. In his enthusiasm for nationalist ideas, he became a lecturer and public figure. He had written the most popular book of the year and was given all kinds of offers to cash in on his good fortune. Under the stress of all these, the essential integrity of his character emerges more than at any other time in his career. Throughout all the furor, he maintained his high sense of duty. Lucrative offers to lecture, profitable opportunities for writing sequels to Looking Backward or any other kind of novel, all these he rejected unless he could see a definite advantage for nationalistic ideas. Nothing could be further from the truth than the charges of some of his contemporaries that he was "posing for notoriety." As his friend, Sylvester Baxter said, "To those who know the retiring modest, and almost diffident personality of the author, nothing could have been more

---

(21) Howells, W.D., op. cit., 256.

absurd." [22] He was like one of the citizens that he
pictured in his Boston of 2000 in his indifference to
personal financial gain. Most of the profits derived from
Looking Backward and his magazine articles on nationalism
were spent on the nationalist cause; for himself he kept
very little.

Under the stress of this active life, his health,
which had never been robust, began to fail. On October
17, 1889, he wrote to his publisher to decline an invitation
to lecture:

Oct. 17, 1889

Dear Mr. Houghton:

I shall certainly give myself the
pleasure of calling on you the first time
I am in Boston long enough to turn around
twice. But as to the lecturing, I fear it
would be no use to discuss that. I have
within a few weeks received enough
invitations to lecture (many of them highly
desirable) in all the big cities, to make
dates for a winter's tour if I accepted them.
I have, however, declined them all, including several propositions for a series
of lectures in California, where the
people seem to be going into Nationalism
en masse. The trouble is my health is not
robust and the first week of travel would
lay me out. Moreover, I should not want to
lecture on this subject for money, and I
could not afford to do it without it. [23]

In May, 1889, a monthly magazine called The Nationalist

---

(22) Baxter, S., "The Author of Looking Backward" in
     1926 edition of Looking Backward, (Boston, 1926), ix.

(23) This heretofore unpublished letter was furnished
     by Mrs. Emma S. Bellamy.

began its career. Devoted to spreading the principles

of nationalism it was edited during its first year by

Henry Willard Austin under the direction of The Nation-

alist Educational Association of which Bellamy was

president. By virtue of this office, he was apparently

the guiding spirit of the magazine and contributed numerous

articles to it. The Nationalist for March,1890 announced

that beginning on May 1, 1890, Edward Bellamy would become

editor-in-chief of the magazine. However, in the April,

1890, issue of The Nationalist the following letter from

Bellamy appeared to show that ill health still plagued him:

> Early in February, Henry Austin, Editor
> of The Nationalist came to see me and strongly
> urged me to become his successor, beginning
> with the May number.
> My regard for Mr. Austin lent great
> weight to his wishes and after considerable
> hesitation I consented.
> I was at that time pretty well used
> up from a two month's tussle with the in-
> fluenza then prevalent, and was in no con-
> dition for work of any kind; but in making
> this engagement with Mr. Austin, and
> through him with the public, I reckoned on
> regaining my ordinary health before it
> should fall due.
> In this expectation I have been
> disappointed. I am now told by my
> physician that if I am to be of use in the
> future, I must take an almost absolute rest
> this summer.
> In view of this advice it would seem
> imperative that I should not assume, at
> least for the present, a duty so responsible
> as that of editing The Nationalist....
> By way of compounding for my broken
> engagement I hope to write a good many
> editorial notes for the Magazine during
> the summer which service, together with
> the Presidency of the Nationalist Educational
> Association...will make me a somewhat active

member of the Editorial Board.

Edward Bellamy [24]

Because of Bellamy's continued ill health, John Storer
Cobb took over the editorship and continued in that capacity
until The Nationalist was discontinued in April, 1891
because of lack of financial support. When his health did
improve, Bellamy decided to start a new journal rather
than to associate himself with the moribund Nationalist.
He therefore became editor of a weekly paper, The New Nation
devoted to criticism of "the existing industrial system
as radically wrong in morals and preposterous economically
and [it] will plan the substitution therefor, as rapidly
as practicable, of the plan of national industrial cooperation, aiming to bring about the economic equality of
citizens, which is known as Nationalism." [25] Bellamy
maintained his active interest in The New Nation until it
perished in 1894 chiefly because of a waning interest in
nationalism.

He apparently began writing his last book, Equality,
shortly after this time. This work---it can hardly even
be called a novel---shows how remote his interest in literature had become. In Looking Backward there had been
enough plot to carry the reader rather pleasantly through

---

(24) The Nationalist, II, (April, 1890), 187.

(25) The New Nation, I, (January 31, 1891), 13.

the economic intricacies of the future. In _Equality_
Bellamy doesn't even bother to coat his economic pill
with the sugar covering of a story; in fact _Equality_ is
little more than an economic treatise devoted to filling
in the gaps in the social structure described in _Looking_
Backward. The transition from an interest in literature
to the study of economics had taken place as early as 1890,
but _Equality_ is the best evidence as to its completeness.
From the standpoint of the student of literature, this
change is regrettable, for Bellamy's early work augured
well for some really great production in the realm of
romance. This point of view is substantiated by a comparison of _Looking Backward_ with _Equality_; the former
succeeded because of definite literary merit, winning its
readers through an unusual plot arrangement. _Equality_
failed to reach any wide audience because it falls entirely
in the realm of economics.

The writing of _Equality_ was too great a tax upon
Bellamy's energy. "His health, never robust, gave way
completely, and the book was finished by an indomitable
and inflexible dominion of the powerful mind over the
failing body which was nothing short of heroic." [26]
Tuberculosis developed, and in September, 1897, Bellamy
with his family went to Colorado in the hope of finding

_____

(26) Baxter, S., _op. cit._, xii.

a cure. He was warmly acclaimed in the West, where his work was well known and where nationalist ideas had met an enthusiastic reception.

A few months in the higher altitude of Colorado made it apparent that there was no cure for him. His one desire was to return to Chicopee Falls. He left Colorado in 1898 and arrived home to spend the last month before his death on May 22, 1898, in the scenes that he loved. In this, Howells sees a larger significance:

> I am glad that he lived to die at home in Chicopee,--in the village environment by which he interpreted the heart of the American nation, and knew how to move it more than any other American author who has lived. The theory of those who think differently is that he simply moved the popular fancy; and this may suffice to explain the state of some people, but it will not account for the love and honor in which his name is passionately held by the vast average, East and West. His fame is safe with them, and his faith is an animating force concerning whose effect at this time or some other time it would not be wise to prophesy. (27)

At his funeral in accordance with Bellamy's own wishes were read passages from Looking Backward, Equality, and "The Religion of Solidarity" an unpublished paper which he wrote in 1874 containing his philosophy of life.

His death occasioned innumerable tributes, for his work was as well known in other countries as in the United

_____

(27) Howells, W.D., op. cit., 256.

States. Even those who thought his ideas impracticable, recognized the essential integrity of their author. He left a deep impression upon the generation in which he lived and did more than any other American of his day to marshall the forces of idealism by giving them a popular expression.

His life had lent a dignity to reform movements and reformers, for his sincerity was undoubted, his high-minded purpose unquestioned. One of the best estimates of his qualities says, "Edward Bellamy was on the whole one of the gentlest and most humane revolutionists that ever lived. He was so mild-mannered in his innovations, so peaceable in thought and life, so sympathetic even with the distorted conditions of human society, that we scarcely know how to classify him." [28] By so obviously not belonging to the wild-eyed, bomb-throwing group of foreign agitators that were beginning to be typed in the popular mind as "reformers", Bellamy's life and work typified a reform that was essentially American.

The following poem shows the unrestrained type of eulogy that Bellamy received from those who believed implicitly in his ideas:

Edward Bellamy
by
Winwood Waitt

The newer day has dawned for him:

_____

(28) "Is the Prophet Dead", an editorial in The Arena, XX, (August, 1898), 285.

The prophet of the greater good
Has joined a nobler brotherhood.

No court of saints or seraphim,
No city of all-blissful peace,
Allured his spirit's glad release.

He thrust aside the mystic veil
And found, beyond Death's "dust to dust",
Convened the Council of the Just.

On planes of keener consciousness,
With poet, sage, and earnest seer,
He scans the fabric patterned here.

"Hail and well met!" The greeting given,
With native, unassuming grace
He holds with these the chosen place,

Wherein his ampler scope of mind
And broadened vision yet shall span
The perfect brotherhood of man---

The ripe fruition of a dream
To crown the toil of centuries!
A social apotheosis! (29)

A far greater tribute, however, came from the pen of

William Dean Howells, who could give an estimate of Bellamy's

life without being overwhelmed by an unrestrained admiration

for his ideas:

> I recall how, when we first met, he
> told me that he had come to think of our
> hopeless conditions suddenly, one day, in
> looking at his own children, and reflecting
> that he could not place them beyond the
> chance of want by any industry or forecast
> or providence; and that the status meant the
> same impossibility for others which it meant
> for him. I understood then that I was in
> the presence of a man too single, too sincere,
> to pretend that he had begun by thinking of
> others, and I trusted him the more for his

---

(29) The Arena, XX, (July, 1898), 133.

confession of a selfish premise. He never
went back to himself in his endeavour, but
when he had once felt his power in the world,
he dedicated his life to his work. He wore
himself out in thinking and feeling about
it, with a belief in the good time to come
that penetrated his whole being and animated
his whole purpose, but apparently with no
manner of fanaticism. In fact, no one could
see him, or look into his quiet, gentle
face, so full of goodness, so full of common
sense, without perceiving that he had ·
reasoned to his hope for justice in the
frame of things. He believed that some now
living should see his dream--the dream of
Plato, the dream of the first Christians,
the dream of Bacon, the dream of More--come
true in a really civilized society; but he
had the patience and courage which could
support any delay. (30)

As Howells indicates, one can disagree with the dream,

Looking Backward, but for the man behind it, there can

be nothing but respect and admiration.

---

(30) Howells, W.D., op. cit., 256.

CHAPTER VII

LOOKING BACKWARD AND NATIONALISM

In retrospect, one can easily demonstrate that
Looking Backward was one of the most opportune books
ever to appear in America. Viewed as it should be against
the background of historical forces making for popular
discontent (already described in Chapter IV), _Looking
Backward_ clearly expresses ideas which were in the minds
of millions of less articulate Americans. In this one
novel were fused most of the reform ideas of Bellamy's
generation, expressed in a form so attractive and with a
method seemingly so capable of attainment, that almost
immediately it became the focal point of all idealistic
schemes. Perhaps most important was the fact that the
book appeared less than two years after the great labor
struggles of 1886, when affairs like the Haymarket episode
in Chicago and the widespread eight-hour strikes, centering
in Chicago, were still fresh in public memory. Later,
while thousands were reading its descriptions of future
peace and prosperity, occurred the bloody strikes in the
Carnegie Steel Works at Homestead, Pennsylvania, and in the
Pullman Plant at Chicago. Small wonder then that to its
millions of readers, _Looking Backward_ seemed to offer the
one way out. Benjamin O. Flower, a fellow-reformer,
accurately analysed the intellectual forces that made this

utopian novel so popular.

> Certain it is that had it not been for
> the rising tide of social and humanistic
> idealism that was opposing the dominant
> materialistic commercialism, and the
> nation-wide hunger for a nobler social order,
> the book would never have approached a sale
> of half a million copies.
> But the soil was prepared for the
> message. Mr. George had doubtless done
> much toward this end, in that he had
> awakened hundreds of thousands of thinkers,
> breaking the moral lethargy that had long
> held the nation in thrall; but a great
> number of his readers had unconsciously
> imbibed so much of the distrust of
> liberty and humanity that had gone hand
> in hand with the onward march of re-
> action and privilege, that they did not
> possess his splendid Jeffersonian faith
> in freedom. Others did not want to do
> much thinking for themselves, and here
> was a problem worked out for them ....
> Hence, while those deeply grounded in the
> individualistic democratic philosophy
> of Mr. George were unaffected, a still
> greater number of those who had first
> been startled out of sodden complacence
> by Progress and Poverty enthusiastically
> acclaimed Looking Backward as a new social
> evangel which they believed had only to
> be read by the millions to be generally
> accepted. (1)

Considering the novel against the background of these social,

economic, and intellectual trends, one can fairly conclude

that in its opportune expression of popular ideas Looking

Backward is second only to Uncle Tom's Cabin in the history

of American literature.

The attitude of Bellamy's contemporaries toward his

---

(1) Flower, B.O., Progressive Men, Women, and Movements of
the Past Twenty-Five Years, (Boston, 1914), 81-82.

novel is not surprising---but the opinions of later critics
are amazing. For instance Edward Weeks, John Dewey, and
Charles Beard in their independently prepared lists of
"The Twenty-Five Most Influential Books Published Since
1885---including books which have influenced both thought
and action", [2] rank Bellamy's novel as second in influence
only to Marx's Das Kapital. Another list compiled for
librarians of "The Twenty-Five Books that Have Changed the
Modern World" [3] gives an important place to Looking Backward. Economic conditions have unquestionably reawakened
interest. There is some ground for a parallel between the
conditions that Bellamy describes and the realities of the
first third of the twentieth century. The Rooseveltian
New Deal is thought by many to be going in the direction
of Bellamy's nationalistic state. These and other factors
have combined to arouse new interest in Bellamy's novel.
While much of this interest will die with an improvement
in economic conditions, Looking Backward will undoubtedly
occupy a prominent and permanent part in the history of
American literature and thought.

The manuscript of Looking Backward was sent off to
Ticknor and Company in October, 1887, and was immediately
accepted for publication, but with certain suggestions as

(2) The complete list may be found in the Atlantic Monthly,
    April, 1935.

(3) Wilson's Bulletin for Librarians for October, 1935, 118.

to changes in the book itself and the possibility of
publishing it anonymously. Both of these suggestions
Bellamy rejected, and something of his own haste to get
his ideas before the public is reflected in his answer:

> Yours at hand proposing to publish
> this new book....
> If you tackled it, how soon could you
> bring it out? I am particularly desirous
> that it should see the light as quickly
> as possible. Now is the accepted time,
> it appears to me, for the publications
> touching on social and industrial questions,
> to obtain a hearing. As to the anonymity
> business, I don't care about that. I
> think the book had better bear the author's
> name. The only reason wherefore I
> suggested anything else was that the
> fiction underlying the plot is rather
> given away by the bold confession of a
> nineteenth-century authority. But probably
> the public will not even notice so fine a
> point as that. (4)

Bellamy goes on to discuss various changes that the reader
for Ticknor and Co. had suggested, and rejects them all.

The original hope of both author and publisher had
been to bring out the novel in time for Christmas, 1887,
but delay in printing held it over until the first of the
year. Bellamy was still reading the proof of the book in
December, 1887. A letter to Ticknor written at the time
reveals his feeling that Looking Backward would attain some
popularity.

> I am not in the main a very favorable
> critic of my own work, but in reading this
> book in proof I have been strengthened in

(4) The entire letter is quoted in Caroline Ticknor's
Glimpses of Authors, (Boston, 1922), 113-4.

> the conviction that if pushed with the
> vigor which no doubt you will use, it is
> calculated to make an impression. (5)

No one could have predicted the amazing success of
Looking Backward. Bellamy himself was deeply gratified
at the widespread interest his ideas aroused. His work
became the literary sensation of the year, and the sales
of _Looking Backward_ mounted steadily over several years.
The following statistics taken from advertisements of the
Houghton Mifflin Company in _The Nationalist_ and _The New
Nation_ give an accurate idea of the immediate popularity
of Bellamy's novel.

```
November, 1889----175,000
December, 1889----210,000
February, 1890----301,000
March, 1890-------310,000
May, 1890---------330,000
July, 1890--------347,000
January, 1891-----371,000
```

The total sales of _Looking Backward_ are difficult to estimate, but they are probably well over a million copies in
the United States. When one realizes that this novel has
been translated into most of the languages of the world,
one begins to realize its widespread influence. But before
examining some of the specific manifestations of this influence, we had better look at the book itself.

Looking Backward purports to be a narrative orginating
in the "Historical Section, Shawmut College, Boston, December

---

(5) _Ibid_, 116.

26, 2000" according to its Preface. Julian West, its narrator, is supposed to be a Professor of History at Shawmut College, and this volume has as its object "to assist persons who, while desiring to gain a more definite idea of the social contrasts between the nineteenth and twentieth centuries, are daunted by the formal aspect of the histories which treat the subject." (6) In order to overcome the lack of interest of ordinary history, the author proposes to put his account in the form of a story. Bellamy consistently maintains this guise by titling his book Looking Backward when from the viewpoint of most of his nineteenth century readers it might more accurately have been called Looking Forward.

The narrative is quite simple. Julian West, a wealthy young resident of Boston, after having spent May 30, 1887, with his fiancée, Edith Bartlett, returns to his home only to find himself troubled with his chronic ailment, insomnia. He calls in Dr. Pillsbury a "Professor of Animal Magnetism", who mesmerizes him. West has had a special sound-proof, subterranean chamber prepared to which he retires on such occasions.

When West awakes he finds himself surrounded by a group of strangers who regard him with great curiosity. Eventually he learns that he has slept 113 years and has awakened in

(6) Bellamy, E., "Author's Preface" to Looking Backward, (New York, 1926), xix.

Boston in September, 2000. He finds himself in the home
of Dr. Leete, a distinguished physician of Boston, with
whom resides his wife and daughter, Edith Leete. In describing the bewilderment and terror of West at finding
himself in this strange new world, Bellamy does much to
make an impossible situation seem real.

From that point forward, the plot moves along very
slowly, because Bellamy's chief interest is in the exposition of the various details of the social system.
These are brought out naturally enough by having Julian
West ask innumerable questions of Dr. Leete. He is
escorted by Edith Leete to all parts of Boston; all the
marvels of science are described in detail. A mild element
of suspense is added by Edith's mysterious knowledge of
various people that had been friends of West until the
reader finally learns that Edith Leete is the great grand-
daughter of Edith Bartlett, West's 19th century sweetheart
who had eventually married someone else.

A novel touch is added to Looking Backward by having
West apparently return to the 19th century so that the
Boston of 2000 seems but a dream. His dissatisfaction with
conditions in the 19th century is intensified by the apparent
glimpse of the future world. The throat-cutting competition
of business and the squalor of Boston are revolting in the
extreme, and he begins to wonder how he can endure living
in this nineteenth century world when he awakes to find

that this has been the dream, and Boston in 2000 is a
reality. This part of Looking Backward Howells found
particularly praiseworthy because as he said "that is
quite as it would happen in life, and the power to make
the reader feel this like something he had known himself
is the distinctive virtue of that imagination which re-
vived throughout Christendom the faith in a millenium." (7)
The book ends with the impending marriage of West and Edith
Leete.

Many critics agree with Heywood Broun's estimate of
the story of Looking Backward when he says, "I cannot confess
any vast interest in the love story which serves as a
thread for Bellamy's vision of a reconstructed society.
But it can be said that it is so palpably a thread of sugar
crystal that it need not get in the way of any reader." (8)
This, however, puts a rather low estimate on those phases
of Looking Backward which are quite independent of social
gospel. While the plot is hardly exciting, millions of
Americans were led to finish Looking Backward not primarily
for its social ideals but because of interest in the events
described and the aura of reality with which Bellamy in-
vested them. One can draw an interesting parallel between
Henry George's Progress and Poverty and Bellamy's novel in

(7) Howells, W.D., "Edward Bellamy" in Atlantic Monthly,
     LXXXII, (August, 1898), 254.

(8) Broun, H., "Introduction" to Looking Backward,
     (Boston, 1926), iv.

that respect. Both preach a social gospel---but Looking Backward has won for itself a far wider audience because of its story. One can see the real importance of the plot element in Looking Backward even better by reading Equality, Bellamy's last book, which might very well be called "Looking Backward without a plot." Equality is dry, uninteresting, and difficult to read, and consequently it has won a hearing only among the limited group of people interested in social reform. One of the most significant facts about Looking Backward is that it made itself read by those who ordinarily would not be concerned with social gospels. This fact, Broun and the other critics completely ignore.

As we have seen, however, Bellamy rewrote Looking Backward in order to give increased emphasis to social ideals, and ultimately the book must stand or fall upon the social system expounded in it. However examined---and despite the fact that Bellamy euphemistically called it Nationalism---the system advocated in Looking Backward is a modified form of socialism. This indeed is one of the novel's great triumphs---it introduces socialism in a form attractive to Americans, possibly because they didn't recognize it as such. Professor Ely remarks,

> A generation ago Edward Bellamy wrote his Looking Backward in which he describes his plan for socialism and called it "Nationalism". I recall hearing a lady speak in high praise of Bellamy's book and in the same breath speak in abhorrence of

socialism, not recognizing that what
Bellamy and his associates were working
for was simply socialism under another
name. (9)

Equally important is the fact that Bellamy's socialism

was far removed from the Marxian variety, which was anathema

in most American circles in the late nineteenth century.

Whether consciously or not, he adopted a form of government

like that in Laurence Gronlund's Cooperative Commonwealth,

which was peculiarly adapted to American conditions.

Historically, America had no horizontal division of classes

pointing to an inevitable class struggle, and Bellamy

wisely omitted any suggestion of a class war from his novel.

In addition to avoiding any Marxian principles, Bellamy

used certain American economic tendencies to indicate what

he believed would be the inevitable trend in all social and

political organization. His was the era of great economic

trusts; the basic fact of organization in Boston of 2000

is the application of monopolistic principles to everything.

> The nation, that is to say, organized as
> the one great corporation in which all
> other corporations were absorbed; it
> became the one capitalist in the place
> of all other capitalists, the sole
> employer, the final monopoly in which
> all previous and lesser monopolies were
> swallowed up, a monopoly in the profits
> and economies of which all citizens shared.
> The epoch of trusts had ended in The
> Great Trust. (10)

---

(9) Ely, R.T. and Bohn, F., The Great Change, (New York,
    1935), 72.

(10) Bellamy, E., op. cit., 56.

To readers beginning to be aware of the great trusts controlling oil products, iron, steel, copper, lead, sugar, coal, and other staples, this idea of the government as "The Great Trust" seemed to be not a socialistic dream but a realistic projection of nineteenth century tendencies out into the future. Unquestionably the chief merit of Bellamy's social structure for American readers was its air of being completely American, both in its avoidance of the less inviting aspects of German socialism and in its use of tendencies already familiar in the United States. In its essence it depicts an American socialism.

The organization of this new society advocated by Bellamy rests completely upon the industrial army, an idea that probably derived from Bellamy's interest in military organization. Into this army all able-bodied citizens enter at the age of twenty-four and remain until they are forty-five, when they are "mustered out" subject to further call only in the event of national emergency. Citizens are permitted the fullest liberty in choosing work on the theory that men do best the things they want to do. The hours of labor are adjusted to compensate for the severity or unpleasantness of the work---and this keeps large numbers from flocking to any one profession.

There is no money in this new civilization but only credit cards entitling each person to a share in the national wealth. Everyone receives an equal share on the principle

that "all men who do their best, do the same." (11)
Bellamy argues that this principle is not contrary to
human nature because those who make great contributions
to civilization receive honor and appreciation from their
fellow citizens sufficient to impell them to new striving.
This factor will seem to many readers the weakest part of
Bellamy's system. Because everyone has security in this
new social structure, crime and its attendant evils have
vanished. Juries, lawyers, and judges have been eliminated;
criminals are treated as if they were mentally ill.

Bellamy's expository method throughout the novel is
to compare constantly the system of the nineteenth century
with this ideal new world. Julian West is ostensibly amazed
all the time at the sanity and practicability of this new
social structure, and he takes every opportunity to contrast
the greed and injustice of his former existence. This sort
of thing is climaxed by having Mr. Barton, the most eminent
preacher in Boston, deliver a sermon---eighteen pages in
length!---in which he contrasts the principles of the new
and the old waysof living. He concludes what to most readers
is a very tiresome part of the book with these rhapsodic
words:

> With a tear for the dark past, turn we
> then to the dazzling future, and, veiling
> our eyes, press forward. The long and

---

(11) Bellamy, E., op. cit., 94.

> weary winter of the race is ended. Its
> summer has begun. Humanity has burst the
> chrysalis. The heavens are before it. (12)

The external trappings of Boston in 2000 have received
more attention from critics than they deserve. Many have
been most impressed with Bellamy's predictions of radio,
which according to Heywood Broun "might almost have been
lifted bodily from an article in some newspaper radio
column." (13) The scientific marvels of the future with
electricity as the universal servant and with all kinds of
rapid transportation are described with apparent reality.
This sort of thing is the most obvious part of any prediction of the future, and since Bellamy himself possessed
no mechanical ability or interest, this phase of Looking
Backward has received unwarranted praise.

Much more important are the parts of the novel showing
the weaknesses of the competitive system of the 19th century
under the ruling doctrine of lassez-faire. Whole sections
of the book are devoted to the periodic depressions caused
by a maladjustment between the agencies of production and
consumption. He describes the unproductive sections of
the populace---advertising men, lawyers, and salesmen.
This phase of Looking Backward is climaxed by the dream,
already described, in which Julian West imagines that he
has actually returned to 19th century Boston and is over-

---

(12) Bellamy, E., op. cit., 292.

(13) Broun, H., op. cit., ii.

whelmed by its outward ugliness and organized injustice.

The basic criticism of the competitive system is moral-
--and it is easy to see Edward Bellamy, thinking of the
future of his own two children, when he penned in the
following words what was his own most serious indictment
of the nineteenth century:

> Do your work never so well,...rise early
> and toil till late, rob cunningly or serve
> faithfully, you shall never know security.
> Rich you may be now and still come to
> poverty at last. Leave never so much
> wealth to your children, you cannot buy
> the assurance that your son may not be the
> servant of your servant, or that your
> daughter will not have to sell herself for
> bread. (14)

Regardless of his views on the practicability of the
social scheme of Looking Backward, no reader can be unaware
that a great and unselfish personality exists behind its
strictures. In his longing for a true equality for all
men, in his zeal for the elimination of poverty, injustice,
and crime, Edward Bellamy emerges as a great American imbued
with the one idea of bringing about the brotherhood of man.
One can feel his strength of purpose and his righteous
indignation in the following passage, perhaps the best
in Looking Backward:

> I cannot do better than to compare society
> as it then was to a prodigious coach which
> the masses of humanity were harnessed to
> and dragged toilsomely along a very hilly and
> sandy road. The driver was hungry, and

---

(14) Bellamy, E., op. cit., 321.

permitted no lagging, though the pace was
necessarily very slow. Despite the
difficulty of drawing the coach at all
along so hard a road, the top was covered
with passengers who never got down, even
at the steepest ascents. These seats on
top were very breezy and comfortable. Well
up out of the dust, their occupants could
enjoy the scenery at their leisure, or
critically discuss the merits of the
straining team. Naturally such places
were in great demand and the competition
for them was keen, every one seeking as
the first end in life to secure a seat on
the coach for himself and to leave it to
his child after him. By the rule of the
coach a man could leave his seat to whom
he wished, but on the other hand there
were many accidents by which it might at
any time be wholly lost. For all that
they were so easy, the seats were very
insecure, and at every sudden jolt of the
coach persons were slipping out of them
and falling to the ground, where they were
instantly compelled to take hold of the
rope and help to drag the coach on which
they had before ridden so pleasantly. It
was naturally regarded as a terrible mis-
fortune to lose one's seat, and the
apprehension that this might happen to them
or their friends was a constant cloud upon
the happiness of those who rode.

But did they think only of themselves?
you ask. Was not their very luxury rendered intolerable to them by comparison
with the lot of their brothers and sisters
in the harness, and the knowledge that their
own weight added to their toil? Had they
no compassion for fellow beings from whom
fortune only distinguished them? Oh, yes;
commiseration was frequently expressed by
those who rode for those who had to pull
the coach, especially when the vehicle came
to a bad place in the road, as it was constantly doing, or to a particularly steep
hill. At such times, the desperate straining of the team, their agonized leaping and
plunging under the pitiless lashing of
hunger, the many who fainted at the rope
and were trampled in the mire, made a very
distressing spectacle, which often called
forth highly creditable displays of feeling

on the top of the coach. At such times
the passengers would call down encouragingly
to the toilers of the rope, exhorting them
to patience, and holding out hopes of
possible compensation in another world for
the hardness of their lot, while others
contributed to buy salves and liniments
for the crippled and injured. It was agreed
that it was a great pity that the coach
should be so hard to pull, and there was
a sense of general relief when the specially
bad piece of road was gotten over. This
relief was not, indeed, wholly on account
of the team, for there was always some
danger at these bad places of a general
overturn in which all would lose their seats.

It must in truth be admitted that the
main effect of the spectacle of the misery
of the toilers at the rope was to enhance
the passengers' sense of the value of their
seats upon the coach, and to cause them
to hold on to them more desperately than
before. If the passengers could only have
felt assured that neither they nor their
friends would ever fall from the top, it is
probable that, beyond contributing to the
funds for liniments and bandages, they
would have troubled themselves extremely
little about those who dragged the coach. (15)

This is Bellamy at his best, for here he is neither enmeshed
in economic theory nor a propagandist, but a skilled literary
artist dominated by a driving emotion. One can wish that
there might have been more of this kind of writing in Looking
Backward and fewer detailed expositions of utopian economics.
Contemporary reviews of the novel took much this same
view of Bellamy's utopia:

Yet it is impossible for a generous
mind to be unmoved by the contrast which
Mr. Bellamy draws between the nineteenth
century, with the fierce struggle for life,
and the twentieth, when the lion and the

_____

(15) Bellamy, E., op. cit., 10 and ff.

lamb lie side by side, the lion with his
claws pared and eating grass....There are
many shrewd observations, some noteworthy attempts at indicating the trend
of present social movements, and above all,
as we have said, an earnest cry for the
peace of human brotherhood,---a cry which
resounds through the book and is far more
effective a sermon to selfish minds than
the vague generalities which fill the actual
sermon preached in the hearing of Mr. West. [16]

American idealists immediately rallied around Looking
Backward and its economic system. Frances E. Willard said
"I do not see why what is in it should not some day come
to pass." [17]   Edward Everett Hale and Thomas Wentworth
Higginson became staunch supporters of Nationalism.
Higginson declared:

It often happens in literature that he who
giveth his life saveth it. When a writer
forgets the doctrine of art for art's sake,
and writes for a great purpose, he sometimes achieves a success beyond expectation.
This was the case when Mrs. Stowe wrote
Uncle Tom's Cabin and Mrs. Helen Jackson
wrote Romona; but there never was a more
striking instance of it than when Edward
Bellamy wrote Looking Backward. [18]

Immediately upon publication of the novel a debate arose
as to whether 2000 was not a ridiculously early date for
this social system to be put into effect. A reviewer in
the Boston Transcript of March 30, 1888, suggested that

---

(16) Atlantic Monthly, LXI, (June, 1888), 846.

(17) The Arena, VI, (August, 1892), 321.

(18) Higginson, T.W., "Step by Step" in The Nationalist,
     I, (May, 1889), 144.

Bellamy should have pushed his system seventy-five centuries ahead. Bellamy answered by pointing to the progress that the last century had seen and concluded:

> Looking Backward was written in the belief
> that the Golden Age lies before us and not
> behind us, and is not far away. Our children
> will surely see it, and we, too, who are
> already men and women if we deserve to by
> our faith and by our works. [19]

This attitude Bellamy maintained until the end of his life, despite the fact that interest in Nationalism had already begun to wane. More realistic admirers were inclined to agree with Edward Everett Hale that "it is not probable that we shall see Mr. Bellamy's arrangements adopted in any less time than he himself gave to this particular solution." [20]

This discussion of the time when nationalism would be attained was mild compared to the controversy that raged over the system itself. No reputable economist would express any belief in the practicability of such a social organization. Three very scathing attacks on its ideas were written by Francis A. Walker, Professor W.T. Harris, and Professor Nicholas Gilman. All three maintained the same point of view. Professor Harris [21] accused any

---

(19) This letter now forms a Postscript to Looking
Backward. The above quotation is from page 337
of the 1926 edition.

(20) Cosmopolitan Magazine, X, (November, 1890), 123.

(21) Harris, W.T., "Edward Bellamy's Vision" in The
Forum, VIII, (October, 1889), 199-208.

such utopia of resting upon two false premises: first,
that in a competitive system the rich grow richer and the
poor grow poorer and more numerous, and second that the
rich grow rich at the expense of the poor. Nicholas Gilman
writing in The Quarterly Journal of Economics for October,
1889, goes on to discuss the people interested in such a
book and the author's fitness to write it. "Nationalism"
he says, "is characterized most of all by a literary
character. It was founded upon the basis of a clever
novel, which itself originated in a metaphor pushed to the
extreme." [22] As for its author,

> But when Mr. Bellamy assumes "in all
> seriousness", the role of prophet, refusing
> to be accepted simply as an intellectual
> stimulator through the imagination, he im-
> poses a painful strain upon our respect.
> When he prophesies "he is a child". The
> author of Looking Backward is so throughly
> a man of letters rather than an orator of
> the millenium, a man of imagination rather
> than of political sense or economic sagacity,
> that his best wishers must desire for him
> the speediest possible collapse of a crusade
> which, as at present organized is much more
> amusing than formidable. The solid repu-
> tation in the field of letters to which
> Looking Backward has properly contributed
> much, can only be weakened by the mere
> notoriety which his estravagant prophecies
> have conferred upon him. [23]

This is indeed a well-founded charge, for Edward Bellamy
was prepared neither by education nor experience to be a

---

(22) Gilman, N.P., "Nationalism in the United States"
in The Quarterly Journal of Economics, IV, (October,
1889), 66.

(23) Gilman, N.P., op. cit., 68.

critic of social and economic institutions. His province
had always been belle lettres, and it is dubious if even
the most keen social sympathy could compensate for an
inadequate grasp of all the ramifications intrinsic in
our economic organization.

However, Looking Backward cannot fairly be judged as
a work of economics alone. It assumed an importance over
and above that. As Laurence Gronlund, a leading American
socialist, conceived of it,

> It has served as a mirror to this one million
> Americans [who have read it], in which they
> saw their own ideas objectively reflected,
> and thus they became for the first time
> conscious of them; moreover, they became
> thereby for the first time aware of the
> great number of people of their own class
> who shared their notions... (24)

The most tangible result of this awareness was the Nationalistic movement, which grew specifically out of the ideas
of Looking Backward.

Nationalism had as its purpose the practical application
of the general ideas expressed in Looking Backward. It
advocated the government's taking over all agencies of
production and distribution through a system described
as "national cooperation". It aims were set forward
succinctly in a "Prospectus" in every issue of The New
Nation, edited by Bellamy:

> The New Nation will criticize the

---

(24) Gronlund, L., "Nationalism" in The Arena, I,
     (January, 1890), 153.

> existing industrial system as radically
> wrong in morals and preposterous
> economically, and will plan the sub-
> stitution therefor, as rapidly as prac-
> ticable, of the plan of national industrial
> cooperation, aiming to bring about the
> economic equality of citizens, which is
> known as Nationalism. (25)

For accomplishing these ends, Nationalist Clubs were
organized in various parts of the United States.

The first of these was The Boston Bellamy Club organized in September 1888, with about thirty members,
including Edward Everett Hale, Thomas Wentworth Higginson,
Frances E. Willard, and Mrs. Mary A. Livermore. Something
of the enthusiastic spirit of this group may be inferred
from one of B.O. Flower's recollections:

> One brilliant member of the club, a lady
> of culture and literary attainments, came
> to my office one afternoon, completely
> intoxicated with the idea of Nationalism,
> which she believed was about to sweep over
> the Republic, transforming a capitalistic
> despotism into an altruistic civilization
> such as only prophets, sages, and poets
> had hitherto caught glimpses of. "The
> Nationalist Club and the Magazine," she
> said, "are the beginning of a movement
> that will soon envelop the country and
> change the old order, for the message is
> so simple and plain, and the benefits are
> so clearly discernible for the millions,
> that when they hear the new truth and see
> how it can be realized, we will have
> practical Christianity for the first time
> in the State, as well as in the hearts of
> men." (26)

---

(25) The New Nation, I, (January 31, 1891), 13. The
complete platform of the Nationalist Party may be
found in the Encyclopedia of Social Sciences.

(26) Flower, B.O., op. cit., 82.

Unfortunately the brotherhood of man didn't spread
through all members of this original Bellamy Club, which
was condemned because of its exclusiveness. Flower recalls "one gentleman who came to my office one afternoon
burdened with grievances against the 'kid-glove Socialists'
as he termed the members of the Club, who thought they
were holier than others." (27) These disgruntled members
formed a more democratic association which they called
the Cold Cut Club, under the leadership of Henry R. Legate.

In December, 1889, the Boston club changed its name
and became the first Nationalist Club with over two hundred
active members and a larger number of associate members.
A directing force was given to the whole movement by a
great meeting in Tremont Temple, Boston, on December 19,
1889. Edward Everett Hale presided, with Bellamy as the
chief speaker. His address, according to the _Boston Post_,
furnished "the most comprehensive and definite statement
yet presented to the public of the grounds of the movement
and the programme which it presents. Its ultimate aim,
frankly avowed by Mr. Bellamy without the use of the term,
is neither more nor less than state socialism in its com-
pletest form..." (28) A writer in _The Nation_ criticized
various details that Bellamy had described in his address,

---

(27) Flower, B.O., _op. cit._, 83.

(28) _Public Opinion_, VIII, (December 28, 1889), 285.

and concluded with the admonition that "the Bellamy kind
of reformers should beware of the dangers of descending
to particulars." [29] Various recommendations as to
organization of other Nationalist Clubs were made and a
program for disseminating information was agreed upon.
The next year----from December, 1889 to December, 1890----
marked the high point of Nationalism.

The anniversary number of The Nationalist, one year
after the publication of Looking Backward, contains the
following information as to the strength and scope of the
movement:

> Today we have over fifty organized
> clubs in fourteen states, and the District
> of Columbia, and while the membership has
> not been as yet fully compiled, it is safe
> to say that there are over 6000 organized
> adherents of Nationalism, working for the
> common end. It is also safe to say there
> are over 500,000 believers, more or less
> in the doctrines of Nationalism. Looking
> Backward is now in its 210 thousandth, and
> selling at the rate of 10,000 a week. It
> is adding converts to our ranks rapidly.
> Since May 1st, 1889, 69,000 copies of this
> magazine have been circulated, and we are
> now called on to print a sixth edition of
> our May number. [30]

A statement as to the exact position of Edward Bellamy
and his novel was issued in the same magazine. Apparently
the fear was prevalent that this nationalistic crusade might
become a movement centered in one man. Furthermore critics

---

(29) The Nation, L, (January 2, 1890), 7.

(30) The Nationalist, II, (December, 1889), 40.

were attacking specific social and economic devices explained in Looking Backward, and advocates of nationalism
probably found some of these charges difficult to meet.
In the light of these facts, the following statement by
Henry W. Austin, Editor of The Nationalist, is significant,
particularly because it must have had Bellamy's consent.

> Realizing that in this age any reform,
> which can be juggled into even the sem-
> blance of a mere one-man following, can
> thus be sidetracked, some of our opponents
> have tried to make out that Nationalism and
> Bellamyism are identical; have attempted
> to foist on the people the idea that
> Nationalists regard Bellamy's delightful
> picture, Looking Backward, as a perfect,
> though pre-natal, photograph of Society
> in the twentieth and succeeding centuries.
> ...Nationalists, as a rule, do indeed
> believe in the broad, general colors of
> that picture....As to many points of
> detail, however, a wide divergence of
> opinion is entertained---and rightly....
> Nor, yet further, does Bellamy wish to
> pose, or be posed, as a guide or leader,
> like Henry George, for instance. Bellamy
> recognizes that the movement is too vast
> to be led or guided by any one man. He
> knows that to ensure a speedy and per-
> manent success, it needs the patient
> focalization of many earnest hearts and
> subtle minds... (31)

Despite this statement, there is little question that
Nationalism and the ideas of Bellamy as set forth in
Looking Backward were one and the same thing in the public
mind.

By the middle of 1890, one hundred and twenty-seven
Nationalist Clubs had been organized in twenty-seven states.

---

(31) The Nationalist, II, (December, 1889), 34.

It is difficult to get any exact estimate of the total
number of members---and of course, thousands who believed
in Bellamy's ideas joined none of these organizations.
The movement was beginning to attract the attention of
other reform groups---and leaders of the trade unions,
crusaders in the woman's suffrage movement, and officers
of the Farmers' Alliance soon found it profitable to
advocate Nationalism.

The columns of The Nationalist during this year were
filled with notices of club meetings all over the country
and with prophecies that the first steps toward Nationalism
would be taken within five years when the government would
take over the railroads and the telegraph. California
welcomed Nationalism more cordially than did any other part
of the country. In June, 1890, there were fifty-five clubs
in that state, and thirty of them located in Los Angeles.
In October, 1890, the nation had over a hundred and fifty
clubs---California still led with sixty-four; New York had
twenty-one, and Massachusetts eleven; the others were
scattered among most of the states in the union. This
marks the climax of Nationalism as a completely independent
movement; thereafter it merged with other reform groups
and began to lose its identity. Representatives of the
Nationalists attended the conference at Cincinnati at which
they endorsed the formation of the new Populist party.
After the Omaha convention of the Peoples Party in July,
1891, The New Nation declared that the earlier ideas of

the Nationalists were incorporated in the new party and
that the plank advocating government ownership of railroads received more applause than any other proposal.
Another meeting of Nationalists was called in Chicago in
1893, but nothing was accomplished, and no later meeting
was held. The dates of the two most important nationalist
magazines shows quite definitely the active period of
Nationalism---The Nationalist published monthly from May,
1889, to April, 1891, and Bellamy's weekly paper The New
Nation from February, 1891, to January, 1894.

The chief weaknesses of Nationalism as a social and
political movement lay in the type of people who were interested in it and its lack of any definite organization.
As already indicated, most of the leading nationalists were
literary people inexperienced in politics, but inspired
by a temporary enthusiasm for a social system set forth in
a novel. Their lack of any organization strong enough to
bring political pressure on influential members of the
government became apparent when they were merged in the
larger reform groups and gradually lost their identity.
This same feature is typical of twentieth century Bellamy
Clubs, which are located in all parts of the world. There
is still no central organization, and no one knows how many
members there are.

The greatest practical accomplishment of the nationalists
was in educating the general public to the possibilities
of government ownership of utilities. Specifically in

their advocacy of municipal ownership of gas, electric light, and water plants by local communities, the nationalists accomplished much. The columns of The New Nation are filled with references to cities which had adopted these measures. In the wider field of national affairs, the Nationalists accomplished nothing beyond the education already mentioned. Government ownership of railways, telegraphs, and other utilities still seems remote. The best analysis of the movement is given by Professor Fred Haynes:

> Its prominence was due to the wide reading of the novel and to the friendship of literary people for its author. Such a basis could hardly be expected to form a foundation for a substantial social movement. Much more thoroughly organized efforts, resting upon long-continued economic studies, have failed as yet, under more favorable conditions, to develop a strong socialist movement in the United States. Certainly a vague enthusiasm for a different social order, generated by an ingenuous literary Utopia, could have only a passing influence. (32)

In literature, one can point to more specific results of Looking Backward and the Nationalist crusade. The following magazines were devoted completely or partially to the advocacy of Nationalist doctrines: The True Nationalist, a weekly paper with Mr. Stansbury Norse as editor, published in New York beginning in 1891; The American

---

(32) Haynes, F.E., Social Politics in the United States, (New York, 1924), 151. Professor Haynes gives by far the best estimate of Nationalism that I have seen.

Nationalist, a monthly journal edited by James Mac-
Donald, published in Las Vegas, New Mexico, beginning in
1891; The True Commonwealth published at Washington, D.C.
in 1890; The Commonwealth and The Pacific Monthly both
from California, were joined in 1889 by a weekly magazine
called Looking Forward published at National City, California; The Dawn edited by Rev. W.D.P. Bliss in Boston
advocated Christian Socialism, but contained much material
sympathetic to Nationalism; The Living Issue a weekly
paper published in Cincinnati under the editorship of
Mary L. Geffs was devoted to Nationalism as it found expression in the Peoples' Party; The Western Advocate of
Mankato, Kansas, a weekly recognizing "Nationalism as the
only practical solution of the industrial and social
problems." [33]; The Sociologic News, published at Brooklyn, New York, with Imogene C. Fales as editor; and The
Nationalist a little monthly paper published by the
Baltimore Nationalist Club. Something of the popular
interest in Nationalism may be inferred from the fact that
the following magazine articles all appeared within six
months:

> Nationalism by Laurence Gronlund in The
> Arena, Jan., 1890.
>
> Looking Backward Again by Edward Bellamy.
> North American Review, March, 1890.

---

(33) The New Nation, I, (August 1, 1891), 435.

Why I am a Nationalist. Burnett G. Haskell.
Twentieth Century, May, 1890.

Nationalism. Thaddeus B. Wakeman. *Open
Court*, May, 1890.

Nationalism. Professor Bernard Moses.
Overland Monthly, June, 1890.

Nationalistic Socialism. J. Ransom Bridge.
The Arena, January, 1890.

The Mask of Tyranny. Wm. Lloyd Garrison.
The Arena, April, 1890.

Books bearing directly on Nationalism were so numerous that a complete list would lie outside the province
of this thesis. A few of them illustrate the seriousness
with which Nationalism was accepted by the general public.
Most typical of these was J. Pickering Putnam's *Architecture under Nationalism* (Boston, 1891), which is an
exposition of the ways in which architecture would benefit
if a nationalist government were set up. In 1896,
Fayette Stratton Giles published *The Industrial Army*
(New York, 1896), a detailed exposition of the fundamental
organization in Bellamy's system. It explains that the
army would be, in effect, a great profit-sharing trust in
which men would serve for five years. Among the other
works of nationalism, the following books and pamphlets
are most important: Bellamy, Edward *Plutocracy or Nation-
alism---Which?* (Boston, 1889); Bellamy *Principles and
Purposes of Nationalism* (Philadelphia, 1889); Bellamy *The
Program of the Nationalists* (New York, 1894); Colville,
W.W.J. *Nationalism; or The Next Step in Civilization*

(Boston, 1890); Cator, T.V. National Ownership of Rail-
roads and Telegraphs (San Francisco, 1892); Claflin,
Sumner F. Nationalism (Boston, n.d.-before 1892); Green,
M.A. Unconscious Nationalism in our Political System
(New Haven, 1890); Griffin, C.S. Nationalism (Boston,
1890); Hunter, R.F. An Exposition of Nationalism (Phila-
delphia, 1892); Huntington, E.S. Nationalism the Only Cure
(Boston, 1890); Mansfield, Dana In Trust for the People
(Boston, 1888); Myrick, Herbert How to Cooperate (Boston,
n.d.); Parsons, Frank The Wanamaker Conference; or, John
Wanamaker and the Nationalists; Putnam, J.P. The Outlook
for the Artisan and his Art (Chicago, 1899).

Many other works indirectly professed Nationalism or
were influenced by it. The extent of this influence is
difficult to estimate, for the nationalist magazines of
the period acclaim any book preaching a social gospel as
"nationalistic". Among those that do concern Nationalism
was Lynn Boyd Porter's Speaking of Ellen, a novel published under the pseudonym of "Albert Ross". Although not
utopian, Speaking of Ellen is filled with nationalist ideas
inserted into a rather ordinary plot. The Nationalist
greeted the book warmly for the good that it would do the
cause. "Essays on these subjects reach the cultured, but
a vivid novel like Speaking of Ellen will do work with
the masses. Many of them will receive their first lessons
in Nationalism through its pages." (34) Actually it is

_____

(34) The Nationalist, II, (February, 1890), 124.

dubious if novels like this reached many who had not been already indoctrinated by <u>Looking Backward</u>. Lucia True Ames's <u>Memoir's of a Millionaire</u> (1890) was another novel motivated chiefly by Nationalism; it was advertised along with <u>Looking Backward</u> and was intended to appeal to those who had been impressed with Bellamy's novel. It advocates among the other things cooperative tenement houses, unsectarian missionaries, suppression of the slave trade in Africa, and prevention of liquor traffic. The motivating character for all these reforms is Mildred Brewster. Reviewers were already tiring of this mingling of economics with belle lettres, as may be seen in <u>The Nation's</u> review of <u>Memoirs of a Millionaire</u>:

> In this age of organized charities and of awakened altruism, no book on the mental, spiritual, or material welfare of the race can be simply a romance. It is an appeal or an argument. <u>Looking Backward</u> creates a hundred Bellamy societies, and we can see no reason why, from the present book, there may not spring up all over the land Mildred Brewster Clubs. (35)

A much more effective novel probably inspired by Bellamy's Nationalism was Katharine Pearson Woods' <u>Metzerott, Shoemaker</u> (1890), published anonymously, which concerns conditions as they are and not as they ought to be. The novel presents socialism in an attractive guise, but the author emphasizes the fact that men must be made perfect by the practise of Christian ethics. <u>Metzerott</u>,

---

(35) <u>The Nation</u>, L, (February 20, 1890), 160.

Shoemaker was praised as a story, rather than as an
economic argument; one reviewer points out that if by
reading this novel "one capitalist [is] converted into
a Socialist, let the story-teller, not the controversialist
or political reformer, take to herself the credit of
victory." (36)

A work in which the principles of Nationalism and
Christianity are fused, is the Reverend F.E. Tower's The
Advancing Kingdom (1891) which points out that the wave
of nationalistic sentiment indicates the approach of the
only true society and that Nationalism is little more
than applied Christianity. Edward Stanton's Dreams of the
Dead (1892) presents a general tone of sympathy for the
downtrodden and the poor and predicts a general social
upheaval. Its preface states that Mr. Stanton is an ardent advocate of Nationalism , and The New Nation recommended the book as excellent reading for all nationalists.
A long epic poem in the manner of Milton called Human
Life; or the Course of Time in the Open Light (1889) gives
a complete history of mankind until the attainment of
universal brotherhood on principles similar to Nationalism.
This was also recommended as excellent reading in the
various nationalist journals.

How much nationalistic ideas affected the major
American authors is difficult to estimate. Howells, Twain,

_____

(36) The Nation,L, (March 13, 1890), 225.

and Hamlin Garland doubtless approved the general spirit of this movement; whether they could agree to the specific methods suggested is questionable. Some critics have intimated that Twain's A Connecticut Yankee was influenced by Looking Backward. Professor Russell Blankenship suggests that "it is a bit significant that Bellamy's work appeared the year before A Connecticut Yankee." [37] The Nationalists fervently hailed Twain's ideas. According to them "its allegorical illustrations will do good Nationalistic service." [38] However, no definite influence can be proved, and there probably was none. We know that Twain was already at work on A Connecticut Yankee in 1886; Paine says, "Mark Twain that year [1888] was working pretty steadily on The Yankee in King Arthur's Court, a book which he had begun two years before." [39] Since Looking Backward was not put into the hands of the publishers until October, 1887 Mark Twain could hardly have known of its ideas before publication. Howells recalls Twain's later enthusiasm for the novel:

> He never went so far in socialism as I
> have gone, if he went that way at all,
> but he was fascinated with Looking

---

(37) Blankenship, R., American Literature, (New York, 1931), 469.

(38) The Nationalist, II, (February, 1890), 116.

(39) Paine, A.B., Editor, Mark Twain's Letters, (New York, 1917), II, 500.

> <u>Backward</u> and had Bellamy to visit him;
> and from the first he had a luminous
> vision of organized labor as the only
> present help for working-men. (40)

Howells himself was not completely committed to Nationalism,
although Professor Walter Fuller Taylor has clearly demonstrated that Bellamy's work influenced the economic novels
of Howells. (41) By April 27, 1890 he had decided against
the nationalist system, as the following letter to his
father shows:

> The Christian Socialists are more to
> my mind than the Nationalists; but I doubt
> if I shall openly act with either for the
> present. The Christian Socialists have
> loaded up with the creed of the church,
> the very terms of which revolt me, and the
> N. seem pinned in faith to Bellamy's dream.
> But the salvation of the world will not
> be worked out that way. (42)

Eventually Howells came out openly for neither Nationalists
nor Christian Socialists---but his novels are filled with
ideas that both groups could accept.

But to see the most specific literary effect of <u>Look-
ing Backward</u> and Nationalism we must turn to the numerous
novels that are either objections to Bellamy's system or
fictionalized sequels to it. These works that show a
direct connection with <u>Looking Backward</u> will be discussed

---

(40) Howells, W.D., <u>My Mark Twain</u>, (New York, 1910), 43.

(41) See "On the Origin of Howells' Interest in Economic
Reform", <u>American Literature</u>, II, (March, 1930), 3ff.

(42) Howells, Mildred (Editor) <u>Life in Letters of
William Dean Howells</u>, (New York, 1928), II, 3.

in Chapter IX. Then finally there is the large group
of utopias which advocate o ther systems for the world's
regeneration. These show no direct derivation from
Bellamy's utopia, but one can hardly question the fact
that they rose in the wake of Looking Backward's
popularity and were thus indirectly motivated by it.
Since so many other works derived directly or indirectly
from Bellamy's novel, the study of his sources presented
in the next chapter is very significant.

CHAPTER VIII

THE SOURCES OF LOOKING BACKWARD

Followers of Edward Bellamy have long hailed him
as one of the great original thinkers of the world.
Typical of this sort of comment is the following statement by a former president of the Los Angeles National
Club. "Bellamy is the Moses of today. He has shown us
that a promised land exists; he has answered, disconcerted,
and put to shame the wise men of the modern Pharaoh, and
has beckoned to us from the house of bondage and the land
of slavery." [1] Sylvester Baxter, a friend of Bellamy,
is even more specific as to the fact that Looking Backward
has no "sources".

> One of the most remarkable things
> about this work is that Bellamy should
> have formed the most complete, well-bal-
> anced, and definite scheme of social
> organization ever presented without
> acquaintance with the literature of the
> subject; without even a preparatory "reading
> up". This seems almost incredible, and
> one who has been a student of such matters
> for years, said that at least six books
> occurred to him that he believed Bellamy
> must surely have read in order to give
> his story its shape. It is a strong
> argument for the truth of his views. In
> working out any problem, the same mistakes
> are rarely repeated, whereas those who
> are on the right road arrive at a common
> conclusion. Therefore, that Edward Bellamy,

---

[1] Peebles, H.P., "The Utopias of the Past Compared
with the Theories of Bellamy" in The Overland Monthly,
XIV (Second Series), (June, 1890), 576.

without previous study, but simply by the
application of a clear-seeing mind to the
problem of the life before him, and reading
directly from Nature's book, should have
reached the same conclusions as the scholars
who have given their lives to the study,
seems indeed a sign of good omen set in the
heavens. (2)

If these rhapsodic utterances are insufficient, we
have Bellamy's own words written shortly after the appearance of Looking Backward in which he specifically denies
any connection with the reform ideas of others. "I never
had, previous to the publication of the work, any affiliation
with any class or sect of industrial or social reformers
nor, to make my confession complete, any particular sympathy
with undertakings of the sort." (3) This declaration has
usually been taken to indicate Bellamy's disapproval of
Marxian socialism. Although he had spent a year in Germany where he had undoubtedly heard of the Marxist philosophy, there is no semblance of Marxian socialism in Looking Backward, for the basic conception of a class struggle
is completely missing from Bellamy's work.

Despite these and other testimonials as to the originality of Looking Backward, a careful analysis of the novel
shows that neither its plot nor its social system is
original with Bellamy. The prominence attained by his

---

(2) Baxter, S., "The Author of Looking Backward" in The
New England Magazine, I New Series, (VII, Old Series),
(Sept., 1889), 98.

(3) Bellamy, E., The Nationalist, I, (May, 1889), 1.

utopian romance has obscured the fact that other American writers preceded Bellamy in this same field of
literature. It has been shown in an earlier chapter
that the birth of his two children in 1884 and 1886
turned Bellamy's thoughts toward some system that would
give them social security. He read widely in works devoted to solving social and economic problems. The ideas
impressed by the various writers unquestionably left an
impression in his mind, and once Looking Backward was
begun, these same ideas found expression, which may have
been unconscious. Two such works to which Bellamy owed
much were August Bebel's Frau and Laurence Gronlund's
The Cooperative Commonwealth. There is every reason to
suppose that Bellamy had read these books, and a careful
reading of Looking Backward shows definite parallels between the ideas expressed by Bellamy and his two pre-
decessors----a fact which will be presented in the excerpts
in the latter part of this chapter.

More difficult to establish is the source from which
Bellamy took the form of novel that he used in Looking
Backward. Pictures of utopian civilization set in the
future or in some remote territory have been popular ever
since Plato's Republic, and many of them derive from that
great prototype. Yet one need not go back so far to find
the source which Bellamy may have used as a suitable
medium for his social doctrine. Only five years before

the publication of Looking Backward, Professor John Macnie

of the University of North Dakota had published The Diothas,

or A Look Far Ahead under the pseudonym of Ismar Thiusen.

That Edward Bellamy had read The Diothas cannot be de-

finitely proved; but we know that he read widely and there

is some probability that he would know of a novel that

had sold several hundred thousand copies. At any rate,

a close comparison of The Diothas with Looking Backward

shows several similarities which can hardly be ascribed

to coincidence.

The Diothas was the only widely circulated and com-

plete novel of a society of the future to precede Looking

Backward in America. To get into this society of the

future, Bellamy used the same type of mesmeric dream that

his predecessor had used. The plots of both novels follow

the same general outline. In Looking Backward, the hero,

Julian West, meets and falls in love with a descendant

of the girl he had loved in the nineteenth century; in

The Diothas, the same thing happens. The nineteenth-

century sweethearts in both books are named Edith. The

climax of each book is attained when the hero "wakens"

from his dream, although here Bellamy used a slightly

different device from that of Macnie. In The Diothas,

Ismar Thiusen wakes from his dream to find himself back

again in the nineteenth century with his dream merely a

vision of the future; in Looking Backward, Julian West

seems to wake from his dream and to be back again amid all of the injustices of the nineteenth century, but we learn later that return has been only a nightmare, and that West actually remains in the society of the twentieth century.

The device by which descriptions of the future society are made logical is the same in each novel---both Julian West and Ismar Thiusen encounter highly educated gentlemen who open their homes to them and answer all of their questions about the new society with the greatest courtesy. In both, the reflections upon the nineteenth century are the same, condemning it as an unstable, inequitable, and blind era marred by competition and injustice.

Many of the details of the two societies are the same. Both novelists use science as the magic wand that will bring comfort to all men. Emphasis is put upon mechanical devices like the telephones and automobiles. For instance, both Bellamy and Macnie describe a rude forerunner of modern radio in similar terms:

> "The telephone is the magician," said Utis. "The concert you heard this morning was performed in a great city of Central Europe, at an hour there belonging in the afternoon. Each continent has its own great musical centre, toward which gravitates whatever arises of genius, talent, or vocal endowment. In that city are produced musical performances on a grand scale. By means of the telephone, these are reproduced at the ends of the earth, in the homes of all willing to pay a small annual sum for the privilege. A whole continent, at times all the continents, will thus, at the same moment, sit in judgment on a new piece or

a new singer." (4)

> She made me sit down comfortably, and,
> crossing the room, so far as I could see,
> merely touched one or two screws, and at
> once the room was filled with the music of
> a grand organ anthem; filled, not flooded,
> for, by some means, the volume of melody had
> been perfectly graduated to the size of
> the apartment. I listened, scarcely breathing,
> to the close. Such music, so perfectly
> rendered, I had never expected to hear. (5)

The description of cooking done in central kitchens is
much the same in both works:

> All cooking, therefore, is done on
> the cooperative plan. About the centre
> of this district is a building, carefully
> fitted up with every appliance and con-
> venience for the preparation of food that
> science or experience has suggested.
> Bills of fare for each day are care-
> fully drawn up, for some time in advance,
> by a special committee. The prescribed
> dishes are prepared with care. You have
> had opportunity to judge how skillfully
> and scientifically our artists can work.
> For we justly regard the skillful preparation
> of food as a fine art, contributing in no
> small degree to the health and happiness
> of our race. Waste of all kinds our
> training causes us to shrink from with a
> dislike almost instinctive. The telephone
> sends in the orders of each household on
> the preceding evening, so that the quantity
> required of each dish can be estimated with
> scientific exactitude. (6)

> If we expect to dine here, we put in our
> orders the night before, selecting anything
> in market, according to the daily reports in
> the papers. The meal is as expensive or as

(4) Macnie, J., _The Diothas or A Far Look Ahead_, (N.Y.,
1883), 83.

(5) Bellamy, E., _Looking Backward 2000-1887_, 112. This
and all other references are to Riverside Library
Edition published by Houghton Mifflin, 1926.

(6) Macnie, J., _op. cit._, 43.

> simple as we please, though of course
> everything is vastly cheaper as well as
> better than would be if prepared at
> home. There is actually nothing which
> our people take more interest in than the
> perfection of the catering and cooking
> done for them, and I admit that we are
> a little vain of the success that has been
> attained by this branch of the service. (7)

The basis of each society is an industrial army in which

men must remain until they attain a certain age---in

Bellamy's novel forty-five, in Macnie's twenty-five. Pre-

ference as to occupation is permitted in each society:

> At seventeen each young man was ex-
> pected to report for duty at a certain
> place. There, unless allowed to return
> home for another year, he was at once
> assigned to some duty, always at a distance
> from his home. According as exigency
> required, any zerdar might become a sailor,
> a miner, a member of the sanitary police,
> and so on. The nature of the training
> they had received rendered them fully
> competent for the management of the
> machinery that had superseded muscular labor
> in every department of life.
> The younger were first assigned to
> comparatively light tasks. I had already
> remarked, with some surprise, that the
> conductors of the city railroads, and other
> similar officials, were all very young men.
> After a year or more at such light tasks,
> they were drafted to heavier labors in some
> other division of the world; regard being
> had, as far as possible, to the preferences
> of the young men. (8)

> Every man for himself in accordance
> with his natural aptitude, the utmost pains
> being taken to enable him to find out what
> his natural aptitude really is. The prin-

---

(7) Bellamy, E., op. cit., 153-4.

(8) Macnie, J., op. cit., 156-7.

> ciple on which our industrial army is
> organized is that a man's natural endow-
> ments, mental and physical, determine what
> he can work at most profitably to the nation
> and most satisfactorily to himself. (9)

This cooperative element is the same in each novel, but both authors are exceedingly careful to avoid any title such as communism or socialism.

In view of all these similarities, one may at least assume that Bellamy had read The Diothas and possibly had used many of the details of its plot and of its future civilization when he came to write Looking Backward. The chief argument against such dependency is Bellamy's own inventiveness, which is so definitely revealed in his earlier short stories. His outstanding characteristic before the publication of Looking Backward had been the invention of fantastic plots to which he gave an air or reality. One can hardly believe that he found it necessary to take the plot for his great novel from Macnie's work; yet the similarities of plot of these two utopian novels do show some borrowing on the part of Bellamy, however unconscious it may have been.

One can be much more definite as to the source of the social system expounded in Looking Backward; without much question it derives from the earliest American work on socialism, Laurence Gronlund's The Cooperative Commonwealth,

---

(9) Bellamy, E., op. cit., 65.

originally published in 1884 and re-issued in 1886.
William Dean Howells spoke of this similarity in his
earliest comment on <u>Looking Backward</u>, for in <u>Harpers</u>
<u>Magazine</u> of June, 1888, he said; "Mr. Bellamy's allegoric
state of A.D. 2000 is constructed almost exactly upon
the lines of Mr. Gronlund's <u>Cooperative Commonwealth</u>; and
it is supposed to come into being through the government
acquisition of the vast trusts and monopolies, just as
the collectivist author teaches." [10] Howells' comment
was ignored by contemporary critics, and twentieth century
commentators are almost unanimous in stressing the originality
of Bellamy's social system. As a matter of fact, <u>Looking</u>
<u>Backward</u> is actually a fictionalized version of <u>The</u>
<u>Cooperative Commonwealth</u> and little more. Gronlund's book
appeared at exactly the time when Bellamy was casting
about for some social system that would give security to
his children. The plan offered by Gronlund stressed the
idea of security for all. Surviving members of the Bellamy
family have assured me that Edward Bellamy had read
Gronlund's book with great interest, although they are not
sure as to the exact date. That he read it sometime between
1884 and 1887 seems to me to be clear because of the internal evidence of the books, because by his own admission
he was thinking seriously about social systems in the years

---

(10) <u>Harper's</u>, LXXVII, (June, 1888), 154.

following the birth of his children, and because after
1887 he was so busy convincing others of the social
system expounded in Looking Backward that he paid little
attention to other social systems. The following detailed analysis is submitted to show the parallels of
these two commonwealths of the future.

The basis of Bellamy's commonwealth is the organization
of society into the ultimate monopoly, government ownership of everything. In one of the most widely quoted
passages in Looking Backward, he explains:

> The nation, that is to say, organized as
> the one great business corporation in which
> all other corporations were absorbed; it
> became the one capitalist in the place of
> all other capitalists, the sole employer,
> the final monopoly in which all previous and
> lesser monopolies were swallowed up, a
> monopoly in the profits and economies of
> which all citizens shared. The epoch of
> trusts had ended in The Great Trust. (11)

The basic idea of Gronlund is exactly the same:

> The Co-operative Commonwealth, then,
> is that future Social Order---the natural
> heir of the present one---in which all
> important instruments of production have
> been taken under collective control; in
> which the citizens are consciously public
> functionaries, and in which their labors
> are rewarded according to results. Is
> it Utopian to expect that all enterprises
> will become more and more centralised,
> until in the fulness of time they all end
> in one monopoly, that of Society? (12)

---

(11) Bellamy, E., op. cit., 56.

(12) Gronlund, L., The Cooperative Commonwealth, 102.
All references, except where otherwise noted, are
to the 1886 edition of The Cooperative Commonwealth,
published in London by Le Bas and Lowry, but widely
circulated in the United States.

Both men conceive of the state as the greatest aid to
the individual's development:

> We have no wars now, and our governments no
> war powers, but in order to protect every
> citizen against hunger, cold, and nakedness,
> and provide for all his physical and mental
> needs, the function is assumed of directing
> his industry for a term of years. No, Mr.
> West, I am sure on reflection you will per-
> ceive that it was in your age, not in ours,
> that the extension of the functions of
> governments was extraordinary. (13)
>
> The future commonwealth will help every
> individual to attain the highest development
> he or she has capacity for. It will lay
> a cover for every one at nature's table.
> "State" and "State help" will be as inseparable
> as a piano and music. (14)

In each of these descriptions of the future, there is
absolute condemnation of the cut-throat competition in-
duced by the growth of monopolies in the late nineteenth
century:

> In the United States there was not, after
> the beginning of the last quarter of the
> century, any opportunity whatever for in-
> dividual enterprise in any important field
> of industry, unless backed by a great capital.
> During the last decade of the century, such
> small businesses as still remained were
> fast-failing survivals of a past epoch, or
> mere parasites on the great corporations, or
> else existed in fields too small to attract
> the great capitalists. Small businesses,
> as far as they still remained, were reduced
> to the condition of rats and mice, living
> in holes and corners, and counting on evading
> notice for the enjoyment of existence. The
> railroads had gone on combining till a few

---

(13) Bellamy, E., op. cit., 60.

(14) Gronlund, L., op. cit., 96.

great syndicates controlled every rail in
the land. In manufactories, every important
staple was controlled by a syndicate.
These syndicates, pools, trusts, or whatever
their name, fixed prices and crushed all
competition except when combinations as vast
as themselves arose. Then a struggle, resulting in a still greater consolidation,
ensued. The great city bazar crushed its
country rivals with branch stores, and in the
city itself absorbed its smaller rivals till
the business of a whole quarter was concentrated
under one roof, with a hundred former proprietors of shops serving as clerks. Having
no business of his own to put his money in,
the small capitalist, at the same time that
he took service under the corporation, found
no other investment for his money but its
stocks and bonds, thus becoming doubly dependent
upon it. (15)

The small employers, the small merchants, are
just as much victims of that cruel kind of
competition as the wage-workers. For every
one of the fleecers lives in a state of
nature with all of his brethren; the hand
of the one is against the other, and no foe
is more terrible than the one who is running
a neck-to-neck race with him every day. The
mammoth factory, the mammoth store is a most
implacable foe. The fierce competition
lessens the profit on each article, and that
must be compensated for by a greater number
of them being produced and sold---that is,
the cheaper the goods, the more capital is
required.
     Precisely, then, for the same reason
that the mechanic with his own shop and
working on his own account nearly has disappeared in the struggle between hand-work
and machine-work, the small employers with
their little machinery, their small capital,
and their little stock of goods are being
driven from the field. (16)

Interdependence and fraternity of men are the keynotes of

---

(15) Bellamy, E., op. cit., 53.

(16) Gronlund, L., op. cit., 43.

these new states:

> You know the story of that last, greatest,
> and most bloodless of revolutions. In the
> time of one generation men laid aside the
> social traditions and practices of bar-
> barians, and assumed a social order worthy
> of rational and human beings. Ceasing to
> be predatory in their habits, they became
> co-workers, and found in fraternity, at once,
> the science of wealth and happiness. "What
> shall I eat and drink, and wherewithal shall
> I be clothed?" stated as a problem beginning
> and ending in self, had been an anxious and
> an endless one. But when once it was conceived,
> not from the individual, but the fraternal
> standpoint, "What shall we eat and drink, and
> wherewithal shall we be clothed?"---its
> difficulties vanished. (17)

> ...the present tendency of the social organism
> in the direction of Socialism, or Interde-
> pendence. Oh, if we could with propriety
> emphasize that central fact on every page of
> this book! For we have not written these pages
> in order to show that the Socialist system
> is a good system. They have been written in
> vain, if it will not have been brought home
> to our readers that the fact that Society is
> moving irresistibly towards Socialism is the
> one important fact; that we are going to have
> the Socialist State whether it is good or bad,
> and that every active individual in our country
> is, consciously or unconsciously, working to
> that end, in some way. This, therefore, in
> the central fact of society and the red thread
> running through these pages as well. (18)

Because of this interdependence, both writers glorify society

and the state as the institutions whose cumulative effect

has made for all progress:

> "How happened it," was Dr. Leete's
> reply, "that your workers were able to pro-
> duce more than so many savages would have

---

(17) Bellamy, E., op. cit., 285.

(18) Gronlund, L., op. cit., 210.

done? Was it not wholly on account of the
heritage of the past knowledge and achieve-
ments of the race, the machinery of society,
thousands of years in contriving, found
by you ready-made to your hand? How did
you come to be possessors of this knowledge
and this machinery, which represent nine
parts to one contributed by yourself in the
value of your product? You inherited it,
did you not?" (19)

It is Society, organized Society, the State,
that gives us all the rights we have. To
the State we owe our freedom. To it we owe
our living and property, for outside of
organized Society man's needs far surpass
his means. The humble beggar owes much to
the State but the haughty millionaire far
more, for outside of it they both would be
worse off than the beggar now is. To it we
owe all that we are and all that we have.
To it we owe our civilization. It is by its
help that we have reached such a condition
as man individually never would have been
able to attain. (20)

These cooperative commonwealths described by Gronlund and

Bellamy are national; the represent the last step but one

in perfection---the extension of cooperation to the whole

human race:

You must understand that we all look forward
to an eventual unification of the world
as one nation. That, no doubt, will be
the ultimate form of society, and will realize
certain economic advantages over the present
federal system of autonomous nations.
Meanwhile, however, the present system works
so nearly perfectly that we are quite content
to leave to posterity the completion of the
scheme. (21)

The Co-operative Commonwealth ---(mark!)

---

(19) Bellamy, E., op. cit., 136.

(20) Gronlund, L., op. cit., 83.

(21) Bellamy, E., op. cit., 143.

the full-grown Society; the normal State-
--will be a social order that will endure
as long as Society itself, for no higher
evolution is thinkable, except Organized
Humanity, and that is but Social Cooperation extended to the whole human race. (22)

Both authors are going to eliminate state lines as having

no place in this new nation:

"Had the organization of the nation
as an industrial unit done away with the
states?" I asked.
"Necessarily," he replied. "The state
governments would have interfered with the
control and discipline of the industrial
army, which, of course, required to be
central and uniform. Even if the state
governments had not become inconvenient
for other reasons, they were rendered
superfluous by the prodigious simplification
in the task of government since your day.
Almost the sole function of the administration
now is that of directing the industries of
the country. Most of the purposes for which
governments formerly existed no longer
remain to be subserved." (23)

The Co-operative Commonwealth will only know
of a Nation with a big, very big N. The
present State-lines of the Union only work
mischief. Parts of New Jersey and Delaware
belong as much to Philadelphia as any part
of Pennsylvania does; and New Jersey, Rhode
Island, and Connecticut are far more in-
timately connected with New York City than
is western New York. (24)

Even the monetary systems of these utopias are identical.

Money has been eliminated in favor of credit cards entitling

the bearer to a certain share of what the nation has pro-

---

(22) Gronlund, L., op. cit., 104.

(23) Bellamy, E., op. cit., 207.

(24) Gronlund, L., op. cit., 158.

duced by its common labor:

> A credit corresponding to his share of the
> annual product of the nation is given to
> every citizen on the public books at the
> beginning of each year, and a credit card
> issued him with which he procures at the
> public storehouses, found in every community,
> whatever he desires whenever he desires it. (25)

> As the products were received or as services
> were rendered, labour-checks will have been
> issued (or perhaps such money as we use now,
> which then, however, will have no other
> function than the checks,----that of being
> tickets, tokens), each check will represent
> so many normal days of common labour, and
> there will during each fiscal year, have
> been exactly as many checks issued as will
> correspond to the days of labour, productive
> or unproductive, actually performed. (26)

All this is possible because consumption and production

are now balanced:

> Even in your day statisticians were able to
> tell you the number of yards of cotton, velvet,
> woolen, the number of barrels of flour,
> potatoes, butter, number of pairs of shoes,
> hats, and umbrellas annually consumed by the
> nation. Owing to the fact that production
> was in private hands, and that there was no
> way of getting statistics of actual dis-
> tribution, these figures were not exact,
> but they were nearly so. Now that every pin
> which is given out from a national warehouse
> is recorded, of course the figures of con-
> sumption for any week, month, or year, in
> the possession of the department of distribution
> at the end of that period, are precise. (27)

> It undoubtedly can by proper foresight and
> abundant statistics accurately adjust the
> supply of all products to the demand for
> them; make Supply and Demand balance each other.

(25) Bellamy, E., op. cit., 87.

(26) Gronlund, L., op. cit., 139.

(27) Bellamy, E., op. cit., 181.

> This function of Statistician will be one
> of the most important within its sphere,
> and the principal way in which it will con-
> trol the workers in their industrial pur-
> suits. We think the Commonwealth will
> thereby be quite successful in keeping
> prices steady, and in making the chance for
> Demand and Supply to play any tricks extremely
> small. We think so, because we see with
> what accuracy the manager of a large hotel
> hits upon the proper quantities of the
> innumerable articles of food required by
> his guests. (28)

Each man will follow his own inclination as to the kind of

work he will do, with greater efficiency to the state re-

sulting:

> Every man for himself in accordance with his
> natural aptitude, the utmost pains being
> taken to enable him to find out what his
> natural aptitude really is. The principle
> on which our industrial army is organized
> is that a man's natural endowments, mental
> and physical, determine what he can work at
> most profitably to the nation and most
> satisfactorily to himself. (29)

> Our Commonwealth, on the other hand, will
> nourish the aspirations it has awakened;
> it will use for its own good talents it
> has matured, and enable every man and woman
> to develop his or her peculiar aptitudes,
> whether it be in brain work or hand-work.
> This fact, that every citizen will be able
> to follow his or her peculiar bent, will
> also itself vastly increase the productive
> result of all social activities, for it is
> well known that a person accomplishes most
> when he works in the line of his greatest
> inclinations. (30)

---

(28) Gronlund, L., op. cit., 141.

(29) Bellamy, E., op. cit., 65.

(30) Gronlund, L., op. cit., 113.

Crime will be eliminated completely and for the same

reason----removal of the motive:

> In your day fully nineteen twentieths of the
> crime, using the word broadly to include
> all sorts of misdemeanors, resulted from
> the inequality in the possessions of in-
> dividuals; want tempted the poor, lust of
> greater gains, or the desire to preserve
> former gains, tempted the well-to-do.
> Directly or indirectly, the desire for
> money, which then meant every good thing,
> was the motive of all this crime, the tap-
> root of a vast poison growth, which the
> machinery of law, courts, and police could
> barely prevent from choking your civilization
> outright. When we made the nation the sole
> trustee of the wealth of the people, and
> guaranteed to all abundant maintenance, on
> the one hand abolishing want, and on the other
> checking the accumulation of riches, we
> cut this root, and the poison tree that
> overshadowed your society withered, like
> Jonah's gourd, in a day. (31)

> And why should anybody care to procure wealth
> dishonestly, when wealth no longer will
> mean power over men? When wealth will not
> be able to coax the meanest of men to be
> your footman and wear your livery? When
> wealth simply will mean more to eat, more to
> drink, and more luxuries?-------Instead of
> the present society saying "Help thyself, or
> go to jail!" the future society will help
> everybody by removing all temptations to
> do what is wrong. (32)

Neither commonwealth will have any need for lawyers or

courts:

> With no private property to speak of, no
> disputes between citizens over business
> relations, no real estate to divide or
> debts to collect, there must be absolutely

(31) Bellamy, E., _op. cit._, 200-1.

(32) Gronlund, L., _op. cit._, 235-6.

no civil business at all for them; and
with no offenses against property, and
mighty few of any sort to provide criminal
cases, I should think you might almost
do without judges and lawyers altogether. (33)

It is evident that in the Co-operative
Commonwealth there will be far less litigation
than now. Every one familiar with business
of our Courts knows that cases arising
from contract contribute by far the largest
part of that business. If these were ex-
tirpated, if our Courts had to deal only
with cases of torts and criminal cases, the
great majority of our high-priced lawyers
now crowded with "business", would have to
seek pastures new. (34)

Although the governments own the newspapers, they will still

be reflectors of individual opinion:

The newspaper press is organized so as to
be a more perfect expression of public
opinion than it possibly could be in your
day, when private capital controlled and
managed it primarily as a money-making
business, and secondarily only as a mouth-
piece for the people. (35)

There will probably in every community be
published an official journal which will
contain all announcements of a public nature
and all the news, gathered in the most
efficient manner by the aid of the national
telegraph service, but no comments.
But we are assured that besides these
there will also be published many private
journals, true champions of principles and
measures. True, the printing-press will be
a collective institution but it will be open
to every one. (36)

---

(33) Bellamy, E., op. cit., 202.

(34) Gronlund, L., op. cit., 179.

(35) Bellamy, E., op. cit., 166.

(36) Gronlund, L., op. cit., 178.

Both authors grant women on equal terms with men:

> The sexes now meet with the ease of perfect
> equals, suitors to each other for nothing
> but love. (37)

> The comming commonwealth will place her on
> an equal footing with man....(38)

Special vocations, for which women are adapted will be

reserved for them:

> Women being inferior in strength to men,
> and further disqualified industrially in
> special ways, the kinds of occupation re-
> served for them, and the conditions under
> which they pursue them, have reference to
> these facts. The heavier sorts of work are
> everywhere reserved for men, the lighter
> occupations for women. (39)

> In other words, instead of free competition
> between the sexes, we contend for special
> vocations for the sexes. (40)

All this means that woman of the future will marry only

for love:

> "One result which must follow from the in-
> dependence of women I can see for myself,"
> I said. "There can be no marriages now
> except those of inclination." (41)

> When wealth ceases to be a means of living by
> the labor of other people, and especially
> when an honorable and easy living is within
> her reach, we may suppose that a woman will
> rarely consent to marry for anything but love,
> will no longer consent to be bought to be a

---

(37) Bellamy, E., op. cit., 265.

(38) Gronlund, L., op. cit., 194.

(39) Bellamy, E., op. cit., 257.

(40) Gronlund, L., op. cit., 195.

(41) Bellamy, E., op. cit., 266.

piece of furniture of any western Turk. (42)

One could quote further parallels between these two systems, but the above show them to be practically identical even as to details such as the type of newspaper and the place of lawyers in the commonwealth of the future. In fact, there are but three differences in the two systems, which Gronlund was careful to point out in the "Preface" to the 1890 edition of The Cooperative Commonwealth:

> It should, however, in justice to the cause, be stated, that there are three ideas in that novel for which socialism should not be held responsible....These are a love for militarism, equal wages, and appointments by the retired functionaries. They are decidedly unsocialistic notions, belong exclusively to Mr. Bellamy, and will be further noticed in the course of this volume. (43)

Gronlund, in his devotion to the cause of socialism, was generous enough to say that "the happiest effect of my book is that it has led indirectly, and probably unconsciously, to Mr. Bellamy's Looking Backward which without doubt has stealthily innoculated thousands of Americans with socialism..." (44) One less interested in spreading socialistic ideas, however, must infer that Bellamy's "nationalism" is merely Gronlund's socialism under another name and clothed in a story of futurity.

---

(42) Gronlund, L., op. cit., 200.

(43) Gronlund, L., "Preface" to 1890 Edition, viii.

(44) Gronlund, L., ibid, viii.

Still another potential source may be offered for
Looking Backward---a work by the German socialist August
Bebel which is variously titled Woman, Woman in the Past
Present and Future, and Woman Under Socialism. In 1890,
Mrs. John B. Shipley (Marie A. Brown), an Englishwoman,
published a pamphlet called The True Author of Looking
Backward in which by citation of parallel passages she
proved to her own satisfaction that Looking Backward was
derived entirely from Bebel's work on socialism. She
says;

> It is difficult to account for the
> fact that none of the English or American
> reviewers of Looking Backward have noticed
> its extraordinary resemblance to Bebel's
> book, barring the former's novel form and
> the transported existence of its hero into
> another age, the two works being identical
> in substance and plan, in their analysis
> of the evils of the present system of
> social economy, and in the remedies
> suggested. (45)

Mrs. Shipley then proceeds to show that while Bebel's
book had been circulated in an English version among
Americans for several years, no reviewer and none of the
nationalists had ever placed credit where it was due, on
the shoulders of August Bebel. She then offers approximately
twenty-five pages of parallel excerpts to show an amazing
similarity not only in the social systems offered but also

---

(45) Shipley, M.A.B., The True Author of Looking
Backward, (New York, 1890), 11.

in the phraseology. (46) Limited space precludes my
making a detailed analysis of the two systems. Suffice
it to say that Mrs. Shipley definitely shows the following
similarities: all property has been taken over by the
state and the profit system has been eliminated; both
men criticize the capitalistic system as engendering greed,
cut-throat competition, exploitation of human labor, with
insufferable periods of depression; both writers show that
the change to socialism or nationalism is brought about
because evils under the capitalist system became so obvious that everyone realized the need for a change; no
crime exists in either of these systems because the
criminal motive has been eliminated; everyone must labor
between certain age limits at work he wants to do; both
systems eventually will become worldwide; and these commonwealths are to permit complete intellectual liberty and
freedom of speech to scholars, literary men, editors, and
teachers. Even such details as community kitchens and
dining rooms, public laundries, and central heating systems
are common to both works.

As an example of the amazing degree of similarity
between the two systems, let me cite a few examples. Not

_____

(46) The translation that Mrs. Shipley used has not
      been available to me; it is possible that she made
      her own translation directly from the German. A
      careful reading of a translation by H.B. Adams
      Walther called Woman in the Past, Present and Future,
      (London, n.d.) reveals the same general phases of
      the system as Mrs. Shipley cites.

even the most ardent follower of Edward Bellamy could
tell which of the following passages was written by the
American utopist:

> Our washing is all done at public
> laundries at excessively cheap rates, and
> our cooking at public kitchens. The making
> and repairing of all we wear are done out-
> side in public shops.

> When in addition to these central
> kitchens, we have central washing establish-
> ments in which clothes are washed, dried,
> bleached and ironed by the help of machinery,
> and if we take into account...that all our
> clothing and underclothing will be manu-
> factured in central factories, we find our
> whole household life radically changed and
> simplified. (47)

Notice the phraseology of these passages:

> Everyone decides for himself in which
> branch he desires to be employed; the large
> number of various kinds of work will permit
> the gratification of the most various wishes...

> Every man [determines] for himself in
> accordance with his natural aptitude, the
> utmost pains being taken to enable him to
> find out what his natural aptitude really
> is. (48)

These quotations may serve to show the general tenor
of the two books. That Bellamy actually read Bebel's book
cannot be definitely proved, but as with Gronlund's The
Cooperative Commonwealth, we may assume that he knew this
work since it was available at the time when he was most

---

(47) The first quotation is from Looking Backward,
(Boston, 1926), 118. Both are quoted by Mrs.
Shipley in The True Author of Looking Backward, 36.
I have quoted directly from her book as the source
of Bebel since there is no earlier edition of
that work available.

(48) Shipley, M.A.B., op. cit., 33.

interested in social reforms and since there are so many
parallels in the two books. In fact, only two differences
can be pointed out: the first is that Bebel insists that
Christianity must have passed out of existence by the
time the socialistic state is attained, because under
Christianity, state and Church are inextricably entwined----
hence Christianity must be eliminated as one phase of the
capitalistic state. Edward Bellamy, the son of a Baptist
minister, obviously could not go so far. The second
difference is a minor one----Bebel sees Germany as the
only place where the socialistic state may be attained;
Bellamy places his in Boston, a location which Mrs. Shipley
derides as ridiculous. Whether one ought to go so far
as Mrs. Shipley in accusing Bellamy of "pillaging" his
ideas from Bebel is questionable, but one must in all
fairness admit that the ideas and expression of the two
works are amazingly alike.

The facts presented in this chapter at least show
that Looking Backward was derivative----whether from Gronlund's
The Cooperative Commonwealth or Bebel's Woman Under
Socialism, I do not know. On the basis of this evidence,
Edward Bellamy should no longer be acclaimed as the great
originator of a movement, as his nationalist followers
hail him, but as the most successful popularizer of a
modified form of socialism in America.

CHAPTER IX

THE ATTACKERS AND DEFENDERS OF LOOKING BACKWARD

The widespread interest in Looking Backward is shown best by the books that attacked or defended its social system. The advocates of Bellamy's utopia were usually nationalists, and their literary method varies hardly at all. They simply expand Bellamy's system by going into more detail, or by carrying it on into the next generation after the death of Julian West. The critics of the system attack it on the general basis that it is undesirable in its regimentation and monotony or that it is impracticable- --because it is against human nature, because it assumes that all men can be equal, or because some other flaw would make the whole structure crumble. Both critics and advocates with but few exceptions used the novel as the best method of reaching a large audience, and in this re- spect they pay tribute, however unconscious, to the success of Looking Backward in spreading its message by means of a story.

One of the best attacks on the social system of Looking Backward was not an attack specifically directed at that work, for it preceded Bellamy's utopia. But Anna Blake Dodd's Republic of the Future, or Socialism a Reality, (1887) raised all of the fundamental objections to utopian

socialism that specific critics of Bellamy were to make. [1]
She shows a socialistic state in which perfect equality
has been attained, but only by a process of downward
levelling. Mediocrity is the chief characteristic of the
inhabitants, boredom their worst affliction. It is a
world in which there is nothing to be struggled for and
where the only effort exerted is to kill time. While
exaggerated, this attitude represents a fundamental criticism of all socialistic enterprises where utility has
become the state's chief criterion. William Morris meant
the same thing when he called Bellamy's Looking Backward
"a horrible cockney dream". [2] and produced his lovely
News From Nowhere to show what an artist's utopia would be.

Oliver Wendell Holmes presented a clever satire on
the fundamental principles of the utopists in The Atlantic
Monthly of February, 1890, later incorporated in Over the
Teacups. He describes the inhabitants of Saturn in their
quest for an ideal life. Their passion for an unattainable
equality, typical of utopians in general, is the target
of Holmes' ridicule:

> "I suppose that now they have levelled
> everything they are quiet and contented. Have
> they any of those uneasy people called
> reformers?"

---

(1) Walter Fuller Taylor in his doctoral dissertation
Economic Unrest in American Fiction 1880-1901 (Chapel
Hill, 1929) classifies this as a "reply" to Bellamy's
book. Since it was published a year before Looking
Backward, it was obviously no reply.

(2) Morris, W., News From Nowhere, Vol. XVI of Collected
Works, (London, 1912), xviii.

> "Indeed they have," said my attendant.
> "There are the Orthobrachians, who declaim
> against the shameful abuse of the left arm
> and hand, and insist on restoring their
> perfect equality with the right. Then there
> are Isopodic societies, which insist on
> bring back the original equality of the upper
> and lower limbs. If you can believe it,
> they actually practise going on all fours,---
> generally in a private way, a few of them
> together, but hoping to bring the world
> round to them in the near future." (3)

Holmes then proceeds to ridicule the monotony and dullness
of ideal commonwealths. His visitor to Saturn notices that
every fourth or fifth person has his mouth wide open.
Upon inquiring he learns that "They are suffering from the
endemic disease of their planet, prolonged and inveterate
gaping or yawning, which has ended in dislocation of the
lower jaw. After a time this becomes fixed and requires
a difficult surgical operation to restore it to its place." (4)
Finally, becoming serious, Holmes offers the following
criticism of standardized utopias:

> Your Utopia, your New Atlantis, and the
> rest are pretty to look at. But your
> philosophers are treating the world of
> living souls as if they were, each of them,
> playing a game of solitaire,---all the pegs
> and all the holes alike. Life is a very
> different sort of game. It is a game of
> chess, and not of solitaire, nor even of
> checkers. The men are not all pawns, but
> you have your knights, bishops, rooks,---
> yes, your king and queen,---to be provided
> for. Not with these names, of course, but

---

(3) Holmes, O.W., "Over the Teacups" in The Atlantic
Monthly, LXV, (February, 1890), 241.

(4) Holmes, O.W., ibid, 241.

> all looking for their proper places, and
> having their own laws and modes of action.
> You can play solitaire with the members of
> your own family for pegs, if you like, and
> if none of them rebel. You can play checkers
> with a little community of meek, like-
> minded people. But when it comes to the
> handling of a great state, you will find
> that nature has emptied a box of chessmen
> before you, and you must play with them so
> as to give each its proper move, or sweep
> them off the board, and come back to the
> homely game such as I used to see played with
> beans and kernels of corn on squares marked
> upon the back of the kitchen bellows. (5)

Answers to specific phases of the system set forth in

Looking Backward began appearing in 1890. One of the first

was Arthur Dudley Vinton's Looking Further Backward (1890).

Written as a series of lectures at Shawmut College by

Professor Won Lung Li, who is Julian West's successor,

Looking Further Backward is a lurid exposition of what its

author regarded as the fundamental weakness of the nation-

alistic system---its lack of an adequate defence. Vinton,

who is evidently a strong army advocate, describes how the

whole world except China became nationalized under Bellamy's

system. The Chinese then built up a tremendous army and

navy, invaded the United States, destroyed New York, sub-

jugated the whole country, and populated it with Chinese. (6)

Thus Professor Won Lung Li is lecturing in Boston to a

group of his compatriots. The sensational aspects of the

---

(5) Holmes, O.W., Ibid, 241.

(6) This idea had previously been used in P.W. Dooner's
Last Days of the Republic (San Francisco, 1880) which
described the conquest of the United States by
Chinese early in the twentieth century. It was
obviously intended to appeal to racial prejudice on
the Pacific coast.

book are, of course, unimportant in so far as criticism of Bellamy's system is concerned. In fact, Vinton distorts the facts of Looking Backward a little, because Bellamy looked forward to the time when all nations would be nationalized---and Vinton's whole novel is based on the fact that some of the nations would not accept this system.

But Looking Further Backward has a more serious criticism of Bellamy's utopia than merely its lack of a system of defense. The charge is made that such a method of organization would build up in the people a dangerous habit of mind characterized by absolute obedience to superiors and resulting in a complete loss of initiative, self-reliance, and the ability to act effectively in time of emergency such as is described in the novel. This general criticism that nationalism organized everything so definitely that no room remained for individual initiative and that in time all creative ability would perish is the basis of several other works. Vinton adds to this a unique idea as the results engendered by the security that nationalism guaranteed all citizens:

> The fact that the nation guaranteed to each child that was born the means of subsistence, had taken away one of the greatest checks of over-population, and as a consequence parents had given their sexual passions full sway, and it was not an unusual thing for mothers to bear children every year. At the beginning of the twentieth century the average number in each family was five, at the beginning of

the twenty-first it had risen to sixteen. (7)

One can imagine the mothers of sixteen children rising in

revolt against this situation and putting an end to it---

but Vinton's general idea is probably well-founded. He

defines his own attitude toward Looking Backward early in

the book:

> Whatever promises to regenerate mankind
> or better the chances for life, liberty,
> and happiness, I am heartily in favor of.
> But a false guide is worse than no guide,
> and a wrong solution of a great human
> problem is worse than no solution; and
> therefore, I have endeavoured in the following
> story, to point out wherein the Bellamy
> Nationalism would prove disastrously weak. (8)

For the most part, Vinton's criticisms are well-founded,

although they are somewhat weakened by the sensationalism

of the story that conveyed them.

A still more valid criticism of Bellamy's work may

be found in Richard Michaelis' Looking Forward (1890).

Michaelis was a German-American, editor of the Freie Presse.

His novel continues the story of Julian West where Bellamy

leaves off. West begins to find out that conditions in

this new world are not as rosy as they seemed when Dr.

Leete described them originally. Fundamentally, human

nature has not changed; selfishness still exists, bringing

with it abuse of office and power. Laborers in the new

---

(7) Vinton, A.D., Looking Further Backward, (Albany, 1890),
     84.

(8) Vinton, A.D., "Preface", op. cit., vi.

world are still enslaved, and since there is no adequate
means of redress in this system, they are no better off
than they were in the nineteenth century. In the closely
geared machinery of Bellamy's state, there are millions
who have nothing to look forward to. The honors and
various systems of reward by means of colored ribbons
are not sufficient to justify initiative and energy on the
part of the individual. West finds out all this and more
from his predecessor at Shawmut College who has been de-
moted to a janitor because he openly preferred the system
of the nineteenth century when each man reaped the reward
for his own efforts. Curiously enough, Michaelis, a
foreign-born American, is the sole critic to point out that
Bellamy's plan is contrary to the spirit of our institutions
and to the actual events of our history, both of which have
tended to work for the greater development and freedom of
the individual. Basically, Michaelis' argument rests upon
the proposition that human nature cannot be made to change
by any external system of government; that there will be
many selfish individuals in Boston in 2000, and that there
will be millions who will not work for the state as they
would for themselves. In his "Preface" he states this
fundamental tenet:

> The surmise, that men and women in a
> communistic state, would put off all selfish-
> ness, envy, hate, jealousy, wrangling, and
> desire to rule is just as reasonable as the
> supposition that a man can sleep one hundred
> and thirteen years and rise thereafter as

fresh and young as he went to bed. (9)
The work concludes with suggestions for reform of the
nineteenth century, so that it avoids the charge of being
entirely destructive in its criticism. Michaelis' answer
to Looking Backward was in turn answered by Ludwig
Geissler's Looking Beyond (1891). This reasserts the
viewpoint of the nationalists by a debate between Professor
Forest, a character taken from Michaelis' novel, and Mr.
Yale, an ardent follower of Bellamy, but the story really
adds little to what Bellamy had originally said. It concludes in a fashion quite irrelevant to the controversial
purpose of the book by describing the tremendous sensation
caused among terrestial inhabitants by the discovery that
the Martians were trying to signal them. As an answer
to the basic flaws that Michaelis had exposed, Looking
Beyond is ineffectual, although The New Nation character-
istically claimed that "Mr. Geissler has not only effectually disposed of Mr. Michaelis, but made a useful and
interesting contribution to nationalistic literature." (10)

Very similar to Michaelis' novel in spirit is the

---

(9) Michaelis, R., Looking Forward, "Preface", IV.
There was a German edition of this work titled
Ein Blick in die Zukunft and an English edition
titled, Looking Further Forward, both Chicago, 1890.

(10) The New Nation, I, (November 21, 1891), 683.

German work [11] of Conrad Wilbrandt translated into English by Mary H. Safford unter the title of Mr. East's Experiences in Mr. Bellamy's World (1891). The book criticizes Bellamy's utopia as essentially impossible because of human nature and accomplishes this through the medium of having a Mr. East see this new world from a viewpoint considerably different from that of Bellamy's Julian West. Like Michaelis, Wilbrandt proposes some specific remedies for the admitted flaws in nineteenth century organization; among these suggestions are such things as the abolition of all legislation favoring other classes and detrimental to labor, the right of union, guaranteed protection against injurious work, and general improvement of living conditions among the laboring classes. From the program, it is obvious that all of Wildbrandt's sympathies are with the laboring classes. Professor Walter Fuller Taylor in discussing the novels of Michaelis and Wildbrandt says "the proposals that have been most nearly effected in recent fact occur in two counter-attacks on Bellamy's Looking Backward." [12] The fact is that all

(11) Looking Backward attracted as much discussion in Germany as in any other country. Among the specific answers to it were Eugene Richter's Zukunftbilder (1891); Ernst Mueller's Ein Rückblick aus dem Jahre 2037 auf das Jahre 2000. Aus den Errinerungen des Herrn Julian West (1891); and Phillip Wasserburg's, who wrote under the pseudonym of "Phillip Laicus", Etwas Später Eine Fortsetzing von Bellamy's Rückblick aus den Jahre 2000. (1891). All these books like Wilbrandt's are critical of Bellamy's whole system.

(12) Taylor, W.F., Economic Unrest in American Fiction 1880-1901, an unpublished doctoral dissertation, (Chapel Hill, 1929), 172.

of the answers to Bellamy are far less radical in their changes; they would alter only the most glaring faults in the social structure----hence in their novels they approached closer to what has subsequently become reality.

An earlier and ineffectual rejoinder to Looking Backward is John Backelder's A.D. 2050, or Electrical Development at Atlantis (1890), which appeared pseudonymously as by "A Former Resident of the Hub". Bachelder takes as his basic idea the fact that competition "acts as a stimulant both to mental and physical activity", [13] and is necessary to the world's progress. Since Bellamy eliminates the competitive element, progress would stop. Actually this is almost the same criticism as that of other authors already mentioned----that the individual must receive an individual reward, and this is possible only under a competitive civilization. A.D. 2050 is filled with marvellous and astounding scientific developments of the future. Rather amusing is the nonchalance with which the novelist projects his hero forward one hundred and ten years: "On retiring that night Morpheus soon took possession of my faculties, and with electric speed I was transferred to the Boston of A.D. 2000." [14] The novel describes the breakdown of nationalism, and then goes on to describe the

---

(13) Bachelder, J., A.D. 2050, (San Francisco, 1890), 22.

(14) Bachelder, J., op. cit., 4.

founding of a new civilization on the recently discovered
island, Atlantis. Here competition, individual initiative
and reward, and scientific progress attain a renascence
after the slough of nationalism. Volapuk is the language
of Atlantis; science its slave. The evils of excessive
competition are eliminated "by limiting the wealth of
any one individual to $100,000". [15] In the same year
(1890), there appeared one of the earliest defences of
Bellamy in F.U. Worley's Three Thousand Dollars a Year,
a pamphlet which describes life in 2001 under the nationalistic government. It takes its title from Worley's
estimate that every person under nationalism would get
a share worth $3,000 a year; about this Bellamy himself
never descended to particulars.

A bitter attack on all of the fundamental ideas of
Looking Backward is contained in J.W. Roberts' Looking
Within, or the Misleading Tendencies of "Looking Backward"
Made Manifest (1893). Something of the virulent attitude
of Roberts is evident in the following excerpt:

> Looking Backward has been the bane of
> this nation. It breeds a notion in the
> minds of thousands that somehow the govern-
> ment will be compelled to do for them what
> God, nature, and society demand they shall
> do for themselves. Its Utopian notions
> have taken root in many minds. Multitudes
> who never saw the book have received its
> teachings second-hand; and been poisoned

(15) Bachelder, J., op. cit., 21.

by them. It is like the fabled basilisk:
its very presence is death. Like the
upas tree, it is fair to behold, but all
who come within its shade are doomed. (16)

Looking Within is carefully modelled on _Looking Backward_----
it contains the same characters (Julian West, Dr. Leete,
and his daughter), the same method of explanation, the
same device of a sermon at the end----but all these things
are here designed to show the impracticable phase of
Looking Backward. Roberts moves his hero ahead into the
future three times----to 1927, 2000, and finally to 2025----
by means of a sleeping draught which can be regulated to
affect the patient for any desired period of time. This
permits Roberts to criticize Bellamy's system in all its
phases as it developed. In 1927, the dangerous conflicts
between capital and labor, the unequal distribution of
wealth and the throat-cutting competition are described
as the motivating forces for a change. Disgusted with all
this, the hero takes his sleeping potion, to wake again
in 2000 when the cooperative system is in full flower.
Roberts finds that Dr. Leete is an impractical dreamer,
who sees only the best phases of the cooperative community.
Actually, nationalism has brought the complete stagnation
of society, a system of slavery, a group of lazy people
living on the efforts of the industrious, and the loss of

(16) Roberts, J.W., _Looking Within_, (New York, 1893),
64.

all initiative. The criticism of nationalism is shrewd:

> Government owns everything, in-
> cluding products of the mental and physical
> powers of her citizens---in fact, owns the
> man himself. He is a mere machine, or a part
> of it; the crank or belt which runs the
> whole affair is the government. Individual
> freedom, in the broad sense that a man is
> master of himself, his time, talents, and
> labor, is not known. If it ever existed,
> it is a thing of the past; it died with the
> surrender of the man to the government.
> Hence there is almost no improvement in
> any direction. (17)

In a sermon matching that in _Looking Backward_, a minister

points out that for food, clothing, and shelter, the citi-

zens under nationalism have bartered their political

heritage, their control of themselves until they are

forty-five years of age, and all manly independence. His

attitude is that they are paying too dear for their whistle.

Again our hero goes to sleep for twenty-five years,

and awakens in 2025, when the ideal civilization has been

attained. This ideal is nothing more than the old system

of the nineteenth century:

> The disease [of nationalism] is inherent
> and incurable. The remedy must be radical.
> We therefore propose to the people of the
> nation, a return to the government of the
> nineteenth century under the old constitution
> of the United States, with such modifications
> as may be deemed wise and expedient. (18)

Looking Within is one of the most valid attacks on Bellamy's

---

(17) Roberts, J.W., _op. cit._, 166.

(18) Roberts, J.W., _op. cit._, 268.

utopia, for it raises the fundamental problem of whether the price of nationalism is not too high when viewed from the standpoint of the individual.

Among the more complete attempts to advocate the ideas of Looking Backward was Young West, A Sequel to Bellamy's Celebrated Novel "Looking Backward" (1894) by Rabbi Solomon Schindler of Boston, an ardent nationalist and the translator of the German edition of Looking Backward. This is like most of the other defences of Bellamy in being simply an amplification and further exposition of his system. The story concerns Julian West's posthumous son, familiarly called Young West, and his life under the cooperative commonwealth. Schindler traces his career through his early education and experiences to the time when he becomes President of the United States by virtue of his discovery of a method of utilizing sewage as fertilizer. On the thread of West's career, Schindler hangs all kinds of observations about the benefits of this social structure and contrasts it with the nineteenth century. His comment on the teaching methods of the twenty-first century as contrasted with those of the nineteenth is typical of his technique:

> If a clear distinction between our
> system of teaching and that of previous
> ages is to be given in a few words, it
> could be formulated into the following
> sentence: Heretofore, the teacher
> questioned the pupil, now the pupil

questioned the teacher. (19)

Children are educated by the state because "we love our children so well that we give them in charge of persons who have made a study of child nature and hence are competent to develop them properly..." (20) A curious idea is added to the nationalism of Young West when some letters of Julian West are discovered by his son. One letter confesses that:

> With all its advantages over my previous life, my present existence does not satisfy me. I miss too many conditions that were dear to me by force of habit. The very absence of worry, of care, oppresses me like a calm on the ocean oppresses the sailor. (21)

From this Schindler draws the following conclusion which was doubtless aimed at Bellamy's critics, who could see nothing attractive about nationalism:

> Your father's confession makes me think of his many contemporaries, who, as we know, dreamed in the turmoil of their time of an order of society similar to ours. Suffering from the evils that sprang from the competitive strife in which they were engaged, they wished for conditions like ours, they wished for economic equality, for a time of peace and universal happiness, resulting from the recognition of every person's right to life, and the enjoyment of life. If they could have realized their

---

(19) Schindler, S., Young West, (Boston, 1894), 77.

(20) Schindler, S., op. cit., 201.

(21) Schindler, S., op. cit., 276.

> wishes of a sudden; if, like your father,
> they could have passed the period of
> transition in sleep and that kingdom of
> heaven, the establishment and realization
> of economic equality would have suddenly
> fallen upon them, they would have become
> as dissatisfied and melancholy as has your
> father, simply because they were not ready
> to pay the price for these new institutions,
> simply because they would not or could not
> have put away the ideas, associations,
> customs and views of life under which they
> had been reared. (22)

Aside from this insistence upon the necessity of changing

slowly and upon the difficulty of nineteenth century critics

judging impartially of such a social organism, Schindler

makes no real addition to Bellamy's ideas.

Another work that advocated nationalism was The Six-

teenth Amendment (New York, 1896) by Stephen H. Emmens

("Plain Citizen"). The author is chiefly concerned with

the way in which nationalism is to be put into practise.

His plan is to organize all citizens into a Legion of

Labor, which is merely another name for Bellamy's Industrial

Army. The citizens are then to pass the Sixteenth Amend-

ment, which is to be phrased as follows:

> The Legion of Labor shall have power
> to nationalize and acquire in the name of
> the Legion of Labor of the United States
> all or any of the real or personal property
> that may at any time exist in the United
> States. (23)

---

(22) Schindler, S., op. cit., 281.

(23) Emmens, S.H., The Sixteenth Amendment, (New York,
     1896), 224.

Emmens in his book was undoubtedly trying to answer
the charges of Bellamy's critics that the nationalist
system was an ideal one but there was no practical way
of putting it in operation.

The same general procedure of amplification was
followed by Bellamy in his sequel to <u>Looking Backward</u>,
<u>Equality</u> (1897). <u>Equality</u> went into great detail about
various aspects of the future, which he had merely sketched
in his earlier novel. Bellamy himself said "<u>Looking Back-
ward</u> was a small book and I was not able to get into it
all I wished to say on the subject. Since it was published what was left out of it has loomed up as so much
more important than what it contained that I have been
constrained to write another book." [24] The novel takes
its title from the fact that Bellamy regards equality of
all men as the basis of his structure. <u>Equality</u> hardly
merits a detailed examination, for fundamentally it contains no vastly different ideas from his earlier novel.
To a social reformer like B.O. Flower <u>Equality</u> was "in
many respects the most noteworthy picture of social democracy which has appeared", [25] but to the average reader
it was lacking in interest and novelty.

<u>Equality</u> provoked more replies from critics. Signifi-

---

(24) Bellamy, E., "Preface" to <u>Equality</u>, (New York, 1934), vii.

(25) Flower, B.O., "The Latest Social Vision" in <u>Arena</u>, XVIII, (October, 1897), 518.

cant is the fact that while Looking Backward had been answered by replies cast in the form of novels, Equality was answered by cold economic analyses. The importance of the story element in each work is correspondingly reflected in the replies to it. Professor George Harris of Andover Theological Seminary in his Inequality and Progress (1897) attacked Bellamy's premise. Professor Harris maintains that it is not equality, but inequality that is the natural condition of mankind; that it is hopeless to try to make all men equal by any external social scheme, and that it is only by holding out greater rewards to those of greater ability that any progress is made. An earlier answer to Looking Backward and to utopianism in general, David Hilton Wheeler's Our Industrial Utopia and Its Unhappy Citizens (1896), had anticipated this point. Mr. Wheeler believes that the world we live in is as close to utopia and to absolute equality as we shall ever get. In his conception our civilization is bounded in the rear by Magna Charta, on the sides by invention and ability, and by evolution in the front. With all these forces to guide us right, he has no fears for civilization. The most serious error of all the utopists, in his opinion, is their belief that utopians are a happy people.

The conservative opinion of utopias in general and Bellamy's novels in particular is best expressed in George

A. Sanders' <u>Reality, or Law and Order vs. Anarchy and
Socialism: A reply to Edward Bellamy's "Looking Backward"
and "Equality"</u> (1898). Sanders calls <u>Equality</u> "the most
subtile, insinuating, captivating exhibition of special
pleading extant in literature. If the reader but grant
the premise, he will be pretty sure to accept the conclusion." (26) This false premise is Bellamy's idea of
the equality of all men; for Sanders, inequality is the
only reality in the world:

> The advocates of Social Democracy,
> Communism, and Anarchy are mistaken, when
> they claim that all men are born equal
> and must remain so for the greatest devel-
> opment in life. In fact, inequality is the
> rule of life, by both birth and culture.
> Using that term in its usual significance,
> all men are not born with equal capacities
> and powers of head, heart, and body; nor
> is it possible for them ever to become
> equal and remain so through the varied
> experiences of life. (27)

Sanders then tries to prove that this is the best of all
possible worlds by citing statistics concerning our
education, wealth, population increase, and industrial
production. His smug complacency in the face of what most
of his contemporaries considered dangerous portents is
astounding:

> Our people are the freest, most contented,

(26) Sanders, G.A., <u>Reality</u>, (Cleveland, 1898) 21.

(27) Sanders, G.A., <u>op. cit.</u>, 32.

> and prosperous people on the face of the
> earth. They live contentedly in the sun-
> shine; most of them have peaceful, happy
> homes, and fully believe that "God's in
> his heaven, all's well with the world". (28)

If this represents the attitude of the capitalists of the
period, it is not surprising that men like Donnelly, Bellamy,
and Howells went to such extremes in portraying the absolute
indifference of the upper classes toward the suffering of
the poor. Reality is significant in representing the viewpoint of the upper classes----a point of view which for
the most part they hardly found even necessary to express.
One is lead to greater sympathy for the ideas of Bellamy
and the rest by reading Reality.

Zebina Forbush in his novel The Co-opolitan (1898)
simply applies Bellamy's ideals to a new locale. The book
describes the founding of an ideal commonwealth in Deer
Valley, Idaho, under a system called "Industrial Cooperation".
The story carries forward from 1897 well into the twentieth
century, when they are attaining their goal, the system
of Looking Backward. "In this the twentieth year of the
Cooperative Commonwealth, the United States is moving swiftly
and quietly to that condition which Bellamy held in Looking
Backward.' (29)

Much the same device is employed by Bradford Peck in

---

(28) Sanders, G.A., op. cit., 68.

(29) Forbush, Z., The Co-opolitan, (Chicago, 1898), 165.

his _The World A Department Store, a Story of Life Under a Cooperative System_ (Lewiston, Maine, 1900). The plot is taken wholesale from _Looking Backward_, and the social structure is merely nationalism under the name of cooperation. Instead of Bellamy's industrial army, Peck substitutes organization after the manner of a department store with which he was more familiar as President of B. Peck and Company of Lewiston, Maine, and Vice President of the Joliet Dry Goods Company of Joliet, Illinois. This novel is one of the most preposterous of all the utopias.

With the beginning of the twentieth century, the controversy over Bellamy's ideas became almost extinct. Only one novel, H.W. Hillman's _Looking Forward_ (Northampton, Mass., 1906), is obviously derived from the discussion of the 'nineties.

In summing up the ideas expressed concerning Bellamy's work, it becomes obvious that the followers of nationalism were able to add nothing new to the social system described in _Looking Backward_. Their works merely continue the story as in Schindler's _Young West_ or Geissler's _Looking Beyond_, or they apply its ideas in some new locality as in Forbush's _The Co-opolitan_ or in some modified form as in Peck's _The World a Department Store_. This shows the completeness of the social scheme which Bellamy erected. His attackers all concentrated upon the same weaknesses. The idea that human nature with its selfishness and love of individual

reward would render the whole system impossible is set
forth in Wilbrandt's _Mr. East's Experiences in Mr. Bellamy's
World_ and Roberts' _Looking Within_. The lack of all incentive to progress under nationalism is also mentioned
in these two works and in Vinton's _Looking Further Forward_
which attacks nationalism's weakness in military defence.
The fundamental fallacy that men are equal is exposed by
Harris' _Inequality and Progress_ and Sanders' _Reality_.
These critics chose their points of attack well, and the
impartial judge of the controversy is likely to feel that
they had the better of it, for their criticisms were never
effectually answered.

CHAPTER X

AMERICAN UTOPIAS, 1888-1900

The success of <u>Looking Backward</u> inspired a legion
of social protests in the form of utopias. In the
thirty-three years previous to its publication, fifteen
rather vague utopias had appeared; in the last twelve
years of the nineteenth century, over sixty utopias
were specifically directed at abuses in society. Aggravated social conditions were partially responsible for
this increased interest in utopia. As has been shown
in Chapter IV, the frontier had vanished by 1890, the
trusts were reaching the zenith of their power, a few
men were amassing a large portion of the nation's
wealth, great masses were herded together in cities,
and cut-throat competition engendered by a laissez-faire
philosophy was the reigning mode of industrial procedure.
A reformer of the time might well have wondered how he
could protest effectively against the enormity of these
abuses. <u>Looking Backward</u> supplied the answer by indicating a medium through which reform ideas could reach
a potential audience of millions. Thus a combination
of unsatisfactory social conditions and one opportune
novel were responsible for the numerous quests for utopia
by Americans from 1888 to 1900. These novels were
peculiarly American, for no similar body of literature
was produced in England---in fact, the only important

English utopian novels of these years were William
Morris' socialistic <u>A Dream of John Ball</u> (1888) and
<u>News From Nowhere</u>, and some of the early romances of
H.G. Wells.

In general, the utopian literature of the period
developed on two main levels. We had the work of such
men as Howells and Bellamy, whose appeal was definitely
to an educated and literary class of readers; at the same
time we had another level typified by the productions of
forgotten novelists like Ignatius Donnelly, Albert
Chavannes, and Solomon Schindler, in whose works reform
was secondary to fantastic adventure set in some future
century. Yet these popular adventure books contained new
theories described in human terms, and because of their
large circulation, were sometimes as significant as the
more intellectual works of Bellamy and Howells, from whom
their ideas were derived.

Before taking up the chronological discussion of
these American utopias, we may well examine the general
qualities of the whole group. Their outstanding characteristic is earnestness; no reader can doubt that most of
these writers believed themselves the sole hope of mankind.
Their appeals to readers for aid, financial or moral, are
almost pathetic. Various obvious methods of spreading
the ideas are incorporated in the stories themselves.
For instance Samuel Crocker's <u>That Island</u> (1892) describes
the struggle between two philosophies of government---

one plutocratic, the other nationalistic; the latter
triumphs because two million copies of a book setting
forth the vices of present day society and pointing the
way to salvation are circulated---the book is That Island!
The anonymous authors of The Beginning (1893) use a plot
which involves the writing of a great book designed to
open men's eyes to the vices of society and conclude by
an appeal to the readers for an expression of their ideas:
"Tell them to send their letters to the publisher for
the book, which we will call The Beginning".[1] Charles
W. Caryl in New Era (1897) inserted a large picture of
himself entitled "One Who Dares to Plan", and to circulate his novel more widely, announced a prize contest for
persons selling the most copies of the book---the author
apparently expected at least a million copies to be sold
in this fashion. "An Open Letter to All Earnest Readers"
in The Practical City (1898), which Warren S. Rehm published under the pseudonym of Omen Nemo, announced that:

> After 5000 copies of The Practical
> City have been sold at one dollar apiece,
> and if proper encouragement is given, all
> net returns from the sale of future copies
> will be used for the furtherance of the
> purposes of this book.
> All earnest persons who wish to join
> in a careful study of the suggestions out-
> lined in The Practical City will please

---

(1) Anonymous, The Beginning, A Romance of Chicago as
It Might Be (Chicago, 1893), 123.

send to us their full address. (2)

Zebina Forbush closes his novel, The Co-opolitan (1898)
with a practical proposal as to the way the cooperative
ideas of his book may be accomplished:

> If one million working men would pay
> ten cents each into a fund to help such a
> plan, it would mean one hundred thousand
> dollars a month, or one million two hundred
> thousand dollars a year. ...The results
> would be marvellous, especially as a dollar
> in the hands of co-operators would prove
> far more efficient than a dollar employed
> in the extravagant and wasteful channels
> of competition. (3)

Bradford Peck in The World, A Department Store (1900)
describes a social organization after the manner of a
cooperative department store and closes with a fervid
plea for funds asking the reader to "be one of us, and
let your posterity know that you are among the first to
establish the Treasury Department of the Cooperative
Association of America". (4) These earnest appeals, direct
or indirect, are typical of a large group of the American
utopias; one cannot doubt after reading them that the
authors believed implicitly in their own ideas and ex-

---

(2) Rehm, Warren S., The Practical City. A Future
City Romance; or A Study in Environment, (Lancaster,
Pa., 1898). The quotation is from the back cover
of this paper-bound pamphlet and has no page number.

(3) Forbush, Z., The Co-opolitan, (Chicago, 1898), 171.

(4) Peck, B., The World, A Department Store, (Lewiston,
Maine, 1900), 312.

pected their readers to carry on a crusade to incorporate
these reforms in our government. However, none of the
books containing these specific demands for aid attained
a large enough circulation to have any tangible result.

Another common characteristic of this group is their
fear of such names as communism and socialism. This
probably derived partially from Bellamy's designation
of his socialistic scheme as "nationalism" and partially
from a widespread dislike of encouraging any "Un-American"
doctrines. Hence Albert Chavannes in describing what is
actually a socialistic state in The Future Commonwealth
says, "We...are not Socialists as you understand the term.
All governments are somewhat Socialistic, some a little
more, others a little less. We are a little more and
have intrusted the Commonwealth with the accumulation
and use of a portion of our capital for the benefit of
our people..." (5) This rather contradictory statement
is typical. Other authors use fine sounding names for
systems that are basically socialistic or communistic.
Henry Olerich's A Cityless and Countryless World (1893)
expounds a system of "practical cooperative individualism";
many, like Albert Chavannes' In Brighter Climes (Knoxville, 1895), Zebina Forbush's The Co-opolitan (Chicago,
1898), and Charles W. Caryl's New Era (Denver, 1897)

_____

(5) Chavannes, Albert, The Future Commonwealth, or
What Samuel Balcom Saw in Socioland, (New York,
1892), 13.

advocate what they describe as "cooperation"; Castello
N. Holford in _Aristopia_ (Boston, 1895) describes "the
Commonwealth of Aristopia" which combines features of
socialism and democracy; Bellamy's word "Nationalism"
is used to describe the system of James M. Galloway's
John Harvey (Chicago, 1897) and B.J. Wellman's _The Legal
Revolution of 1902_ (Chicago, 1898); "Fraternia, a
cooperative colony" is the name given the social system
of Caroline A. Mason's _A Woman of Yesterday_ (New York,
1900); Alcanoan Q. Grigsby in _Nequa, or the Problem of
the Ages_ (Topeka, 1900) uses Howells' term "Altrurian"
to describe a country based on the golden rule. Ignatius
Donnelly in _Caesar's Column_ (Chicago, 1890) describes
anarchy in full sway, but disavows any intention of advocating that philosophy by saying "neither am I an
anarchist; for I paint a dreadful picture of the world-
wreck which successful anarchism would produce". [6]
No author denominates his system as socialism; several
remark that parts of their utopias are "socialistic",
but they are unwilling to have the whole system so classified and hide behind names like "cooperation" and the
others already mentioned.

A study of the panaceas suggested by the utopists
who followed Bellamy reveals many fantastic and amusing

---

(6) Donnelly, I., _Caesar's Column_, (Chicago, 1890), 3.

remedies, and a few that are extremely rational; they
are all significant in indicating what the citizen of
the late nineteenth century believed to be the crying
evils of his own day. The tendencies chiefly deprecated
in these works were the growing hostility of capital and
labor, increasing urbanization, the trend toward monopolies,
and above all, the possession of a large part of the
nation's wealth by a small portion of its population.

Bellamy regarded unequal distribution of wealth as
the greatest menace to American civilization, and to
eliminate it, he constructed an ideal commonwealth in
which wages were equal and all citizens shared alike.
In decrying this trend, Looking Backward was the prototype of numerous other novels, chief among which were
Ignatius Donnelly's Caesar's Column (1890), Alvarado
Fuller's A.D. 2000 (1890), Albert Chavannes's The Future
Commonwealth (1892), William Dean Howells's A Traveller
from Altruria (1894), Solomon Schindler's Young West
(1894), C.N. Holford's Aristopia (1895), Alexander Craig's
Ionia (1898), A.A. Merrill's The Great Awakening (1899),
and Bradford Peck's The World, a Department Store (1900).

To solve this problem of unequal distribution,
various plans are offered by the novelists. Some would
set a limit beyond which no man can own property, as in
Holford's Aristopia; others would restrict inheritances
or the amount of land that one man can own as in Fuller's

A.D. 2000 (Chicago, 1890). Interest is denounced by
all as a device responsible for putting wealth and power
into the hands of a few. The utopists abolish it, either
by doing away with money entirely or by specifically
forbidding savings to be put out at interest. In general,
the authors are sympathetic with the laboring classes,
although many of the writers were themselves from the
upper strata of society.

The specific suggestions for social reform are too
many and too varied to enumerate; included among them
are such heterogeneous remedies as the single tax, birth
control, eugenics, calendar reform, abolition of the gold
standard, a four-hour working day, a universal language,
and innumerable schemes for governmental participation
in business. Some of these ideas are so completely fool-
ish that one wonders how they ever got into print. For
instance, Henry Olerich in A Countryless and Cityless
World (1893), expounds a Fourieristic system which would
divide the population evenly throughout the country, thus
eliminating the cities, which many believed to be the
curse of mankind. Just how this was to be done equitably,
Olerich leaves unexplained.

Science plays an important role in all of these
American utopias; we had no followers of Butler and Morris
in ruling out machines. All these ideal commonwealths
rest on the assumption that men will someday have much

leisure because machines will do their work. Imaginations ran riot as to what electricity and other forms of power would do in the future commonwealth---but even then, these authors were often unable to surpass what has become reality in the forty years since they wrote. Predictions of airplanes, television, radio, power from the sun, and electric clocks are commonplace. The speed of vehicles in the future is a favorite subject for speculation, the estimates running from airplanes that go several hundred miles an hour to Albert Adams Merrill's prediction in his The Great Awakening (1899) that in the twenty-second century "horseless carriages" would go "twelve miles an hour and sometimes fifteen". [7] Chauncey Thomas proved an even poorer prophet in The Crystal Button (Boston, 1891) when he described an automobile ride in the forty-ninth century:

> An inquiry addressed to the driver brought the response that, while coasting down the hillside, they had for a short space made a record of twenty-one and one-tenth miles per hour, but that this was now reduced to eighteen and four-tenths. [8]

More pertinent to the social structures they describe, are their estimates of the number of hours a day men would have to labor with marvelous machines to aid them.

---

(7) Merrill, A.A., The Great Awakening, the Story of the Twenty-Second Century, (Boston, 1899), 41.

(8) Thomas, C., The Crystal Button, or the Adventures of Paul Prognosis in the Forty-Ninth Century, (Boston, 1891), 194.

Typical is the estimate in Grigsby's <u>Nequa</u> (1900):

> The standard day's labor was but
> two hours; and yet with the aid of
> machinery, ten persons harvested a strip
> of grain one hundred feet wide and
> thirty miles in length, delivering the
> same at the elevators in sacks, while
> another ten prepared the soil and put
> in another crop. All the other work was
> carried on in the same labor-saving manner,
> and this two hours of labor was deprived
> of every feature of drudgery and became
> only agreeable exercise. [9]

Other estimates are higher, but an average of all would
be about four hours. Many follow Bellamy in allotting
shorter hours to the less pleasant tasks---although if
one accepts their descriptions of the joys of work, one
finds it difficult to imagine an unpleasant labor.

The novels themselves are rather poorly written---
with the exception of works by Bellamy, Howells, Donnelly,
and one or two others. Samuel Crocker has one of his
characters in <u>That Island</u> say, "Well! Well! papa; I never
knew you guilty of such neglect to mamma and I before". [10]
This kind of writing was probably suited to the vast
majority of the readers of these utopias. Many of the
books themselves are paper bound and sold for a quarter,
so that they were not intended to reach an intellectual
or educated class. Many of them were issued in such series

---

(9) Grigsby, A.Q., (Jack Adams), <u>Nequa, or the Problem
    of the Ages</u>, (Topeka, 1900), 164.

(10) Crocker, S., ("Theodore Oceanic Islet"), <u>That
     Island. A Political Romance</u> (Oklahoma City,
     1892), 66.

as The Library of Progress Series published by Charles
H. Kerr and Company of Chicago in which the anonymous
The Beginning (1893), S. Byron Welcome's From Earth's
Center (1894), B.J. Wellman's ("A Law Abiding Revolution-
ist") The Legal Revolution of 1902 (1898), and Zebina
Forbush's The Co-opolitan (1898) were issued. The
Charles H. Kerr Company of Chicago and the Arena Pub-
lishing Company of Boston specialized in utopian novels.
A large number of the writers had to pay to get their
ideas before the public. All of the following books
were apparently issued at the author's expense: D. Herbert
Heywood's The Twentieth Century (1890); M. Louise Moore's
Al-Modad (1892); Henry Olerich's A Cityless and Country-
less World (1893); Frank Rosewater's '96: A Romance of
Utopia (1894); Albert Chavannes' In Brighter Climes (1895);
Albert W. Howard's The Milltillionaire (1895); Charles
W. Caryl's New Era (1897); Warren S. Rehm's The Practical
City (1898); and Bradford Peck's The World, A Department
Store (1900). This indicates something of the passionate
belief these men had in their own ideas.

The novelists are little known. It is difficult to
find out anything about some of the men, probably because
the writer of a utopia may not be primarily a literary
man. Hence someone like Bradford Peck of Lewiston, Maine
or Samuel Crocker of Oklahoma City, or Henry Olerich of
Holstein, Iowa, or Castello N. Holford of Wurtsboro, N.Y.

might have an idea for the salvation of mankind and publish a utopia, the only book that he ever wrote. A few men prominent in other fields of endeavor produced utopias, among them Simon Newcomb, the inventor, who wrote His Wisdom, the Defender (1900); John Jacob Astor whose A Journey in Other Worlds appeared in 1894; General M.D. Leggett of the staff of General McClelland in the Civil war wrote A Dream of a Modest Prophet (1890). Minor literary people upon witnessing the success of Looking Backward turned to what seemed a remunerative form of literature; in this class may be grouped novelists like Mary Agnes Tincker author of San Salvador (1892); A.P. Russell who wrote Sub-Coelum in 1893; Byron A. Brooks who wrote Earth Revisited (1894); and W.N. Harben who published The Land of the Changing Sun in 1894. Among the more prominent utopists of the period are Bellamy, Howells, Joaquin Miller, and Ignatius Donnelly---these four represent the only literary men in the group that even a scholar might be expected to know. The investigator's task is made more difficult by the authors' desire to conceal their identity. At least fifteen of them hide behind such names as "Omen Nemo", "An Untrammeled Free Thinker", "Theodore Oceanic Islet", "M. Auburre Hovorré", "Plain Citizen", "Lord Commissioner", "Anon Moore", "A Law-Abiding Revolutionist", and "Myself and Another". This may represent a fear of adverse criticism or a hesitancy at being identified with a type of litera-

ture considered not quite respectable. Others use it
as a device for consistency by which one of the characters in the narrative seems to tell the story. Regardless of who they were in private life, these men in their
novels are definitely on the side of labor and the downtrodden. The viewpoint of capitalism and big business
was seldom expressed, probably because their exponents
saw no need for catering to popular opinion.

The utopias began appearing in significant numbers
about two years after Looking Backward was issued---
apparently the novelists realized that this was an ad-
vantageous type of fiction in the latter part of 1889
and wrote their utopias for publication in the early
'nineties. The years of the Populist Party and the
reform movements culminating in the Bryan crusade saw
the largest number of utopias, although they continued
in some volume until the end of the century. They represent the transitional medium for the expression of discontent between the rather inchoate criticisms of the
'seventies and 'eighties and the Muck-raking movement
of the first years of the twentieth century. The utopias
permitted reform sentiments to coalesce and to get themselves expressed, but after a decade, men became weary
of this quest of a dream world located nowhere and turned
to more practical reforms in municipal government, federal
laws, and big business.

The feeling of many an American reformer in the
last decade of the nineteenth century was expressed by
B.O. Flower Editor of the Arena when he wrote:

> Now however we are in the springtime
> of another period of awakening and advance.
> Again we find the world's thought in a state
> of flux. Change is written over all portals.
> A larger vision of earth and heaven than
> the brain of the people was capable of con-
> ceiving at any previous period is dawning
> upon humanity. (11)

As to the method of getting these sentiments expressed,
The Arena had been explicit in an earlier editorial, "The
Highest Function of the Novel":

> The exigencies of the hour demand the
> employment of every available agency for
> breaking the shackles of unjust laws, for
> emancipating the brain of the people, for
> granting absolute equality and justice to
> woman, for the abolition of child slavery,
> and establishment of a system of universal
> education for the young; for supplanting
> our present barbarous treatment of criminals
> by one founded on justice, love, and good
> sense, one that is in accord with a civilized
> age, by raising the public standard of
> right and justice so that a crime committed
> by a man will be as heinous in the eyes of
> the people as the same offence committed
> by a woman. To accomplish these and kin-
> dred reforms, to quicken the public con-
> science, to awaken the multitude, to make
> the people think, act, and grow morally
> great---all this, it seems to me, should
> engross the heart, brain and soul of the
> true novelist, making him the herald of
> a better state, the champion of the world's
> helpless and oppressed millions. (12)

---

(11) Flower, B.O., "The Latest Social Vision" in The
Arena, XVIII, (October, 1897), 517 .

(12) The Arena, I, (April, 1890), 630.

There were critics who maintained that this attitude
merely generated further discontent among the "oppressed
millions". The reformer's answer to such charges was
forthcoming:

> ...Would it not be nearer history to say
> that general dissatisfaction had generated
> utopian writings rather than that they had
> generated dissatisfaction?
> ...It is this horizon of a black past and
> a blacker future which has given birth to
> anarchy as a science. ...The state of the
> future as reflected in modern romance is
> not the evidence of popular despair but
> the shadow of coming events. (13)

This belief that the utopias were reasonably accurate
portrayals of future events was part of the utopists'
credo. Whether they were correct can be shown only by
an examination of the individual utopias that appeared
between 1888 and 1900.

The only other utopian work to be published in the
same year as Looking Backward was Edward Everett Hale's
How They Lived in Hampton, an expanded version of a story
called "Back to Back" originally published in Harper's
and reprinted in 1877 in Harper's Half-Hour Series. Hale
describes a vaguely located industrial town where a
cooperative plan based on the golden rule, applied Christianity, and the Rochdale system of cooperation, meets with
wonderful results. Cooperation is applied first to the
woolen mill where "recognizing, then, that for making

(13) The New Nation, II, (January 23, 1892), 57.

woolen cloth, and bringing it to a fit market, three coadjutors were necessary,----capital, work, and the directing skill which should enable capital to use the workman's industry----they agreed that these three agencies should share equally in the profit of the article produced." [14] This plan had such obvious advantages as attracting skilled workmen, paying them better and eliminating child labor. Gradually this principle is applied to everything in Hampton until the whole town is organized on a cooperative basis with cooperative stores, banks, schools, and libraries. Hale's novel is an isolated phenomenon and is typical of his earlier writings; it cannot be considered as part of the utopian movement following Bellamy.

John Ames Mitchell's The Last American (1889) was another solitary utopia removed from the main group in the hue and cry after Bellamy. It is further distinguished by being completely satirical. Written by the founder of Life, The Last American goes ahead to 2591 when American civilization has completely disintegrated. The novel purports to be the journal of a Persian who has rediscovered America and with his companions is exploring the ruins of "Nhu Yok" in an attempt to reconstruct American civilization of the nineteenth century. The Last American

---

(14) Hale, E.E., The Works of Edward Everett Hale, (Boston, 1900), IX, 252.

is rather a diverting satire on American life and manners
without any attempt to expound an integrated plan for
social and economic improvement.

The first large group of utopias appeared in 1890
when Bellamy's influence was very strong. Of the nine
novels published in that year, four are either attacks
on Bellamy's ideas or defences of his system. [15] Indirect influences of Bellamy can be seen in the other
novels of that year---Donnelly's Caesar's Column, Fuller's
A.D. 2000, Heywood's Twentieth Century, and Leggett's
A Dream of a Modest Prophet.

Ignatius Donnelly's Caesar's Column is one of the
most important and most powerful of all these American
utopias. Its author is perhaps best known for his
efforts to prove that Bacon was Shakespeare, although
he was prominent in Minnesota politics as a member of
Congress from 1863 to 1869. Caesar's Column describes
the complete collapse of civilization in 1988, as the
result of society's being split into two classes---one
fabulously rich by virtue of inventions and special
privileges, the other desperately poor. A secret society
overthrows the regime of the wealth, and there follows
a reign of terror, which for sheer bloodiness and horror

---

(15) These novels, discussed in the preceding chapter
are Bachelder's A.D. 2050, Michaelis' Looking
Further Forward, Vinton's Looking Further Backward, and Worley's Three Thousand Dollars a Year.

exceeds anything in American literature. The book takes
its name from Caesar Lomellini, leader of the terrorists,
who declares that he will pile up the dead from New York's
streets, pour cement over them, and carve his name on
this gruesome memorial. "...It shall be a column---
Caesar's Column---by G-d. It shall reach to the skies.
And if there aren't enough dead to build it, why we'll
kill some more..." [16] After this revolution, a few
men escape to a settlement in South Africa where the hero
forms them into an ideal community based on Donnelly's
own ideas of reform such as cooperation, universal education, woman's suffrage, abolition of the gold standard,
state ownership of all agencies of production and communication, and the abolition of interest on loans. The
general principles of this ideal commonwealth are similar
to Bellamy's, but Donnelly is unique in insisting that
there is only one end of society if certain tendencies
continue---a titanic death struggle between the classes.

Caesar's Column is imbued with Donnelly's pessimistic
attitude toward nineteenth century society. "Who is it
that is satisfied with the present unhappy condition of
society? It is conceded that life is a dark and wretched
failure for the great mass of mankind. The many are
plundered to enrich the few." [17] His hatred of a system

---

(16) Donnelly, I., Caesar's Column, (Chicago, 1890), 319.

(17) Donnelly, I., op. cit., 4.

that allows one man to attain millions while thousands
eke out a bare livelihood is more virulent than that of
any other novelist . "In short, the most utterly useless,
destructive and damnable crop of country can grow is---
millionaires." [18] His solution for all this is socialistic: "Government---national, state and municipal---
is the key to the future of the human race....We have
but to expand the powers of government to solve the enigma
of the world." [19] His general principle would be to
abolish all laws which "gave any man an advantage over
any other man; or which tended to concentrate the wealth
of the community in the hands of the few...." [20]
Caesar's Column combines a sensational plot with vigorous
reform ideas; the result is a novel that for sheer power
is memorable, although its sensational aspects are carried
to extremes.

Lieutenant Alvarado M. Fuller's A.D. 2000 concerns
an inventor who discovers a method of putting himself
asleep for a long period of time; in 1887 he tries it on
himself and awakes in 2000---the exact dates used by Bellamy,
to whom the book owes much. Fuller is more concerned with
the scientific than the political aspects of this new

---

(18) Donnelly, I., op. cit., 114.

(19) Donnelly, I., op. cit., 115.

(20) Donnelly, I., op. cit., 106.

world and describes various electrical devices, radios, and rapid means of transportation. This is the only American utopia advocating calendar reform, similar to the thirteen-month calendar advocated by George Eastman. "The year, as now divided, consists of 13 months of 28 days each, and one day over." [21] The political system is apparently nationalism. "The government owns the railroads and likewise the telegraph system. Furthermore, each city owns its own water supply and electric-light plant. It will thus be seen that the people, and not the capitalist, own and govern the country." [22]

A very complete novel of the future is General Mortimer D. Leggett's A Dream of a Modest Prophet, which uses the conventional device of a dream journey to Mars. Since this planet is 3000 years ahead of the earth in time and since it has passed through all of the stages that the earth is now going through, terrestial inhabitants are expected to learn much by Martian experience. The novel is highly colored by religious sentiments, but it also describes political and social organization. The Martians proceed on the theory that the best government is that which governs least. Allusions to nineteenth century affairs are numerous; for instance, the inhabitants of Mars long ago found that civil service was inefficient

---

(21) Fuller, A.M., A.D. 2000, (Chicago, 1890), 148.

(22) Fuller, A.M., op. cit., 270.

because the poorly qualified men were willing to stay
in a rut and hold their jobs, while the good men left
the government for better positions demanding more
initiative. Labor-saving devices on Mars are so far
advanced that "the people were hopefully looking forward
to the time when machines would be so perfected as to
allow the operators to supervise them with but little
interruption of reading and study." (23) In describing
the early history of Mars, Leggett sees all the vices
that the nineteenth century reformer decried:

> In that age Mars had many large cities.
> Idle people seeking employment, and idle
> people who desired to live without employment,
> flocked to these, and everywhere the cities
> were the gardens for the cultivation of
> vice and crime. Large wealth was accumulated
> in the hands of the few all over the planet,
> and poverty and want belonged to the many.
> The few lived in luxury, the many in
> want...(24)

These are the evils that the great majority of utopists
use as the basic criticism of nineteenth century life.
Coming from General Leggett of Civil War fame and first
president of the Brush Electric Company, they may have
carried additional weight for nineteenth century readers.
A Dream of a Modest Prophet is one of the most readable
American utopias, marred only by its excessive use of

---

(23) Leggett, M.D., A Dream of a Modest Prophet,
(Philadelphia, 1890), 2.

(24) Leggett, M.D., op. cit., 32.

religious sentiments and its tendency toward theological disputes completely irrelevant to the main thread of the story.

H.B. Salisbury's Birth of Freedom (1890) might well be included among the continuations of the Bellamy theme except for the diversity of subjects treated. The novel relates the popular dissatisfaction, the subsequent revolution, and the ideal social conditions that follow when a socialistic system is applied to New York, the scene of the book. A working day of four hours is the average in this new world, in which a credit system similar to that of Bellamy is used. The plot has a conventional romance of the type used by Macnie in The Diothas and Bellamy in Looking Backward and concludes with a description of a colossal historical pageant depicting the birth of freedom.

A fifty-page prospectus of D. Herbert Heywood's The Twentieth Century. A Prophecy of the Coming Age also appeared in 1890. Whether Heywood's novel ever attained complete form or not is questionable, but the following synopsis from his prospectus gives some idea of its strange and chaotic nature:

> The only book of its kind ever written.
> A Vivid portrayal of the world's progress
> in Mechanics, Education, Science, and
> Social Conditions---the Changes in the
> Earth's Surface and Climate---Classic
> New England---The West a Blooming Garden-
> --The Rocky Mountain Deserts Reclaimed.
> Divorceless Chicago---Free Love. Mournful

San Francisco, bewailing her lost
Chinese. Happy New York, the Bulls and
the Bears at Sing Sing. (25)

Surely the world lost something when these chapters on

"Divorceless Chicago" and "Happy New York, the Bulls and

Bears at Sing Sing" remained unpublished. (26)

The stream of utopias somewhat lessened in 1891,

although at least five titles were added. In addition to

Geissler's Looking Beyond which has been discussed in

the preceding chapter, there were William Simpson's (Pseud.

"Thomas Blot") The Man from Mars, His Morals, Politics

and Religion; Amos K. Fiske's Beyond the Bourn; Chauncey

M. Thomas' The Crystal Button; and "Birch Arnold's" The

New Aristocracy. (27) The most complete utopia of these

---

(25) Heywood, D.H., The Twentieth Century. A Prophecy
of the Coming Age, (Boston, 1890), 49.

(26) Whether Cyrus Cole's The Aurorophone, (Chicago,
1890) should be discussed as a utopia is dubious.
The work is rather juvenile, describing the invention of an aurorophone, a device for sending
and receiving telegraphic messages from the planets,
where dwell beings further advanced than men.
The chief emphasis is on the scientific marvels
of the book, although there is some discussion
of governmental systems. A futurity story of
this same year was William Hosea Ballou's The
Bachelor Girl: A Novel of the 1400 (New York,
1890). A search of several libraries has revealed no copy of this work.

(27) Henry James' translation of Alphonse Daudet's
satiric utopia, Port Tarascon was circulated in
America in 1891. Walter H. McDougall's The Hidden
City (New York, 1891) is included on many lists
of American utopias. It is a sensational romance
of a man dropped from a balloon into a lost city
of the past where the inhabitants worship him as
a god. Since the book contains no serious discussion of political or social organization, I
have not included it.

three is Simpson's The Man from Mars, which in general outline resembles Leggett's A Dream of a Modest Prophet. This visitor to Mars finds it further advanced than the earth and learns from the Martians how all terrestial difficulties may be solved. Unequal distribution of wealth is indicated as the worst phase of our social structure; this has been brought about by certain individuals' getting a monopoly on land---hence in Mars the ideas of Henry George have borne fruit and the government owns all land. "No representative government can exist long without a system which prevents the monopoly of its territory by wealth." (28) Other phases of nineteenth century life condemned are interest on money, industrial monopolies, and the fact that learning goes completely unrewarded. To avoid these things, Martians have a cooperative system of production and universal education. The Man from Mars has too little plot to carry the reader's interest along; it is actually little more than a long comparative lecture on terrestial and Martian civilizations.

Chauncey Thomas' The Crystal Button is notable chiefly for the way in which it anticipates many of the scientific aspects of Bellamy's futurity story. The Crystal Button was written between 1872 and 1878, but was not published

---

(28) Simpson, W., The Man from Mars, His Morals, Politics and Religion, (San Francisco, 1891), 122.

until 1891---and only then because of the insistence
of George Houghton, who edited it. Its story concerns
Paul Prognosis who is injured by a blow on the head and
recovers consciousness in Boston in 4872. A millenium
has been brought about through the efforts of John Costor,
who preached the gospel of truth and exacted the following
pledge from innumerable people:

> I will try from this moment hence-
> forth to be true and honest in my every
> act, word and thought; and this crystal
> button I will wear while the spirit of
> truth abides with me. (29)

To facilitate this spirit of truth and unselfishness,
the government has taken over the ownership of all land,
for

> As we now look upon it, air, water,
> sunshine, and land, are peculiarly the
> people's own, and it is with great diffi-
> culty that we can understand a state of
> society in which individuals were permitted
> to exercise any control over them. (30)

The Crystal Button emphasizes the mechanical aspects of
the future and abounds in descriptions of airplanes, fast
railways, television, methods of deriving power from the
sun, and the widespread use of aluminum. In this phase
it differs slightly from Looking Backward, but as Houghton
remarks in his "Preface", "its general scheme so closely

---

(29) Thomas, C., The Crystal Button, or the Adventures
of Paul Prognosis in the Forty-Ninth Century,
(Boston, 1891), 158.

(30) Thomas, C., op. cit., 246.

resembles that of Mr. Bellamy's book that it would be difficult to convince the public of its priority---a task I should shrink from undertaking, although I know it to be a fact." [31] The novel ends with the usual device of having Prognosis awake from his dream, imbued with a desire to find people worthy of wearing the crystal button.

A less definite utopia is Amos K. Fiske's Beyond the Bourn. The story is projected to another planet by tracing the mental wanderings of an injured man as he lies between life and death. The planet has attained perfection through eugenics, a universal language, birth control, and utilization of the forces of nature. When the terrestial visitor inquires whether their government is communistic or socialistic, he is told that there is no formal government but that "this state of comparative perfection has been attained by growth and development in individual character...". [32] Similarly vague is "Birch Arnold's" A New Aristocracy which prophesies the coming of an unselfish idealism which is to transform the world in the future.

In 1892 the literary quest for utopia was in full

---

(31) Houghton, G., "Preface" to The Crystal Button, ix.

(32) Fiske, Amos K., Beyond the Bourn, (New York, 1891), 103.

cry with at least eight futurity stories appearing. (33)
The ideas of the People's Party began to influence utopias
and Ignatius Donnelly's The Golden Bottle and Henry L.
Everett's The People's Program reflect the Populist platform. Donnelly announced that his book was "intended to
explain and defend, in the thin disguise of a story, some
of the new ideas put forth by the People's Party". (34)
The Golden Bottle is one of the more significant utopias
because it expresses so many of the reform ideas current
in the West. The story employs a dream mechanism to describe an ideal state in which the Populist Program is in
effect although attained only through much confusion and
turmoil. Ephraim Benezet of Kansas dreams that a spirit
gives him a bottle of a liquid which will change base
metals to gold. With this, Benezet lends enough money
at 2 per cent interest to pay off all the farm mortgages
in his native Butler County in Kansas. His efforts are

(33) Sometimes listed as a utopia of this year is
William Richard Bradshaw's The Goddess of
Atvatabar (New York, 1892). This describes
the discovery at some time in the twentieth
century of the continent of Atvatabar on the
inner surface of the earth, where all kinds of
mechanical devices are used and where life can
be restored by a "soul-force". The emphasis is
largely on scientific marvels rather than on
social organization. A similar emphasis on pseudo-
science is to be found in Robert D. Braine's
Messages from Mars; by Aid of the Telescopic Plant
(New York, 1892), a story of interplanetary
communication.

(34) Donnelly, I., The Golden Bottle, (New York, 1892),
3.

then extended to the national scene where his literally
unlimited wealth is used in behalf of the poor laboring
classes. A gigantic class struggle as in Caesar's
Column looms up between the Plutocrats and the common
people. Finally the people triumph and Benezet is elected
President. Then Benezet wakes up to discover that all
this has been a dream---but Donnelly is quick to point
out the allegorical significance of the whole story---
it is essentially an argument for greenback currency.
"The Golden Bottle represents the power of government to
create its own money. With that power it will do all
that you dreamed the Bottle did. It will make money so
abundant that the credit system will cease, debts will
disappear." [35] The novel expresses the viewpoint of
western farmers typified by an excessive hatred of millionaires and Wall Street and a belief that greenback currency
issued in large amounts was the key to all problems.
Donnelly's opinion of the Supreme Court will sound strangely
familiar to the 1936 reader:

> A lot of lawyers, mainly selected by
> the great corporations, sit upon a bench,
> with old women's gowns upon them with
> power to nullify House, Senate, President,
> and people. Oh, it is a beautiful con-
> trivance to arrest progress and shackle
> liberty! [36]

---

(35) Donnelly, I., op. cit., 308.

(36) Donnelly, I., op. cit., 145.

Virulent almost libellous attacks are made upon specific individuals. A cooperative railroad built by the people has the following effect on Jay Gould:

> Our great four-track trunk line across the continent, with its north and south branches, could not do the business that crowded upon it; and Jay Gould went out and hung himself. And all the people said--- Amen! (37)

This excessive hatred of capitalism and capitalists is Donnelly's worst fault, because he carries it so far as to be humorous rather than effective.

A device similar to that used by Hale in his Ten Times One is Ten is employed by Henry L. Everett in The People's Program. Youths of all nations band themselves together in Geometrical Leagues, in which every member is pledged to enlist ten other people to advance the cause, a combination of Nationalist and Populist principles. Everett is convinced that laboring men should woo literature as an aid:

> The labor unions should cultivate the literary method of increasing the numbers of their friends and members. The lecture platform and literature pertaining to the labor movement should be everywhere employed to rouse the people to the importance of united action, and to persuade them that they can vastly improve their opportunities and enjoyments in life. (38)

---

(37) Donnelly, I., op. cit., 172.

(38) Everett, H.L., "Preface" to The People's Program. The Twentieth Century is Theirs, (New York, 1892), v..

Since most of these utopias represent the viewpoint of the laboring classes, Everett ought to have been well satisfied with the literary fare offered to the public.

The usual emphasis on inequality of wealth is found in Albert Chavannes' novel The Future Commonwealth in which Samuel Balcom, a young American, visits Socioland, a commonwealth in Africa where poverty and millionaires are unknown because the government controls all the important agencies of production. The visitor from the United States remarks that "probably more dissatisfaction is felt among us on account of the inequality in the distribution of wealth than from any other cause". [39] This leads the way to the explanation of the ideal commonwealth, reported by Balcom in a series of letters to a friend in America.

A journey to Mars is described in Francis Worcester Doughty's Mirrikh, or A Woman from Mars. A group of New Yorkers exploring in Thibet inhale a gas which separates soul from body, permitting it to roam at will among the planets. One of them visits Mars where he finds a civilization much further advanced than that on earth. The work is mystical and puts some emphasis on Swedenborgian ideas.

The conception of a struggle between the forces of

_____

(39) Chavannes, A., The Future Commonwealth, or What Samuel Balcom Saw in Socioland, (New York, 1892), 10.

special privilege and popular opinion is at the base of
Samuel Crocker's That Island. This romance concerns an
island whose history is intended to portray the past and
the future of the United States. There had been a struggle
between the White Caps (Labor) and the Yellow Caps (Capital) in which the latter had emerged victorious and enjoyed all sorts of privileges. The apathy of the White
Caps led to the formation of a new party, the Blue Caps,
who advocate the nationalizing of numerous industries.
That all this is intended seriously is made clear by the
publisher's notice that "our firm is desirous of flooding
the country with this work, and will offer special in-
ducements to those desirous of selling it". [40] The
book is poorly written, childish in its conceptions, and
deserves the oblivion to which it has been consigned.

Mary Agnes Tincker's San Salvador describes a small
utopian colony vaguely located in the north of Italy,
where the emphasis is completely on the individual's
development. "We take care of the individual, and the
state takes care of itself." [41] San Salvador is so
general in its descriptions that it leaves no impression
on the reader's mind. One is inclined to agree with The
Nation's reviewer who remarked that "the simple annals

---

(40) Crocker, S., ("Theodore Oceanic Islet"), That
Island. A Political Romance, (Oklahoma City,
1892), 4.

(41) Tincker, M.A., San Salvador, (Boston, 1892), 98.

of a social state where plain living and high thinking
prevail naturally seem insipid". (42)   The same emphasis
on providing the individual with the proper means of
development is set forth in Ai by Charles Daniel.   Hardly to be considered as a complete utopian novel, Ai
is best described by its own subtitle as "a social vision".
The story, which is chaotically told, projects ahead to
1950 and centers around the life of Ai who becomes Bishop
of Philadelphia as the result of a revolution.   He uses
all his resources for the benefit of the poor and finally
brings about a modified brotherhood of man.   The author's
ideas as to the improvement of society are summed up in
his characterization of Ai:

> To influence the individual was the
> one purpose of his life, and he tried to
> have others act on the same principle;
> and thus, he maintained, would society
> be influenced. (43)

Ai is difficult to classify, for it is partly utopian,
partly religious, and partly fantasy. (44)

---

(42) The Nation, LIV, (May 26, 1892), 402.

(43) Daniel, C., Ai.   A Social Vision, (Philadelphia,
1892), 267.

(44) A similar difficulty in classification applies
to M. Louise Moore's ("An Untramelled Free-Think-
er") Al-Modad, or Life Scenes Beyond the Polar
Circumflex (Cameron Parish, Louisiana, 1892) which
is listed by Allyn Forbes and others as a utopia.
The novel relates the adventures of Al-Modad on
earth and finally in a strange civilization on
the inner surface of the earth where men have
strange psychical powers.   While there is some
serious description of social organization in this
new world, the major emphasis is placed on its
sensational pseudo-scientific aspects.

The People's Party's program motivated at least one of the utopias of 1893. The anonymous novel <u>The Beginning, A Romance of Chicago As It Might Be</u> states its position in a Preface:

> Our small debating club of workingmen was discussing the question as to whether the People's Party's platform, if adopted by the country and put in force would benefit the great mass of workingmen, that is, raise the masses.
> We proved to our own satisfaction that it would not. (45)

The novel attempts to supply a substitute program. Its basic idea is that universal education is the key to future happiness. The authors propose to support these educational enterprises by a six per cent tax on all wills probated. As people become educated, they will gradually come around to the application of state socialism to all things; the novel shows this happening in Chicago in the future.

The only Fourieristic novel of the whole group is Henry Olerich's <u>A Cityless and Countryless World</u> in which a visitor from Mars is propelled to the earth by means of a rocket and proceeds to explain the superior Martian system. Their life is based on "the practical cooperative idealism" in which all work for the common good, receive the same wages, and live in great cooperative houses.

---

(45) Anonymous, <u>The Beginning, A Romance of Chicago As It Might Be</u>, (Chicago, 1893), 3.

"We have no credit system, and no interest, as you can see. For in a world where everyone has all the money he wants...credit is unnecessary." (46) The influence of Fourier is found in the living conditions of the people; one thousand of them dwell in a great apartment located on a plot of land 6 by 24 miles so that the population is evenly divided over the land. This is really a system of Phalanxes. Other parts of the system derive from Bellamy.

A.P. Russell's Sub-Coelum. A Skybuilt Human World is the most cloying of all the American utopias. Located somewhere under the sky, is this world where all is sweetness and light, where happiness reigns supreme, and where there is no hard work to do. Even the oysters are described as growing larger in Sub-Coelum! As to the way all this is attained or as to the governmental system which maintains it, the author is vague. Typical of the easy generalities of the novel is the following excerpt:

> In the ordinary sense, the plebeian and the aristocrat did not exist in Sub-Coelum. Society was so constituted, and men were so governed by exceptional conditions, that such distinctions were not recognized. Extremes met on the same plane....The uses of labor, or money, of intelligence, and of character, were held to be inseparable. (47)

(46) Olerich, H., A Cityless and Countryless World; An Outline of Practical Cooperative Individualism, (Holstein, Iowa, 1893), 178.

(47) Russell, A.P., Sub-Coelum, A Sky-Built Human World, (Boston, 1893), 74.

Another Martian journey, this time by airplane,
is recorded in the pseudonymous Unveiling a Parallel
(Boston, 1893) by "Two Women of the West". This novel
is a plea for equality of the sexes and subordinates all
other utopian ideals to that purpose. The terrestial
visitor to Mars finds after several months study that
the happiness of the planet rests solidly on a single
standard of morals for men and women. As we are to infer
from the title, a similar felicity will be forthcoming
on earth as soon as we adopt a similar attitude.

In 1893, comparatively few utopias appeared; (48)
but 1894 more than made up the deficiency. At least nine
futuristic romances appeared in that year, making it the
high point of the whole movement. Most important of the
utopias of 1894 was William Dean Howells' A Traveller from
Altruria, the best American utopia after Bellamy's novel.
Howells avoided all of the cheap tricks and pseudo-scien-

---

(48) In addition to those discussed in this chapter,
J.W. Roberts' Looking Within had answered Bellamy.
C.E. Niswonger's The Isle of Feminine (Little
Rock, Arkansas, 1893) is included by Forbes and
other bibliographers. This is not a utopia, but
a story of an island where women reign supreme.
I have been unable to locate a copy of Fayette
Stratton Giles's Shadows Before, or, A Century
Onward (New York, 1893) which from its title
and from a reading of the author's other work,
I infer to be a utopia. That others have had
a similar difficulty is evidenced by Frances
Theresa Russell's vague statement "In 1893 the
list is augmented by Fayette Giles's Shadows
Before, which tries to throw an extra shade on
Bellamy" (Russell, F.T., Touring Utopia, (New
York, 1932), 219.)

tific predictions of the other utopists. His plot is simple and constitutes the most effective social satire presented in any American utopia.

Howells reverses the process of projecting individuals out into space or time, and simply has his traveller, Mr. Homos, come to America from Altruria, which he doesn't bother to locate geographically. Mr. Homos meets a widely representative group as a summer resort including the Author, the Banker, the Manufacturer, the Lawyer, the Minister, and the Professor. The Altrurian's point of view is original and free from traditional ideas about society; this gives Howells an opportunity for a detached criticism of America, which is the chief concern of the novel. The organization of Altruria is not described until the last part of the book and even then only in a general way as a combination of applied Christianity and Bellamy's social structure.

Into the mouth of Reuben Camp, a farm boy, Howells has put his bitterest indictments of American conditions. Camp is the only person who can listen to the Altrurian's explanations with understanding; the Banker, the Manufacturer, and the rest are so fogged by tradition or so enwrapped in their own interests that they see none of the social evils surrounding them. Howells places particular emphasis on the dangers of our urban life, the closing of our public domain, the lowering living standards of American laborers, and the unequal distribution

of wealth. Howells had a clearer conception of the

changes in American life brought about by the end of

the frontier and other conditions than any other utopist;

in describing the difference between America in the 1850's

and the 1890's he says:

> If a man got out of work, he turned
> his hand to something else; if a man failed
> in business, he started in again from some
> other direction; as a last resort he went
> West, pre-empted a quarter section of
> public land, and grew up with the country.
> Now the country is grown up; the public
> land is gone; business is full on all
> sides, and the hand that turned itself to
> something else has lost its cunning. The
> struggle for life has changed from a free
> fight to an encounter of disciplined
> forces, and the free fighters that are
> left get ground to pieces between organized
> labor and organized capital. (49)

Urbanization constituted a great menace in Howells' mind,

and according to his Altrurian "it was the intolerable

suffering in the cities that chiefly hastened...the rise

of Commonwealth" (50) ---the new social order in Altruria.

The reason why Bellamy's followers hailed Howells

as one of them may be seen in the description of Altruria:

> We have, of course...no money in
> your sense. As the whole people control
> affairs, no man works for another, and no
> man pays another. Everyone does his share
> of labor and receives his share of food,

---

(49) Howells, W.D., A Traveller from Altruria, (New
York, 1894), 212.

(50) Howells, W.D., op. cit., 281.

> clothing, and shelter, which is neither
> more nor less than another's. If you
> can imagine the justice and impartiality
> of a well-ordered family, you can con-
> ceive of the social and economic life
> of Altruria. We are, properly speaking,
> a family rather than a nation like
> yours. (51)

Howells is more effective in pointing out the flaws in
our social structure than he is in offering a better plan.
His satire is devastatingly logical; his constructive
criticism too vague and too insistent upon society as
"the one big happy family". But Howells was not so much
concerned with the solution of our problem as he was with
getting them started. A Traveller from Altruria is the
only important satirical utopia of the period. Cleverly
conceived and simply executed, it presents a better
picture of the flaws of the Gilded Age than any other
utopia. In a letter to his wife written after a lecture
in Oswego, N.Y., Howells laughingly remarked, "Just think
of their using The [sic] Traveller from Altruria as a
text-book in the State Normal School!" (52) But if the
text was selected to make the students think seriously
about the problems of their own age, no better book could
have been chosen.

A most complete utopia of the same year was S. Byron
Welcome's From Earth's Center, one of the few novels of

---

(51) Howells, W.D., op. cit., 287.

(52) Howells, Mildred, Editor, Life in Letters of
William Dean Howells, (New York, 1928), II, 76.

the period to advocate the single tax. The story concerns several young men who, in an expedition to the South Pole, are caught in a strong current and are sucked down into the inner surface of the earth where they find an ideal civilization called Centralia. The hero, Ralph Spencer, falls in love with one of Centralia's beauties and marries her after a courtship which has consisted chiefly of long explanations by his fiancee of the political, social, and economic institutions of Centralia---even including descriptions of Centralian weddings in which bride and groom give presents to the guests. Utopia indeed!

From Earth's Center is unusual in insisting upon the decentralization of government, and Centralia's basic principle is "that the nation must not meddle with anything the states can do, the states must not interfere with anything that the city can do, the city must not undertake to perform anything that the ward can do; and none of the four must touch that which the individual or private company can perform". [53] The book also differs from other American utopias in affirming the necessity of competition. Spencer is informed that "governmental operation of any public service ever tried here has proved inefficient and been superseded by private

_____

(53) Welcome, S.B., From Earth's Center. A Polar Gateway Message, (Chicago, 1894), 114.

enterprises". (54) To accomplish this, Centralia uses
a system of letting out by contracts on a competitive
basis all those functions which are ordinarily thought
to be governmental. But all their reforms are sub-
ordinate to the single tax. "All other reforms or im-
provements would avail the lower classes nothing as long
as land-values were allowed to go into the pockets of
landlords." (55) The secret of Centralia's progress is
the tax on land in the form of rent----for all land is
publicly owned. In this respect, From Earth's Center
is typical of numerous other American utopias in advocating one reform as fundamental to an ideal organization, although in its choice of a reform and its
emphasis upon competition it differs decidedly from the
other utopias.

Two utopias in which the scientific element pre-
dominates but with some emphasis on political and social
organization are John Jacob Astor's A Journey in Other
Worlds and Byron A. Brooks' Earth Revisited. Astor
conceives of a struggle between the classics and science
and wishes that books would go ahead to what we do not
know instead of reiterating the past so constantly. His
world of 2000 is a miracle of efficiency with science
at the helm; most sensational of all his predictions is

(54) Welcome, S.B., op. cit., 89.
(55) Welcome, S.B., op. cit., 256.

his description of the way in which the earth attains
an equable climate by having the water pumped out at
the poles alternately, thus straightening the earth's
axis. Brooks' Earth Revisited dwells on the same type
of marvel, but adds to it a description of the Brotherhood of Man as the foundation of his future society.

A novel concerned with the possible effect of the
dumping of a great quantity of gold on the world's
currency systems is Henry Richardson Chamberlain's 6000
Tons of Gold (Meadville, Pa., 1894). The book is
reminiscent of Donnelly's The Golden Bottle, but has a
completely different conclusion. Robert Brent exploring
in South America receives a gift of six thousand tons
of gold from an Indian tribe. Brent takes the gold to
the United States, stores it in a private vault, and
tries to use it for the good of humanity. He gives
millions to charities, drives the "bears" out of the
stock market, and attempts all kinds of philanthropies.
He succeeds only in upsetting the whole financial structure
of the country, raising prices so that the poor are almost starved. Finally as the only way out, Brent puts
his gold on a warship and dumps it into the Atlantic
Ocean. 6000 Tons of Gold is one of the novels preceding
the currency struggle of 1896 and is designed apparently
to show the dangers of an arbitrary basis for a currency.
Frank Rosewater's '96; A Romance of Utopia, which is

more romance than utopia, according to its title page aims at presenting "A Solution of the Labor Problem, A New God, and a New Religion". The reader, lost in the chaotic narrative, is likely to be skeptical of the author's success. The setting is in a fantastic African valley where two cities, the circular Tsor and the rectangular Tismoul, are located. Inequality is Tsor's chief characteristic: Tismoul is based on American democracy of the kind to be found here in 1896 with suffrage permitted only to the educated. In Tismoul there are cooperative kitchens, public dining halls, and all the usual accoutrements of utopia. When Tsor is wrecked by its internal strife caused by the competitive system, Tismoul instructs her to the better way of life. The book ends with the two cities happily merged and named Utopia. Because of its fantastic elements '96, belongs mostly in the realm of romance, but the descriptions of the ideal commonwealth in Africa make it partially utopian.

A deeply religious and highly mystical novel which is as much a utopia as it is anything else is Joaquin Miller's strange work The Building of the City Beautiful. The story begins in Jerusalem with the meeting of Miriam, a Jewess, and John Morton. Disappointed with the efforts of a rich Jew to reform the human race, each starts out to build his own ideal city. Morton goes to the mountains

overlooking San Francisco and tries to build according
to Biblical precepts but finds that he cannot overcome
man's innate selfishness. He is then mysteriously transported to where Miriam has constructed her "city beautiful", to descriptions of which the last half of the
book is devoted. Miller sees in society the same evils
that the other utopists depicted. "The curse of society
is the granting of special privileges which are the
survivals of the divine right of force and fraud." (56)
According to the author, "there are two ways to cure
this evil: Extend the same favors to all, or withhold
them from the few. We believe in the latter method,
which is more truly in harmony with the Declaration of
Independence". (57) The social and political details of
this ideal city are not worked out, because Miller becomes immersed in Biblical ideas. His ideal city is to
him an application of the Sermon on the Mount. One
curious inconsistency of the work is that while it describes the building of a great city, the author is opposed
to cities and has Miriam say, "But cities, great cities,
as a rule, should not be....No, I would sweep great cities
like New York and London from the face of the earth". (58)

(56) Miller, J., The Building of the City Beautiful,
     (Chicago, 1894), 131.

(57) Miller, J., op. cit., 149.

(58) Miller, J., op. cit., 176-7.

Like most of Miller's other works, <u>The Building of the</u>
<u>City Beautiful</u> is a strange chaotic mixture of beauti-
ful descriptions, trite statements, and egotistical
utterances.

With at least nine utopias appearing in 1894, (59)
a diminishing interest in utopia occurred the next year
as reflected in the appearance of only four rather unimportant utopias in 1895. The most original of these
was Castello N. Holford's <u>Aristopia</u>, an attempt to re-
write history as it might have been. Aristopia is a
colony which broke away from the original Virginia settlement in 1607 and pursued its own course with certain
reform ideas. Curiously enough the first reform undertaken in this new colony was a revision of the English
language "to make the conjugations of all verbs, the
comparison of all adjectives, and the plurals of all
nouns quite regular in all the printing done in this
new nation". (60)   Holford's idea in constructing his
ideal commonwealth is that unequal distribution of wealth

---

(59) Included on most lists of American utopias is
Walter Browne's <u>2894, or The Fossil Man: A</u>
<u>Midwinter Night's Dream</u> (New York, 1894). A
search of a dozen libraries has revealed no
copy of this futurity novel. A similar situation
prevails with Edward T. Bouve's <u>Centuries</u>
<u>Apart</u> (Boston, 1894) and William N. Harben's
<u>The Land of the Changing Sun</u> (1894).

(60) Holford, C.N., <u>Aristopia</u>, (Boston, 1895), 84.

is the besetting evil of America. To avoid this he
provides that "in the Commonwealth, there should be
no private ownership of land" [61] because that gave
one man power over another; furthermore "no person should
leave more than ten thousand dollars to one heir". [62]
By these two devices, he thinks that the future history
of mankind might be more happy.

In 1895, Albert Chavannes was still trying to per-
suade his fellow citizens that his ideas were worth
adopting, despite the fact that his earlier novel The
Future Commonwealth (1892) had made no impression. After
mentioning the lack of success of his earlier books in
his "Preface" to In Brighter Climes, Chavannes declares:
"I have sugar-coated the pill and offer it once more to
the public, fondly hoping that in its new guise it will
meet with a more ready acceptance". [63] In Brighter
Climes, a sequel to The Future Commonwealth, describes
the flight of Charles and Mary Morril from the unemploy-
ment and hard times of America to Socioland in Africa,
where a cooperative system is in effect. Cooperation
"is Communistic as to production and Individualistic as
to distribution". [64] Here in the equal opportunities

---

(61) Holford, C.N., op. cit., 94.

(62) Holford, C.N., op. cit., 98.

(63) Chavannes, A., "Preface" to In Brighter Times, or
Life in Socioland, (Knoxville, 1895), 1.

(64) Chavannes, A., op. cit., 169.

of Socioland the Morrils find the happiness they have
been seeking.

The inevitable journey to Mars, which was at least
an annual occurrence, was supplied in 1895 by Willis
Mitchell's The Inhabitants of Mars, Their Manners and
Advancement in Civilization and Their Opinion of Us (Malden,
Mass., 1895). Badly written and filled with fatuous
ideas, this novel adds nothing to what other utopists
had already contributed concerning that always more advanced planet which the earth must emulate. The author's
particular interest seems to be in settling the vexing
conflict between science and religion.

Among the utopias of 1895 was a pamphlet called The
Milltillionaire which Albert W. Howard issued under the
name of "M. Auburré Hovorré". The book conceives of
the nineteenth century tendency toward unequal distribution
of wealth as being carried in the far future to its
ultimate end. "Now, behold the Milltillionaire not only
King to the Millionaire (an indigent being in comparison)
but Lord o'er the Earth, having with his unlimited wealth
possessed himself of all landed property of all civil
countries..." (65) The Milltillionaire has established
a sort of beneficent despotism in which all others share
alike through his kindly arrangements and through the

---

(65) Howard, A.W., The Milltillionaire, (No date or
place of publication given; The Library of Congress Bibliography lists the book as (Boston,
1895?)), 3.

wonders of science which are described in some detail. The reader is puzzled as to whether The Milltillionaire is offered as a serious contribution to social thought of whether it is merely a fantasy. (66)

The Bryan campaign was the motive for at least two utopian novels in 1896. The first, Ingersoll Lockwood's 1900, or The Last President, told the story of the chaos that followed the election of Bryan to the presidency in 1900. Democracy is shown as breaking up completely as the result of Bryan's efforts. Just exactly what is intended in John Lockwood's Hi-Li, The Moon Man is diffi-cult to say. Hi-Li, a giant from the moon, is shown wrecking New York City, with all kinds of guns rendered useless against him. Finally he is destroyed when he stumbles on "the protruding cranium of William McKinley, statesman of the United States; especially of Canton, Ohio". (67)

---

(66) More clearly a fantastic romance is Professor John Uri Lloyd's Etidorpha (Cincinnati, 1895), which is usually included in lists of utopias.
    Henry L. Call's The Coming Revolution (Boston, 1895) is not a novel, but it does project ahead to the future in its last chapter called "The New Republic".

(67) Lockwood, J., Hi-Li, The Moon Man, (Brooklyn, 1896), 49.

The other utopias of 1896 (68) followed the more conventional paths already delineated. An Ideal Republic, or The One Way Out of the Fog by Corwin Phelps is another description of an ideal commonwealth in Africa settled by American farmers whose mortgages have been foreclosed. The author believes the national bank system and the gold standard the causes of inequality of wealth. By solving the problem of money the ideal republic is attained. The novel is marked by the same hatred of millionaires that characterizes so many of the American utopias.

One of the most lurid tales is contained in James Cowan's Daybreak, A Romance of an Old World, which describes the moon crashing into the earth, permitting two men to board it and to travel to Mars where they climb off when the moon crashes into that planet. Here they find a highly advanced civilization from which money,

---

(68) In addition to the complete utopias discussed, several scientific futurity stories appeared in 1896. Most important of these was "In Sargasso" Missing (New York, 1896) by Julius Chambers, onetime editor of The New York World. This describes the discovery of a race living in the calm of Sargasso sea. While the major emphasis is placed on the more sensational aspects of the story, there is some description of the communal organization employed by these people. More definitely in the Jules Verne tradition is Robert W. Chambers' The Maker of Moons (New York, 1896). I have been unable to locate a copy of the anonymous The Crystal City (Boston, 1896) which is sometimes included on lists of utopias and pseudo-scientific fiction.

private property, and all social distinctions have been
eliminated. The hope is advanced that the earth may
some day attain a similar felicitous organization. Finally with some deference to the reader's credulity, the
author states that the whole thing has been merely a
dream. Daybreak is conventional in form and conception
and differs from the other novels only in its ridiculously sensational device for transferring characters
to Mars.

Four complete utopias appeared in 1897 including
Bellamy's Equality. (69) The most detailed of these was
Charles W. Caryl's New Era which has all kinds of diagrams
and pictures of the "New Era City". This city is to be
designed in 239 circles radiating from a center where
the government buildings are located.

Caryl has planned such details as what class is to
live in a certain circle and how much rent is to be paid.
All this is to be effected by a system of cooperation.

---

(69) Several other books of 1897 might be called
"utopian" in the broadest sense of the word, although they expound no complete ideal commonwealths. Dr. Ellis Paxton Oberholtzer's The
New Man (Philadelphia, 1897) is a rather
philosophic treatise on society projecting ahead
into the future in its last chapter and viewing
all things optimistically.
More definitely sensational than constructive
in their purposes are Frona E.W. Colburn's Yermah
the Dorado. The Story of a Lost Race (San Francisco, 1897); Alfred Smythe's Van Hoff; or the
New Planet (New York, 1897); and William Windsor's
Loma: A Citizen of Venus (St. Paul, Minnesota,
1897).

The plot is unfolded in dialogue, and the book might be considered as a drama in three scenes. The first shows a Mr. Sutta, who plans to utilize the money he has made in a Colorado gold mine, journeying east to get the backing of wealthy men. At a meeting of millionaires, Sutta refuses to be corrupted by bribes. Finally a gigantic mass meeting is held in Faneuil Hall, Boston, where the New Era plan is enthusiastically endorsed by Edward Bellamy, Frances Willard, Count Tolstoi, B.O. Flower, and Emma Goldman. The novel is poorly written and rather childish in its attempt to dazzle readers with pictures and descriptions of the New Era City, but is an excellent example of the intense seriousness with which the average utopist was imbued.

Another cooperative system is expounded in James M. Galloway's ("Anon Moore") <u>John Harvey, A Tale of the Twentieth Century</u>. This describes what is known as The Nationality---an area comprising the states of Utah, South Dakota, Nebraska, Kansas, Colorado, Wyoming, Arizona, New Mexico, and a large part of Texas---where a socialistic commonwealth has been organized by John Harvey. Finally, the forces of special privilege in the United States come into physical conflict with The Nationality, but war is narrowly averted when the common people of the East decide that this cooperative system is the best means of organization for them. The Nationality was made possible by the generosity of its founder,

John Harvey, who discovered a huge quantity of gold, but instead of using it for his selfish interests, built a great irrigation canal to make this whole area productive. A romantic element is added to the work by the love affair between Harvey's daughter and the narrator, an English lord. John Harvey is similar to Donnelly's novels in prophesying a gigantic class struggle, which in this instance is also a geographical cleavage between the equal human rights of the West and special privilege in the East. In The Nationality under a cooperative system "society becomes one great family, working in harmony for a common end, and each enjoying to the extent of his wish and ability all good and desirable things".[70] Contrasted with this is the vicious inequality of the East:

> The entire business of the Eastern states was under the control of a few giant corporations and trusts, which dictated the manner in which it was conducted, and reaped the profits arising from it.... The essential object of these great trusts, or corporations, was the amassing of enormous wealth for those owning and controlling them; and being devoid of the moral characteristics and responsibilities of individuals, the means they employed to attain this object were often more iniquitous in character and pernicious in effect.[71]

Surely this was a utopia designed for western readers.

---

(70) Galloway, James M., John Harvey, A Tale of the Twentieth Century, (Chicago, 1897), 153.

(71) Galloway, J.M., op. cit., 251.

The final utopia of 1897 was the pseudonymous A Prophetic Romance by "Lord Commissioner" which describes the far remote future. The tale abounds in scientific wonders and tells of the visit of the Lord Commissioner of Mars to the earth. He and the President of the United States travel all over the world by airplane observing the miracles of television and modern transportation. The author's own ideas are reflected in the insistence upon vegetarianism throughout the novel. In the future all "slaughter-dens" are converted into beautiful orchards, and forests and animals are no longer "murdered" for the satisfaction of the appetite. A Prophetic Romance is a stereotyped futurity story with all of the usual trappings of scientific marvels and the customary love story to give unity.

In 1898 [72] the revival of interest in Bellamy's ideas was marked by the two works already discussed in

-----

(72) Several futurity novels of 1898 are sometimes listed as utopias. Among these are Oto Mundo's The Recovered Continent; A Tale of the Chinese Invasion (Columbus, Ohio, 1898) and Stanley Waterloo's Armageddon (Chicago, 1898) both of which concern future wars. Waterloo's novel is notable chiefly for a rather accurate forecast of the World War which he conceived of as a struggle between the Anglo-Saxons on the one hand and the Latins and Slavs on the other. Curiously, Germany is shown deserting the Anglo-Saxon cause and is defeated by the Anglo-American forces.

I have been unable to obtain a copy of Joseph E. Badger's The Lost City (Boston, 1898) which may be utopian.

Chapter IX, Forbush's Co-opolitan and Sanders' Reality.
Three other utopias appeared: Alexander Craig's Ionia,
Land of Wise Men and Fair Women; Warren S. Rehm's ("Omen
Nemo") The Practical City; and Bert J. Wellman's The
Legal Revolution of 1902, which was published pseudonymously
as by "A Law-Abiding Revolutionist". Wellman's novel
is one of the most complete and impressive of the
American utopias, and rivals Donnelly's novels in its
virulent hatred of millionaires. The story begins with
the conventional description of the atrocious conditions
in the nineteenth century. Finally a group of reformers
circulate petitions among the people asking for a
Constitutional Convention to amend the constitution.
When the convention is called, amendments providing for
income taxes, inheritance taxes, and direct election of
the president and members of the senate are passed.
Finally amid much turmoil, the party of the people succeeds
in jamming through the Nineteenth Amendment providing
that the government shall confiscate any individual's
property amounting to more than half a million dollars.
This precipitates a Marxian class struggle between millionaires and the people, until the popular triumph brings
about a cooperative socialism.

The Legal Revolution of 1902 describes a sort of
petitioner's paradise. "One petition which was circulated,
and received many signatures, even asked that Lyman

Gage be hanged, and another asked that the same punish-
ment be administered to Mark Hanna. 'Hang Hanna' became a by-word with the boys on the streets." (73)
Possibly the strangest proposal of all the utopias was
the circulation of "petitions that women be prohibited
from wearing bloomers"! (74) The author's fundamental
purpose in all this is to show that anything can be
done by an aroused electorate and by strictly legal
means. Actual personages take part in this struggle
for reform, notably John Wanamaker, Eugene Debs, Edward
Bellamy, Tom L. Johnson, and William Jennings Bryan, who
is elected president in 1900. For a clear picture of
the things in society which nineteenth century reformers
most resented, one can recommend The Legal Revolution of
1902 as one of the best American utopias.

A description of an ideal city of the future reminiscent of Caryl's New Era is contained in Warren S.
Rehm's little pamphlet The Practical City. Its author
is a man of one idea---that "land sharks" are the source
of all evil. He is determined that "in the future
organization of towns and communities land sharks will
not play such an important role". (75) His plan is to

---

(73) Wellman, B.J., The Legal Revolution of 1902,
     (Chicago, 1898), 68.

(74) Wellman, B.J., op. cit., 69.

(75) Rehm, W.S., The Practical City. A Future City
     Romance; or a Study in Environment, (Lancaster,
     Pa., 1898), 6.

have the community itself buy the land and sell it direct to the citizen at cost. He then goes on to describe his ideal city with very specific details as to its size, street layout, and general arrangement. In conclusion, he says rather vaguely, "We hope that you will meet many noble men and women, the happy parents of manly boys and womanly girls". [76]

Alexander Craig's *Ionia, Land of Wise Men and Fair Women* transports a young Englishman to a utopia in the remote Himalayas. Here dwells a people whose happiness derives from four basic laws.

> The first makes the soil of the country and property of the people as a whole, and has prevented the formation of a landed aristocracy. The second provides that no person shall become possessed by inheritance of more than a certain limited amount of wealth, and has preserved us from the dangers of plutocracy. [77]

The other two laws provide that all criminals be put to death and that "those who are unworthy to be progenitors of succeeding generations shall be debarred from the privilege of parenthood..." [78] *Ionia* is a rather charming utopia, gaining by contrast with some of its virulent, class-conscious contemporaries.

One would expect the proximity to the twentieth

---

(76) Rehm, W.S., *op. cit.*, 35.

(77) Craig, A., *Ionia. Land of Wise Men and Fair Women*, (Chicago, 1898), 200.

(78) Craig, A., *op. cit.*, 201.

century to inspire numerous novels about the future in 1899. Actually, Albert Adams Merrill's The Great Awakening, The Story of the Twenty-Second Century was the only one to appear. Merrill uses the conventional device of having his hero fall asleep to awaken in 2199 in an ideal civilization. The author ascribes all of the difficulties of the nineteenth century to the gold standard, which capitalists could control. In the new system currency is issued only on the basis of the actual wealth produced. Aimed likewise at eliminating the concentration of wealth in the hands of a few is their prohibition of interest on money. "With us a man can live only on his principal; in no way can he get interest. Interest on money implies on its face a scarcity of what of all things should be common---a circulating medium." [79] Among other features of this rather remote civilization are a system of eugenics, a four-hour working day, the universal use of electricity, and widespread travel by aeroplanes. The Great Awakening is similar to numerous other utopias in seeing one remedy--where the abolition of the gold standard---as the panacea for all ills.

In 1900, the final year of this study, at least six utopias appeared. Bradford Peck's The World A Department

_____

(79) Merrill, A.A., The Great Awakening, The Story of the Twenty-Second Century, (Boston, 1899), 116.

Store has already been discussed as one of the continuations of Bellamy's ideas. It is one of the most
absurd and ungrammatical of all utopias. A more serious
social criticism is Alcanoan Q. Grigsby's ("Jack Adams")
Nequa, or the Problem of the Ages, the chief weakness
of which is its ridiculously melodramatic plot. It concerns Altruria, a land on the inner surface of the earth,
which is further advanced than the outer world but has
had a parallel history. Their great philospher Krystus
(Christ) had succeeded in putting the Golden Rule into
actual practise, and thus competition and inequality
have been eliminated. The travellers are particularly
impressed that "nowhere did we see vast clouds of smoke
such as vitiate the atmosphere in the large cities and
manufacturing districts of the outer world". [80] The
governmental system is a cooperative one, with all
citizens sharing equally in the wealth produced. The
usual emphasis is put on scientific development, the
two-hour working day, and the general happiness pervading
Altruria. To scholars, the following description of an
Altrurian library may seem the most attractive feature
of all utopias:

> Books are all numbered and catalogued,
> so the visitor has but to press the number
> on an electric keyboard, and it is delivered

---

(80) Grigsby, A.Q., Nequa, or the Problem of the Ages,
(Topeka, 1900), 145.

> at once by a pneumatic tube. The attendants
> return the books to their proper places
> in the same rapid and quiet manner. No
> noise, bluster, or confusion anywhere.
> Everything is reduced to system, and moves
> along like clock work. (81)

Of all the utopias of 1900, (82) two are important because they indicate an awakening of a skepticism about
the underlying ideas of utopists. Mr. Caroline A. Mason's
A Woman of Yesterday is not a complete utopia, but in
its last chapters its characters go to a utopian colony
called Fraternia, in the foothills of southwestern North
Carolina. Here a system of cooperative living similar
to that in many American utopias is described. Finally
Fraternia fails; Mrs. Mason supplies the chief criticism
of all such utopian experiments when one of the characters
questions Gregory, the leader of Fraternia, about their
failure:

> "Then do you feel, Mr. Gregory, that
> the message of brotherhood, of equality,

---

(81) Grigsby, A.Q., op. cit., 238.

(82) I have been unable to find a copy of Milan C.
Edson's Solaris Farm which is listed in various
bibliographies of utopias.
  Professor Simon Newcomb's His Wisdom, The
Defender (1900) is written from the viewpoint of
a future historian looking back on the years
following 1941, when Professor Campbell of Harvard
develops an anti-gravitational substance called
etherine. With this and several other inventions,
Campbell issues an edict telling all the nations
to disarm. Upon their refusal, he attacks with
all his appliances of warfare and enforces an
era of peace with himself as "His Wisdom the
Defender".

cannot be spread by such means as we tried in Fraternia?" Anna asked timidly, and yet without fear.

"I believe that such isolated, social experiments, for many years at least, will be as ours has been, premature and ineffective. They are symptoms rather than formative agencies. They have significance as such, but are otherwise unproductive." (83)

The last utopia of 1900 was <u>Toil and Self</u> which Edward A. Caswell issued under the pseudonym of "Myself and Another". Whether Caswell intended it as such, <u>Toil and Self</u> is a realistic commentary on the whole group of utopias that preceded it. The book takes us ahead to 2400 and is arranged as a series of ten lectures by Professor Winter of Yale University explaining the events that occur between the nineteenth century and the twenty-fifth. The author's fundamental idea is that any utopia must accept human nature as it always has been, and presumably as it always will be. He insists that

> Altruism and philanthropy are merely products of civilization, the outgrowth of intellectual progress and of religious teaching. Without selfishness humanity could not exist. It is a primal necessity of the intricate mechanism of life that each specimen should zealously, sedulously, and persistently look out for himself. Life would be chaos and misery, were it not for this law. (84)

He insists that any governmental system must take into account this innate selfishness, and he shows how various

---

(83) Mason, C.A., <u>A Woman of Yesterday</u>, (New York, 1900), 364.

(84) Caswell, E.A., <u>Toil and Self</u>, (Chicago, 1900), 10.

systems have failed because they did not consider this
essential. Early in the twentieth century a cooperative
system with labor and capital sharing equally in the
profits is tried. Under this cooperative organization
all went well for a time. "Toil aided self---was blended
with it." (85) But when a depression occurred, the
selfishness of the laborers manifested itself in their
refusal to share losses as well as profits. Then a system
of universal education is inaugurated in order to eradicate selfishness. This failed, too, because "the individual is never ready to make any personal sacrifice
to benefit the mass". (86)

Late in the twenty-first century, a wealth young
philanthropist and his idealistic bride put the ideas
of Edward Bellamy into actual practise in an attempt to
solve humanity's problems. This nationalistic organization
fails because men's selfishness causes them to resent
a system that makes all men equal in rank and in pay and
because men won't work for the state as well as they would
for themselves. Other systems are tried in the intervening centuries with no great success until Professor
Winter lecturing in 2400 tells his students by way of
conclusion:

> Costumes and manners, and theories
> and customs, and habits and rules, and laws

---

(85) Caswell, E.A., op. cit., 45.

(86) Caswell, E.A., op. cit., 45.

> and conventions and creeds, have changed---
> but human nature has not. It started out
> with the great fundamental law of life, the
> law of selfishness, and it will end with
> it. There may be movements to curtail or
> modify it, but over them and through them
> will ever rule supreme that motive, and
> the barriers to it will be like straws
> before the resistless force of a deep and
> mighty river sweeping oceanward. We may
> look forward, and with keenest eye or glass
> discover naught else, and looking backward
> we can read no other lesson. We decry it,
> and denounce it, and deplore it, but we
> must never ignore it, for looking forward,
> or backward we see S E L F as the pillar
> of flame which will always guide men through
> the wilderness of life until there is no
> man left to live. (87)

It is altogether appropriate that this study of utopias

should conclude on this note of skepticism, for that was

the predominant attitude toward them in the last years

of the nineteenth century. The public had become

surfeited with this type of fiction. Furthermore, the

Bryan campaign had drawn off much of the reform sentiment

into other channels, and most important, the rapidly im-

proving economic conditions of the last years of the

century had eliminated the chief motive of a quest for

utopia. The tendency of the first decade of the twentieth

century was toward more practical reform as expressed in

the muck-raking of Steffens, Tarbell, and Sinclair.

By that time the utopian novel had made a definite

contribution to American thought. It had awakened the

---

(87) Caswell, E.A., op. cit., 153.

masses---for it was a type of literature that appealed
to the uneducated and laboring classes---to the social
and economic and political problems of life. By offering
solutions---most of which were far too easy---the novels
at least educated men to the possibility of change.

To the literary historian, the utopian novel represents a bypath, somewhat removed from the main current
of American literature. The utopist was treading the
narrow common ground between literature and economics.
When the two fused as in the work of Bellamy and Howells,
a novel deserving a permanent place in American literature
was the result. Concerning the majority of utopias, a
truthful critic must agree with the reviewer who remarked
that "the worst thing about the future...will be its novels". [88] This lack of literary excellence constitutes
no reason for ignoring them. The very fact that at least
seventy of them appeared in a dozen years to be read by
millions [89] is sufficient indication of their importance.
When the definitive history of American thought in the
Gilded Age is written, the utopian novel should offer a

---

(88) The Nation, XVII, (October 23, 1873), 278..

(89) In addition to these American utopias, numerous
     translations of foreign works were being read.
     Among the more important of these were Theodore
     Hertzka's Freeland (1889) and Freeland Revisited
     (1894); Eugene Richter's Pictures of the Social-
     istic Future (1889); Robert Blatchford's Sorcery
     Shop and Merrie England; William Morris' News
     from Nowhere (1890); and the earlier romances
     of Wells.

very important means of determining what the American
people were thinking and dreaming of in that period.

CHAPTER XI

CONCLUSION AND SUMMARY

This history of American utopias from the Civil
War to the beginning of the twentieth century has
shown a large body of fiction, heretofore unnoticed,
which is significant to the literary historian, the
sociologist, and the economist. The dreary phases of
corruption in politics, depravity in public taste, and
greed in business, have long been emphasized as the
leading traits of The Gilded Age and the "Mauve Decade";
but when an integrated picture of the period is finally
presented, these utopias will show that coexistent with
the worst aspects of nineteenth century life, there
were a constant desire for improvement and unselfish,
however impractical, attempts to distribute more
equitably the good things of life.

As we have seen, these later American utopias had
no connection with the idealism of the eighteen-forties
as manifested in various communities. The ideas of
Fourier, which had dominated the earlier period, found
expression in only one novel of the 'nineties---Henry
Olerich's A Cityless and Countryless World (1893). The
Civil War cut cleanly across the reform ideas of the
two periods, and together with such conditions as the
later closing of the frontier, combined to give them a

completely different expression---in idealistic communities before the Civil War, in utopian romances
afterwards.

An examination of English utopias in the same general period shows a number of futuristic romances,
chiefly satirical in purpose, but with no specific influence on American utopists. Lytton's The Coming Race
and Samuel Butler's Erewhon are the most important English
utopias preceding Bellamy's Looking Backward; nothing
similar to them is to be found in America. After Looking
Backward, the American utopia influenced the English in
the novels of H.G. Wells and motivated News from Nowhere
by William Morris. It becomes apparent therefore that
our utopias were nurtured entirely in American soil.

The conditions that produced these descriptions of
ideal commonwealths were economic. Most important of
all was the increasing inequality in the distribution
of wealth. Added to this were the rising hostility between capital and labor, the cut-throat competition
engendered by the laissez-faire philosophy, the growing
urbanization, and the closing of the frontier. All
these combined to create a definite feeling of discontent
among a large section of the American populace and are
specifically attacked in the works of the idealists.

From 1865 to 1888, some fifteen isolated utopias
or futurity stories appeared. Immediately after the

Civil War, the ideal was religious and involved descriptions of life after death offered as consolation to the families of soldiers killed in the war. In the eighteen-seventies, interest was beginning to turn toward earthly conditions, and Henry George's Progress and Poverty (1879) doubtless did much to provoke thought about economic solutions. In the early 'eighties, Professor John Macnie's The Diothas (1883) was one of the first novels to depict a complete civilization of the future, and is further important because of its similarity to Looking Backward.

American utopias would probably have remained isolated and vague, had not Edward Bellamy's Looking Backward (1888) appeared at the most opportune time and given a directing and unifying force to the quest for utopia. The success of Looking Backward rests partially upon its story and partially upon the apparently innocuous form of socialism it presented. Appearing at the most opportune moment when labor disturbances and social injustices occupied America's attention, this novel won an audience of millions here and abroad, many of whom were convinced that it pointed an easy path to the millenium. The organization of the Nationalist Party in the 'nineties and the existence today of numerous Bellamy Clubs are sufficient testimony to the power of this novel. Written by a man impelled with an un-

selfish zeal for social betterment, <u>Looking Backward</u>
gave the clearest expression to the reform ideas of
its generation. It is the best of the American utopias
and one of the two or three most opportune books ever
to appear in America.

Because <u>Looking Backward</u> was so widely imitated
and discussed, the question of whether Bellamy's ideas
were original or derivative becomes important. The
author and his fellow Nationalists asserted that the
book was entirely original, but comparison of its plot
and ideas with those of other works shows that <u>Looking
Backward</u> may have had very definite sources. Its
similarity in plot to Macnie's <u>The Diothas</u> (1883) is
amazing. An examination of <u>The Cooperative Commonwealth</u>
(1884) by Laurence Gronlund forces one to conclude that
<u>Looking Backward</u> is little more than a fictionalized
version of Gronlund's socialistic commonwealth. Another
potential source is August Bebel's <u>Frau</u>. Since <u>Looking
Backward</u> was written in 1886 and 1887, and since Bellamy
had been reading widely in works devoted to social
problems, there is every reason to suppose that he knew
these works. The parallel passages cited in Chapter
VIII of this thesis show rather definitely that Bellamy
borrowed much and that his chief claim to fame is not
so much as an original thinker but as a popularizer of
a modified form of socialism in America.

The widespread interest in Looking Backward is
well attested by the number of attacks and defences
of its social system. Both critics and advocates pay
a tribute to Bellamy's success in winning an audience
for his ideas by using the novel as their medium. The
defenders of his system add little to what Bellamy
himself had done. They merely continue the story of
Julian West as did Solomon Schindler in Young West (1894)
or apply its ideas to some new locale as in Zebina
Forbush's The Co-opolitan (1898) or in some modified
form as in Bradford Peck's The World a Department Store
(1900). All the attacks centered on the same general
weaknesses of the nationalistic system. The idea that
human nature with its selfishness and love of individual
reward would render the whole system impossible is set
forth in J.W. Robert's Looking Within (1893). The lack
of all incentive to progress under nationalism is shown
in Arthur D. Vinton's Looking Further Forward (1890).
The fundamental fallacy that all men can be made equal
is exposed in George Harris' Inequality and Progress
(1897) and in G.A. Sanders' Reality (1898). The impartial reader is likely to feel that Bellamy's critics
had rather the best of it, particularly since none of
their charges were effectively met even by his own
amplification of his early utopia in Equality (1897).

The other utopias that appeared between 1888 and

1900 were unquestionably motivated by the popularity
of Bellamy's novel although they do not specifically
concern his nationalistic system. They appeared in
increasing numbers and reached a climax in 1894. After
that there is a dimunition of interest in ideal commonwealths, although books describing them continued to
be published at the rate of five or six a year until
the end of the century. Three reasons can be offered
for this diminishing interest: first, the public had
become surfeited by the number of utopias; second,
economic conditions improved in the last years of the
'nineties and removed what had been the chief motive
for utopias, economic insecurity; third, the Populist
program and the Bryan campaign of 1896 had drawn off
reform sentiment into other channels. The next step
beyond the quest for utopia was the muck-raking movement
for which the reform sentiments of utopians paved the
way.

As we have noted, the American utopias were not
great in literary qualities. Only Bellamy's <u>Looking</u>
<u>Backward</u> and Howells' <u>A Traveller from Altruria</u> are
certain to win a permanent place in American literature.
All of the other writers, with the possible exception
of Ignatius Donnelly and Joaquin Miller, are now as
obscure as they deserve to be. The temperament of the
American reformers during these years lent itself to an

earnest exposition of an ideal commonwealth rather than
to a clever satire on American conditions. Their plans
of salvation had depended too much on some one idea to
be very practical; their method of expression was too
careless to give them any permanence. They represent
a by-path off the main literary highway. Yet the fact
that some seventy or more of these novels were read by
millions of Americans over a dozen years is sufficient
proof that they were of importance in their own day and
that they are of significance to the American historian,
political, economic or literary.

A CRITICAL BIBLIOGRAPHY OF AMERICAN UTOPIAS, 1865-1900

It has seemed best to arrange this bibliography chronologically in order to show the development of interest in American utopias. On the list are included three types of works generally called "utopian": the complete utopia describing in detail a new form of society; the utopian satire; and the futurity story with some element of utopian idealism. Books erroneously listed as utopias by other scholars are included.

Wherever possible the place of publication and the publisher's name are given. In some instances a search of a dozen important libraries has revealed no copy of the book; yet it seems desirable to include the title even though I have not read it, for in each instance I have a review or some information which indicates that it is a utopia. Such titles are marked #.

1868

Radical Freelance, Esq. (Pseud.), The Philosophers of Foufou-ville. New York; G.W. Carleton. A utopian satire directed at Fourieristic communities.

1869

Hale, E.E., Sybaris and other Homes. Boston; Fields, Osgood and Co. A vague sort of utopian life is depicted.

Phelps, E.S., The Gates Ajar. Boston; Fields, Osgood and Co. A description of a heavenly utopia designed to console relatives of soldiers killed in the Civil War.

1870

Anonymous, Lifting the Veil. New York; Scribners. The future life in heaven.

(Hale, E.E.), Ten Times One is Ten, The Possible Reformation, by Colonel Frederic Ingham. Boston; Houghton Mifflin Co. A utopia attained through the influence of one good character.

Holcombe, W.H., In Both Worlds. Philadelphia; J.B. Lippincott Co. Another story of the perfect life after death.

1874

Trammell, William D., _Ca Ira_. New York; United States
Publishing Co. A prophecy of the future with
attempts to solve the labor problem.

1880

Dooner, Pierton, W., _Last Days of the Republic_. San
Francisco; Alta California Publishing Co.
Utopian and scientific.

#Gaston, Henry A., _Mars Revealed; or Seven Days in the
Spirit World_. San Francisco; A.L. Bancroft
and Co.

1883

(Macnie, John), _The Diothas; or, A Look Far Ahead_, by
Ismar Thiusen. New York; G.P. Putnams. A
complete utopia.

Phelps, E.S., _Beyond the Gates_. Boston; Houghton Mifflin
Co. Another glimpse of life in heaven.

1884

Cridge, Alfred Denton, _Utopia; or, The History of an
Extinct Planet_. Oakland, California;
Winchester and Pew, Printers. A pamphlet
describing ideal life on a planet further
advanced than the earth.

1886

(Allen, H.F.), _The Key of Industrial Cooperative Govern-
ment_, by Pruning Knife. St. Louis. An
exposition of a cooperative plan.

1887

Dodd, Anna Bowman, _The Republic of the Future, or
Socialism a Reality_. New York; Cassell and
Co. A complete utopia intended to show the
fallacies of socialism.

1888

Bellamy, Edward, _Looking Backward_. Boston; Ticknor and
Co. A complete utopia.

1888 (cont.)

Hale, E.E., How They Lived in Hampton. Vol. IX of The
Works of Edwin Everett Hale, Boston; Houghton
Mifflin Co., 1900. A utopian colony.

1889

Mitchell, John Ames, The Last American. A utopian satire.

1890

(Bachelder, John), A.D. 2050. Electrical Development
at Atlantis, by A Former Resident of the Hub.
San Francisco; The Bancroft Co. An answer to
Looking Backward.

#Ballou, William Hosea, The Bachelor Girl: A Novel of
the 1400. New York; Lovell Publishing Co.
A futurity story that may possibly be utopian.

Cole, Cyrus, The Aurorophone. Chicago; Chas. H. Keer
and Co. A story of interplanetary communication with some utopian ideas.

(Donnelly, Ignatius), Caesar's Column, by Edmund
Boisgilbert. Chicago; F.J. Schulte and Co.
A complete utopia.

Fuller, Alvarado M., A.D. 2000, Chicago; (n. n.). A
complete utopia.

Heywood, D. Herbert, The Twentieth Century. A Prophecy
of the Coming Age. Boston; no publisher's
name given. A forty-page prospectus of a
utopia which never appeared.

Leggett, M.D., A Dream of a Modest Prophet. Philadelphia;
J.B. Lippincott Co. A complete utopia on Mars.

Michaelis, Richard, Looking Further Forward. Chicago;
Rand, McNally and Co. An attack on Looking
Backward.

Vinton, Arthur Dudley, Looking Further Backward, Being
a Series of Lectures Delivered to the Fresh-
man Class at Shawmut College by Professor Won
Lung Li. Albany; The Albany Book Co. An
attack on Looking Backward.

1890 (cont.)

(Worley, Frederick U.), Three Thousand Dollars a Year:
        Moving Forward or How We Got There, by
        Benefice. Washington, D.C.; J.P. Wright,
        Printer. A utopian pamphlet advocating Bellamy's
        system.

1891

(Bartlett, J.W.B.), A New Aristocracy, by Birch Arnold.
        Detroit, Mich.; The Bartlett Publishing Co.
        Partially utopian.

Fiske, Amos K., Beyond the Bourn. New York; Fords,
        Howard and Hulbert. A complete utopia.

Geissler, Ludwig A., Looking Beyond. New Orleans; L.
        Graham and Sons. A defence of Looking Backward.

McDougall, Walter H., The Hidden City. New York; Cassell
        Publishing Co. A sensational romance; not
        utopian though so listed on several biblio-
        graphies.

(Simpson, William), The Man from Mars, His Morals, Politics
        and Religion, by Thomas Blot. San Francisco;
        Bacon and Co. A complete utopia.

Thomas, Chauncey M., The Crystal Button, or The Adventure
        of Paul Prognosis in the Forty-Ninth Century.
        Boston; Houghton Mifflin Co. A complete utopia.

Wilbrandt, Conrad, Mr. East's Experiences in Mr. Bellamy's
        World. New York; Harpers. A German utopia
        attacking Bellamy's ideas; widely circulated
        in America in translation by Mary H. Safford.

1892

Bradshaw, William R., The Goddess of Atvatabar. New
        York; J.F. Douthitt Co. A futurity story with
        major emphasis on scientific aspects of life.

Braine, Robert D., Messages from Mars; by Aid of the
        Telescope Plant. New York; J.S. Ogilvie.
        Interplanetary communication; it may contain
        some utopian elements.

Chavannes, Albert, The Future Commonwealth, or What Samuel
        Balcom Saw in Socioland. New York; True
        Nationalist Publishing Co. A complete utopia.

1892 (cont.)

(Crocker, Samuel), <u>That Island. A Political Romance</u>, by
Theodore Oceanic Islet. Oklahoma City; C.E.
Streeter and Co. A complete utopia.

Daniel, Charles, <u>Ai. A Social Vision</u>. Philadelphia;
Miller Publication Co. A social vision of the
future; partially utopian.

Donnelly, Ignatius, <u>The Golden Bottle, or The Story of
Ephraim Benezet of Kansas</u>. New York and St.
Paul; D.D. Merrill and Co. A complete utopia.

Doughty, Francis W., <u>Mirrikh, or a Woman from Mars</u>. New
York; Burleigh and Johnston. Chiefly scien-
tific marvels, but partially utopian.

Everett, Henry L., <u>The People's Program; The Twentieth
Century is Theirs</u>. New York; (n. n.) A complete utopia.

(Moore, M. Louise), <u>Al-Modad, or Life Scenes beyond the
Polar Circumflex</u>, by An Untrammelled Free-
Thinker. Cameron Parish, Lousiana; published
by the author. A futurity story with some
utopian characteristics.

Tincker, Mary Agnes, <u>San Salvador</u>. Boston; Houghton
Mifflin Co. A description of a vague utopian
colony.

1893

Anonymous, <u>The Beginning, A Romance of Chicago As It
Might Be</u>. Chicago; Chas. H. Kerr and Co., Vol.
6 of The Library of Progress. A complete
utopia opposing Populist ideas.

#Giles, Fayette, S., <u>Shadows Before, or A Century Onward</u>.
New York; Humbolt Publishing Co. Apparently
utopian.

Niswonger, Charles E., <u>The Isle of Feminine</u>. Little
Rock, Arkansas; Brown Printing Co. Not a
utopia although listed as such on various
bibliographies.

Olerich, Henry, <u>A Cityless and Countryless World; an
Outline of Practical Co-operative Individualism</u>.
Holstein, Iowa; published by the author. A
complete utopia based on Fourier's ideas.

1893 (cont.)

Roberts, J.W., _Looking Within. The Misleading Tendencies of "Looking Backward" Made Manifest_. New York; A.S. Barnes and Co. An attack on _Looking Backward_.

Russell, A.P., _Sub-Coelum, A Sky-Built Human World_. Boston; Houghton Mifflin Co. A very vague utopia.

"Two Women of the West" (pseud.), _Unveiling a Parallel_. Boston; Arena Publishing Co. A utopia advocating female suffrage.

1894

Astor, John Jacob, _A Journey in Other Worlds_. New York; D. Appleton and Co. Emphasis is largely on science in the future, but the book is partially utopian.

#Bouve, Edward T., _Centuries Apart_. Boston; Little Brown and Co.

Brooks, Byron A., _Earth Revisited_. Boston; Arena Publishing Co. A rather indefinite utopia emphasizing the brotherhood of man.

#Browne, Walter, _2894; or, The Fossil Man: A Midwinter's Night Dream_. New York; Dillingham Co.

Chamberlain, Henry R., _6000 Tons of Gold_. Meadville, Pa; Flood and Vincent. A utopia showing the effect of a large flow of gold on our currency system.

#Harben, William N., _The Land of the Changing Sun_. Allyn Forbes in _Social Forces_ VI; 188 list this as a utopia.

Howells, William D., _A Traveller from Altruria_. New York; Harpers. A utopian satire.

Miller, Joacquin, _The Building of the City Beautiful_. Cambridge and Chicago; Stone and Kimball. Partly religious fantasy and partly utopian.

Rosewater, Frank, _'96; A Romance of Utopia_. Omaha; The Utopia Co., A complete utopia.

1894 (cont.)

Schindler, Solomon, Young West, A Sequel to Edward
Bellamy's Celebrated Novel "Looking Backward".
Boston; Arena Publishing Co. A further
exposition of Nationalism in a utopia.

Welcome, S. Byron, From Earth's Center. A Polar Gateway Message. Chicago; Chas. H. Kerr and Co.,
Volume 10 of The Library of Progress. A complete utopia advocating Henry George's single
tax.

1895

Call, Henry L., The Coming Revolution. Boston; Arena
Publishing Co. Not a novel: the last chapter
describes an ideal republic.

Chavannes, Albert, In Brighter Climes, or Life in Socioland. Knoxville, Tennessee; Chavannes and Co.
A complete utopia.

Holford, Castello N., Aristopia. Boston; Arena Publishing
Co. A utopia rewriting history as it might
have been.

(Howard, Albert W.) M. Auburré Hovorré, The Milltillionaire.
No place or date of publication given;
Bibliography of the Library of Congress lists
it as 1895 (?). A utopian pamphlet.

Lloyd, John Uri, Editorpha. Second edition. Cincinnati;
The Robert Clarke Co., 1896. A fantasy; very
little utopanism.

Mitchell, Willis, The Inhabitants of Mars, Their Manners
and Advancement in Civilization, and Their
Opinion of Us. Malden, Mass.; C.E. Spofford
and Co. A journey to Mars, partially utopian
and partially scientific.

Wheeler, David H., Our Industrial Utopia and Its Unhappy
Citizens. Chicago; A.C. McClurg and Co. Not
a novel, but an examination of utopian ideas.

1896

Chambers, Julius, "In Sargasso" Missing. New York; The
Trans-Atlantic Publishing Co. Chiefly scientific, but with some utopian elements.

1896 (cont.)

Chambers, Robert W., The Maker of Moons. New York;
        Putnams. Sensational story, rather than a
        utopia.

Cowan, James, Daybreak, A Romance of An Old World. New
        York; George H. Richmond and Co. A complete
        utopia.

(Emmens, Stephen H.), A Plain Citizen, The Sixteenth
        Amendment. New York; (n. n.). Advocates a
        nationalistic system in the future; not a novel.

Lockwood, Ingersoll, 1900, or the Last President. New
        York; The American News Co. A futurity story
        used as anti-Bryan propaganda.

Lockwood, John, Hi-Li, The Moon Man. Brooklyn. A
        pamphlet using futurity story for political
        propaganda against Byran.

Phelps, Corwin, An Ideal Republic, or The One Way Out
        of the Fog. Chicago; (n. n.). A complete
        utopia.

1897

Bellamy, Edward, Equality. New York; D. Appleton and Co.
        A complete utopia.

Caryl, Charles W., New Era. Presenting Plans for the
        New Era Union. Denver; published by the author.
        A complete utopia.

#Colburn, Frona, E.W., Yermah, the Dorado. The Story of
        a Lost Race. San Francisco; W. Doxey.

(Galloway, James M.), John Harvey, A Tale of the Twen-
        tieth Century, by Anon Moore. Chicago; Chas.
        H. Kerr and Co. A complete utopia.

Harris, George, Inequality and Progress. Boston; Houghton
        Mifflin Co. An attack on Bellamy's novels; not
        a novel.

Lord Commissioner (pseud.), A Prophetic Romance, Mars
        to Earth.

Oberholtzer, Ellis Paxson, The New Man. Philadelphia;
        Levytype Co. A philosophic work which projects
        ahead a few years in its last chapter; not a
        novel.

1897 (cont.)

#Smythe, Alfred, <u>Van Hoff; or the New Planet</u>. New York;
    American Publishers. Apparently interplanet-
    ary; it may be utopian.

#Windsor, William, Loma; <u>A Citizen of Venus</u>. St. Paul,
    Minn.; Windsor and Lewis. Interplanetary and
    possibly utopian.

1898

#Badger, Joseph E. Jr., <u>The Lost City</u>. Boston; Dana,
    Estes and Co. Sometimes listed as a utopia.

Craig, Alexander, <u>Iona, Land of Wise Men and Fair Women</u>.
    Chicago; (n. n.). A complete utopia.

Forbush, Zebina, <u>The Co-opolitan</u>. Chicago; Chas. H. Kerr
    and Co. An expansion of Bellamy's ideas.

Mundo, Oto, <u>The Recovered Continent; A Tale of the</u>
    <u>Chinese Invasion</u>. Columbus, Ohio; Harper-Osgood.
    A sensational story of the future invasion of
    America. Hardly utopian.

(Rehm, Warren S.),<u>The Practical City. A Future City</u>
    <u>Romance; or a Study in Environment</u>, by Omen Nemo.
    Lancaster, Pa.; The Lancaster County Magazine.
    A complete utopia.

Sanders, George A., <u>Reality; or Law and Order vs. Anarchy</u>
    <u>and Socialism</u>. Cleveland; The Burrows Brothers
    Co. An attack on utopian ideas; it is not a
    utopia, although frequently listed as such.

Waterloo, Stanley, <u>Armageddon. A Tale of Love, War, and</u>
    <u>Invention</u>. Chicago; Rand, McNally and Co. A
    prophecy of the last great war; not utopian.

(Wellman, B.J.), <u>The Legal Revolution of 1902</u>, by A Law-
    Abiding Revolutionist. Chicago; Chas. H. Kerr
    and Co. No. 27 of the Library of Progress.
    A complete utopia.

1899

Merrill, Albert Adams, <u>The Great Awakening. The Story</u>
    <u>of the Twenty-Second Century</u>. Boston; (n. n.).
    A complete utopia.

1900

(Caswell, Edward A.), Toil and Self, by Myself and
Another. Chicago; Rand, McNalley and Co.
A complete utopia offered as criticism of
all earlier utopias.

#Edson, Milan C., Solaris Farm. Washington, D.C.;
published by the author. Listed by Forbes
as a utopia.

(Grigsby, Alcanoan Q.), Nequa, or The Problem of the
Ages, by Jack Adams. Topeka, Kansas; Equity
Publishing Co. A complete utopia.

Mason, Caroline, A Woman of Yesterday. New York;
Doubleday, Page and Co. Not a utopian novel,
but the latter part of the story concerns a
utopian community.

Newcomb, Simon, His Wisdom, the Defender. A description
of how world peace is to be attained in the
future. Partially utopian.

Peck, Bradford, The World A Department Store. A Story
of Life Under the Cooperative System. Lewiston,
Maine; published by the author. A complete
utopia.

GENERAL BIBLIOGRAPHY

GENERAL WORKS ON UTOPIAS

Hertzler, J.O., The History of Utopian Thought; New York; Macmillan Co., 1923.

Kaufman, Moritz, Utopias: or, Schemes of Social Improvement; London; C.K. Paul and Co., 1879.

Masso, Gildo, Education in Utopias; New York; Columbia University Press, 1927.

Mumford, Lewis, The Story of Utopias; New York; Boni and Liveright, 1922.

Scudder, Vida D., Social Ideals in English Letters; Boston and New York; Houghton Mifflin Co., 1898.

Wagenknecht, Edward, Utopia Americana; Seattle; University of Washington Bookstore, 1929.

Wells, Herbert G., A Modern Utopia; London; Nelson, 1905.

Weygandt, C., A Century of the English Novel; New York; The Century Co., 1925.

BIBLIOGRAPHIES---GENERAL AND UTOPIAN

Adams, Raymond, A Booklist of American Communities in mimeographed form, Chapel Hill, 1935.

Baker, Ernest A. and Packman, James, A Guide to the Best Fiction; New York; The Macmillan Co., 1932.

Bibliography of American Utopias 1884-1900, appended to Article by Allyn Forbes in Social Forces VI; 188-189.

List of References on Utopias; a typewritten manuscript in the Library of Congress, 1922.

HISTORICAL BACKGROUND

Bailey, J.O., _Scientific Fiction in English, 1817-1914_;
Chapel Hill: an unpublished doctoral dissertation,
1934.

Beard, Charles A. and Beard, Mary R., _The Rise of American
Civilization_; New York; The Macmillan Co., 1930.

Bebel, August, _Woman in the Past, Present and Future_,
translated by H.B. Adams Walther; London; (n.n.)
(n.d.).

Beard, Charles A., _Contemporary American History_; New York;
The Macmillan Co., 1914.

Beer, Max, _Social Struggles and Socialist Forerunners_;
London; L. Parsons, 1924.

Bellamy, Edward, _Dr. Heidenhoff's Process_; New York; D.
Appleton and Co., 1880.

   Miss Ludington's Sister; A Romance of Immortality;
   Boston; Houghton Mifflin Co., (n.d.).

   Six to One: A Nantucket Idyl, published anonymously;
   New York; G.P. Putnams, 1878.

   The Blindman's World, and Other Stories;
   Boston; Houghton Mifflin Co., 1898.

   The Duke of Stockbridge; New York; Silver,
   Burdett and Co., (n.d.).

Blankenship, Russell, _American Literature as an Expression
of the National Mind_; New York; H. Holt and Co.,
1931.

Bogart, Ernest L., _Economic History of the American
People_; New York; Longmans, Green and Co., 1930.

Carlton, Frank Tracy, _Organized Labor in American History_;
New York; D. Appleton and Co., 1920.

Cooke, Delmar Gross, _William Dean Howells; a Critical
Study_; New York; E.P. Dutton and Co., 1922.

Davis, Jerome, _Contemporary Social Movements_; New York
and London; The Century Co., 1930.

De Voto, Bernard A., Mark Twain's America; Boston;
    Little, Brown and Co., 1932.

Dewey, Davis R., National Problems, 1885-1897; New York;
    Harper and Brothers, 1907.

Ely, Richard T. and Bohn, Frank, The Great Change;
    New York; Thomas Nelson and Sons, 1935.

Firkins, Oscar W., William Dean Howells; a Study; Cam-
    bridge; Harvard University Press, 1924.

Flower, B.O., Progressive Men, Women, and Movements of
    the Past Twenty-Five Years; Boston; The New
    Arena Publishing Co., 1914.

Franklin, Fabian, People and Problems; New York; H. Holt
    and Co., 1908.

Garland, Hamlin, A Son of the Middle Border; New York;
    The Macmillan Co., 1917.

George, Henry, Jr., The Life of Henry George; New York;
    Doubleday and McClure Co., 1901.

Gronlund, Laurence, The Cooperative Commonwealth; London;
    Le Bas and Lowry, 1886.

Hale, E.E. Jr., The Life and Letters of Edward Everett
    Hale; 2 vols., Boston; Little, Brown and Co.,
    1917.

Haworth, Paul L., America in Ferment; Indianapolis; Bobbs-
    Merrill Co., 1915.

Haynes, F.E., Social Politics in the United States; Boston
    and New York; Houghton Mifflin Co., 1924.

Higginson, Mary Potter, Thomas Wentworth Higginson; the
    Story of His Life; Boston; Houghton Mifflin
    Co., 1914.

Hillquit, Morris, History of Socialism in the United
    States; Fourth edition. New York and London;
    Funk and Wagnalls, 1906.

Holmes, Oliver W., Over the Teacups; Boston; The Jefferson
    Press, 1890.

Howells, Mildred, Editor, The Life in Letters of William
        Dean Howells; 2 vols. Garden City, N.Y.;
        Doubleday, Doran and Co., 1928.

Howells, William Dean, My Mark Twain; New York; Harper
        and Brothers, 1910.

Kirkland, Edward C., A History of American Economic Life;
        New York; F.S. Crofts and Co., 1932.

Orth, Samuel P., The Armies of Labor. Vol 40 of The
        Chronicles of America; New Haven; Yale Uni-
        versity Press, 1921.

Paine, Albert Bigelow, Mark Twain, a Biography; New York;
        Harper and Brothers, 1912.

        Editor, Mark Twain's Letters, 2 vols. New York;
        Harper and Brothers, 1917.

Parrington, V.L., The Beginnings of Critical Realism in
        America 1860-1920; New York; Harcourt, Brace
        and Co., 1930.

Shipley, Marie A.B., The True Author of "Looking Backward";
        New York; John B. Alden, 1890.

Russell, Frances Theresa, Touring Utopia, the Realm of
        Constructive Humanism; New York; Dial Press, 1932.

Smith, Goldwin, Essays on Questions of the Day; Second
        revised edition. New York; Macmillan Co., 1897.

Taylor, Walter Fuller, Economic Unrest in American Fiction
        1880-1901; Chapel Hill; an unpublished doctoral
        dissertation, 1929.

Ticknor, Caroline, Glimpses of Authors; Boston; Houghton
        Mifflin Co., 1922.

Walker, Hugh, The Literature of the Victorian Era:
        Cambridge; The University Press, 1921.

MAGAZINE ARTICLES

Austin, H., "Edward Bellamy", National Magazine, IX,
        (October, 1898), 69-72.

Baxter, Sylvester, "The Author of Looking Backward",
    The New England Magazine, (September, 1889), I,
    New Series, 92-98.

Bellamy, Edward, "How I Came to Write Looking Backward",
    The Nationalist, I, (May, 1889), 1-4.

Carlson, W.A., "Professor Macnie as a Novelist", The
    Alumni Review of The University of North Dakota,
    (December, 1934), 4.

Carlton, Frank T., "An American Utopia", The Quarterly
    Journal of Economics, XXIV, (February, 1910),
    428-433.

Cleghorn, S.N., "Utopias Interpreted", Atlantic Monthly,
    CXXXIV, (July, August, 1924), 55-67, 216-224.

Calthorp, D.C., "Folly of Utopianism", Engineer CXXXI ,
    (April 29, 1921), 462-463.

Flower, Benjamin O., "The Latest Social Vision", Arena,
    XVIII, (October, 1897), 517-534.

Forbes, Allyn B., "The Literary Quest for Utopia", Social
    Forces, VI, (December, 1927), 179-188.

Gilman, Nicholas P., "Bellamy's Equality", The Quarterly
    Journal of Economics, XII, (October, 1897), 76-82.

    "Nationalism in the United States", The Quarterly
    Journal of Economics, IV, (October, 1889),
    50-76.

Gronlund, Laurence, "Nationalism", The Arena, I, (January,
    1890), 153-165.

Harris, W.T., "Edward Bellamy's Vision", The Forum, VIII,
    (October, 1889), 199-208.

Hawthorne, Julian, "A Popular Topic", Lippincott's Magazine,
    XLV, (June, 1890), 883-888.

Howells, William Dean, "Edward Bellamy", Atlantic Monthly,
    LXXXII, (August, 1898), 253-256.

Marriott, J.W., "Modern Utopians in Conflict", Hibbert
    Journal, XIII, (October, 1914), 124-137.

Merriam, Alexander R., "Some Literary Utopias", Hartford
Seminary Record, VIII, (May, 1898), 203-226.

Mumford, Lewis, "Fashions Change in Utopia", New Republic,
XLVII,)June 18, 1926), 114-115.

(Paget, Violet), "Modern Utopias" by Vernon Lee (Pseud.),
Fortnightly Review, LXXXVI, (Dec., 1906), 1123-
1137.

Peebles, H.P., "The Utopias of the Past Compared with the
Theories of Bellamy", The Overland Monthly,
(Second series), XIV, (June, 1890), 574-577.

Sempers, C.T., "Utopian Dreams of Literary Men", Harvard
Monthly, III, (Dec., 1886), 95-104.

Shuttleworth, H.C., "Utopias, Ancient and Modern", Monthly
Packet, XC, (July-Dec., 1895), 22-27, 174-178,
310,315, 401-406, 544-548, 655-660.

Smith, Goldwin, "Prophets of Unrest", Forum, IX, (August,
1890), 599-614.

Sparks, E.E., "Seeking Utopia in America", Chatauquan,
XXXI, (May, 1900), 151-161.

Taylor, Walter Fuller, "On the Origin of Howells' Interest
in Economic Reform", American Literature, II,
(March, 1930), 3-14.

Walker, Frances A., "Mr. Bellamy and the New Nationalist
Party", Atlantic Monthly, LXV, (February, 1890),
248-262.

Wheatley, Richard, "Ideal Commonwealths", Methodist Review,
LXXV, (July, 1893), 581-597.

MAGAZINES

Atlantic Monthly, Boston; XVII - LXXXVI; January, 1866
to December, 1900.

Public Opinion, Washington; IX - XXXIV; 1890-1900.

The Arena, Boston; I - XXII; Dec., 1889 - Dec., 1900.

The Athenaeum, London; 1865 - 1888.

The Nationalist, Boston; I - III; May, 1889 - May, 1891.

The Nation, New York; I - LXX; July, 1865 - July, 1900.

The New Nation, Boston; I - II; January, 1891 - December, 1892.